Events Design and Experience

Books in the Series

Management of Event Operations
Julia Tum, Philippa Norton and J. Nevan Wright

Innovative Marketing Communications: Strategies for the Events Industry
Guy Masterman and Emma. H. Wood

Events Management (second edition)
Glenn A J Bowdin, Johnny Allen, William O'Toole, Rob Harris and Ian McDonnell

Events Design and Experience
Graham Berridge

Marketing Destinations and Venues for Conferences, Conventions and Business Events
Rob Davidson and Tony Rogers

Human Resource Management for Events
Lynn Van der Wagen

Events Design and Experience

Graham Berridge

Routledge
Taylor & Francis Group

LONDON AND NEW YORK

First published by Butterworth-Heinemann

First edition 2007

This edition published 2011 by Routledge
2 Park Square, Milton Park, Abingdon, Oxon OX14 4RN
711 Third Avenue, New York, NY 10017, USA

Routledge is an imprint of the Taylor & Francis Group, an informa business

Notice
No responsibility is assumed by the publisher for any injury and/or damage to persons
or property as a matter of products liability, negligence or otherwise, or from any use or
operation of any methods, products, instructions or ideas contained in the material herein.

British Library Cataloguing in Publication Data
A catalogue record for this book is available from the British Library

Library of Congress Cataloguing in Publication Data
A catalogue record for this book is available from the Library of Congress

ISBN-13: 978-0-7506-6453-0
ISBN-10: 0-7506-6453-3

Typeset by Charon Tec Ltd (A Macmillan Company), Chennai, India

Contents

Series editors

Glenn A. J. Bowdin is Principal Lecturer in Events Planning at the UK Centre for Events Management, Leeds Metropolitan University where he has responsibility for managing events-related research. He is co-author of *Events Management*. His research interests include the area of service quality management, specifically focusing on the area of quality costing, and issues relating to the planning, management and evaluation of events. He is a member of the Editorial Boards for Event Management (an international journal) and Journal of Convention and Event Tourism, Chair of AEME (Association for Events Management Education), Charter Member of the International EMBOK (Event Management Body of Knowledge). Executive and a member of Meeting Professionals International (MPI).

Don Getz is a Professor in the Tourism and Hospitality Management Program, Haskayne School of Business, the University of Calgary. His ongoing research involves event-related issues (e.g. management, event tourism, events and culture) and special-interest tourism (e.g. wine). Recent books include *Event Management and Event Tourism* and *Explore Wine Tourism: Management, Development, Destinations*. He co-founded and is a member of the Editorial Board for Event Management (an international journal).

Professor Conrad Lashley is Professor in Leisure Retailing and Director of the Centre for Leisure Retailing at Nottingham Business School, Nottingham Trent University. He is also series editor for the Elsevier Butterworth-Heinemann series on Hospitality Leisure and Tourism. His research interests have largely been concerned with service quality management, and specifically employee empowerment in service delivery. He also has research interest and publications relating to hospitality management education. Recent books include *Organisation Behaviour for Leisure Services*, *12 Steps to Study Success*, *Hospitality Retail Management* and *Empowerment: HR Strategies for Service Excellence*. He has co-edited, *Franchising Hospitality Services* and *In Search of Hospitality: Theoretical Perspectives and Debates*. He is the past Chair of the Council for Hospitality Management Education. He is a Chair of the British Institute of Innkeeping's panel judges for the NITA Training awards, and is advisor to England's East Midlands Tourism network.

Series preface

The events industry, including festivals, meetings, conferences, exhibitions, incentives, sports and a range of other events, is rapidly developing and makes a significant contribution to business and leisure related tourism. With increased regulation and the growth of government and corporate involvement in events, the environment has become much more complex. Event managers are now required to identify and service a wide range of stakeholders and to balance their needs and objectives. Though mainly operating at national levels, there has been significant growth of academic provision to meet the needs of events and related industries and the organisations that comprise them. The English speaking nations, together with key Northern European countries, have developed programmes of study leading to the award of diploma, undergraduate and post-graduate awards. These courses focus on providing education and training for future event professionals, and cover areas such as event planning and management, marketing, finance, human resource management and operations. Modules in events management are also included in many tourism, leisure, recreation and hospitality qualifications in universities and colleges.

The rapid growth of such courses has meant that there is a vast gap in the available literature on this topic for lecturers, students and professionals alike. To this end, the **Elsevier Butterworth-Heinemann Events Management Series** has been created to meet these needs to create a planned and targeted set of publications in this area.

Aimed at academic and management development in events management and related studies, the **Events Management Series**:

- provides a portfolio of titles which match management development needs through various stages;
- prioritises publication of texts where there are current gaps in the market, or where current provision is unsatisfactory;
- develops a portfolio of both practical and stimulating texts;
- provides a basis for theoretical and research underpinning for programmes of study;
- is recognised as being of consistent high quality;
- will quickly become the series of first choice for both authors and users.

Preface

Completing the final touches of this book coincided with the final of the FIFA 2006 World Cup, the second biggest event in the world. According to most commentators the event was organised wonderfully well with the whole of Germany and its' host cities joining the celebration and providing not only a football tournament but also a cultural festival par excellence. Cities that hosted matches played their part with free festivals and exhibitions and the whole event was, to coin a phrase, a true celebration of global football's finest. The World Cup also saw the real breakthrough of 'vicarious events' or 'vicarious spectating' with most of the major cities showing the games live on large screens located in or around the main city centres. In some places numbers watching these live transmissions were estimated at over 50,000. Although not the first time this had happened the 2006 World Cup was the first time it had been an integral part of the design of such an event. But then in the final moments of the tournament itself a strange thing happened. With the World Cup Final match between France and Italy concluded, the officials prepared the podium in the centre of the stadium for the presentation of the winners and losers medals. France collected theirs and Italy theirs and then, inexplicably, the proceedings stuttered. Fabio Canavarro, the Italian captain, was left waiting almost in state of suspended animation as he prepared to act out the final and pinnacle moment of the event, the lifting of the World Cup itself. The players readied themselves for that moment of optimal pleasure, when as winners, they alongside fellow countryman in the stadium and around the world watching on TV, would cheer in exalted delight as the captain hoisted the trophy aloft. And they waited. And they waited a bit more. Finally, in one of the most bizarre conclusions to a major sporting presentation, an Italian squad member (believed to be the reserve goal keeper) sidled up to the trophy, grabbed it and thrust it into Canavarro's arms. He duly did the rest. After some 5 years of planning and organising was this final act deliberately designed to unfold in this way? The question we have to ask is: Was it really in the organisers' mind to have this, the optimal experiential moment of the World Cup for players and spectators alike, to be carried off in such unbecoming circumstances? The hoisting of a trophy is the symbolic finale of many such sports events and provides the conclusion to what has often been a long and arduous endeavour by the players to reach this pinnacle of success. As such it should be seen as a key experiential moment in the unfolding of the whole event, much like the 'kiss' after wedding vows, and is therefore an occasion that should be carefully and deliberately designed since it is providing the culminating and defining moment for the winners.

This example illustrates the importance of such pivotal occasions for event experiences for they help provide memorable moments that often form the basis of our recollections of them.

It also shows that if we do not plan and consider every minutiae of an event then it is easy for such occasions to be disrupted and for the flow of the experience to be, albeit momentarily, interrupted. In modern society such pivotal moments are features of events all over the world, and are becoming more so as the value and presence of events is becoming more recognised both for individuals and society. In this relatively golden period for the industry more than ever events are used to showcase someone (celebrity events, weddings, birthday parties, awards), something (new product, brand, service) or some place (country, region, city, town, attraction). Many events today seek to make a stunning visual impact, something that is commonly referred to as the 'wow' factor. The term is sometimes erroneously used suggesting that there is only one single 'wow' moment when in fact there can often be several but serves its purpose to help highlight that an event contains elements of spectacle that enthuses, and possibly even enraptures, those attending. It can be the total impact of a single event or the result of several occasions within an event but what is clear is that to create such an impact requires careful and detailed planning to design the requisite outcome. The experience of either participating or attending such events is becoming increasingly framed by recognition of the components that create these occasions. As such they are carefully and deliberately designed. The components used largely reflect the purpose and concept of the event and can consist of many and numerous elements within the event. It is the study of these deliberately designed event occasions and the components used to create them that are the focus of this book.

This book is nominally divided into three sections. Chapters 1–4 provide the underpinning rationale for the study of events. Chapter 1 re-visits attempts to define events and explores the characteristics of event management and there is a case study on designing an event for different stakeholder. Chapter 2 provides a brief overview of the main focus of event management literature, in particular examining the general event texts that deal with event organisation and impact. There is also a preliminary discussion on the role of design in event literature. In Chapter 3 the discussion moves on to explore the emergence of the events industry looking at the significance of the Millennium and Olympics as a vital boots in the industry's new found recognition and highlights key trends in specific events sectors. The emergence of event management education is outlined in Chapter 4. These chapters are by nature introductory and are not meant to be definitive on any of the topic areas. They serve only to highlight some of the key points about the study of event management that enables this book to be written. Chapters 5–8 are concerned with exploring and analysing ideas on experience and design for events. The study of experience is explored within the context of leisure and tourism in Chapter 5 as a way of understanding how the notion of experience can be applied to active and passive occasions, whilst Chapter 6 looks at the definitions of design and its applicability for event management, arguing that it should be seen as an integral part of the whole process of managing an event. It includes a case study on participatory design and a Discovery Channel launch. The emergence of the experience industry or economy is the focus of Chapter 7 that examines the core concepts of experience and offers examples of how event experiences can be studied. Bringing the two ideas of experience and design together is the subject of Chapter 8 with further observation on how specific experiential elements of an event can be designed. Chapters 9–11 are concerned with the analysis of events. Chapter 9 introduces symbolic interaction and explains its use as a tool for developing experiential foresight in event design and for analysing event experiences via case study on Formula 1, whilst Chapter 10 applies the model of symbolic interaction to study event experiences through the six different elements of experience. Finally, the meaning and interpretation of events is considered in Chapter 11 by explaining and applying the concept of semiotics to events and event communications. There are several learning activities and case studies used to illustrate key points and these increase in number and depth as the reader progresses through the chapters.

There are several occurrences at events, much like the one described above, that have influenced me to attempt this study. I frequently wondered how was it that I could turn up to an event and come away feeling unhappy about what I had experienced. In studying these events I persuaded numerous researchers to analyse and evaluate their experiences with me. Their responses often confirmed by own analysis of some of these events, that they too experienced emotions of displeasure, disappointment and sometimes even anger at the way the event had been organised. They also experienced emotions of enormous pleasure as well, or optimal arousal as studies of experience tend to call it. In investigating this further I realised that academic critical analysis of these event experiences was not in great supply and that the approach to the study of events adopted a fairly conventional route, a route that was traditionally positivist and often lacking in critical insight into the way an event had been designed. I wondered, if all events were good, then why is that I have attended several events and not felt this to be the case. Why have I come away with the feeling that the experience of attending, participating or working at a particular event has been less than perfect? In some cases the experience had been so poorly designed that it was little more than a charade to call it an organised event and in some others I left feeling that not only had value-for-money not been had, but that the events were simply commercial merchandising opportunities disguised as events, consequently they were poorly designed and executed, presumably put together on a whim but with sufficient business acumen to attract people via effective communication strategies. In some cases I was appalled at what I saw as the most glaring and obvious design flaws in the event, where, amongst other things sound, text, image and lighting competed with each other rather than complemented each other.

Such uncertain experiences seemed at odds with the emergence of what O'Sullivan and Spangler call the 'experience industry' or Pine and Gilmour refer to as the 'experience economy'. The concept of experience has developed into various models for studying and explaining aspects of marketing whereby a product or service are 'imbued with additional qualities', qualities above and beyond their actual real time usage. It has also been applied as a concept for describing some of the features of events and the experiences of guests or participants who attend. This means that a Gala Night or Awards Ceremony or Prom is seen as not only as an 'event function' but is created and construed as an experience (occurrence, occasion or moment) specifically designed to illicit a positive and meaningful feeling of well being for those attending. This feeling should be one whereby they have, in some way, been internally reached or touched; emotionally, physically and psychologically by what their senses have noted and that some element of this experience has been the result of interaction with other people or objects. The focus of this book is to critically unravel the way some of those experiences have been designed. During the next 11 Chapters many ideas on events design and experience will be introduced some of which appear to contradict each other and some of which appear to be of little relevance to event management.

The purpose of this book is not to create a definitive model for analysing event experiences but rather through the help of selected case studies to show how a number of concepts can be applied to the study of the design and experience of events. Some of the concepts overlap, for instance the idea of interaction is a feature of symbolic interaction and experiential theory. The tools are provided to help the reader begin their own process of analysing event experiences and to understand why elements of an event have been designed in such a way.

One way to explore the experience of an event (or any other kind of activity) is to obtain responses of those at the event, and there are several methods of experiential analysis ranging from immediate experience, immediate recall to post reflection. This often results in satisfaction responses, which after all is a reasonable tool to evaluate an event, but tends to be very much a quality based or customer service exercise looking at issues around promptness of service in the cafeteria, cleanliness and response of staff to queries, etc. And whilst it can be used for deeper insight it is rarely used to explore issues of design, environment or ambience. A common feature of modern events (especially larger exhibitions, conventions or conferences) is to have a stand of computers where visitors to the events can complete a simple multiple-choice questionnaire on the event and its organisers and sponsors. The list of questions tends to produce valuable statistics that can no doubt be later used for market research, but this type of evaluation of the event barely touches upon the design of the event or the nature of experience at the event. Another way to study event experiences is to apply theoretical tools to vicariously study the event, that is to look at the signs inherent in the event setting and attempt to understand some of the meanings and messages behind what we see and to interpret these. This observation requires that we understand the significance that different elements have to play in creating the environment and enables us to critically examine how these elements have been constructed so that we can ask questions about their effect. In this way we can begin to explore some of the thematic elements that have been introduced and deconstruct their meaning and the experience created.

At the root of this point is the idea that an event, for some stakeholders but not all, is an activity that is, at that point, meant to be unique and memorable. And outside of business events, visits to or participation in them is for most people part of their leisure experience, their freely chosen use of time. What we want from that time is of course something pleasurable and enjoyable. Who has ever heard of either an event or activity offering you the chance to not have an enjoyable time? For business events the aspect of enjoyment may be removed, but the feeling of pleasure in relation to event experience can be maintained. This would be of a less celebratory nature than a leisure event, but nevertheless people involved in either conference, exhibitions, business meetings or expos should be able to derive some measure of a pleasurable experience where the event has created the right environment for their reason for being there to flourish.

The point here is not that all events impact on us in such a way, but that events are, can and should be carefully designed and communicated experiences and that recipients of the event should be able to extrapolate the meaning they are presented with and use it for pleasure, gratification or other purposes. The symbolic values inherent in an event, whilst not necessarily contributing to our immediate culture, should contribute to our immediate sense of experience. Events can be understood and analysed on several levels. They can also be designed with several different layers and, as such, experienced on several different overlapping levels. In terms of its actual internal planning and organisation, its design and environment created, the experience of multi-recipients and the symbolic experience associated with an event. The question for event management is what these communicated experiences actually are and how do they manifest themselves in the design of any chosen event?

This basis of this book rests upon three simple premises:

1 all event environments are created;
2 all experiences within event environments are purposefully designed;
3 all stakeholders are the direct recipients of the designed experiences.

List of figures

List of tables

List of case studies

Part One

Study of Events: Rationale

Chapter 1
Defining events

Learning outcomes/objectives

- Be aware of the development of event definitions
- Be able to understand what is meant by the term 'events' or 'event'
- Be able to describe a range of event types
- Be able to classify events through genres
- Be able to appreciate the hierarchy of events in terms of their size

Introduction

Numerous authors have attempted to define events so, in theory, we should be clear what constitutes an event. However, with the emergence of event textbooks there has been an emergence of different definitions. For those working in the industry, and although they may work in one of the numerous sub-categories of event management types, there is probably a fairly clear idea of what factors constitute an event if not what actually defines one. For those commissioning an event such clarity is less certain. As one managing director said 'whenever I get a new client the first thing I do is sit down with them and discuss what we both understand an event to be'. This approach is not atypical and reflects a need to establish at the outset what an event is and what specific activities are to be embraced within it. We might also add that very often the definition from a client perspective changes, and the management company needs to either adapt its approach or direct the client towards their understanding of an event. There is no radical change implied here but more a change in emphasis so either side, client and company are working to the same remit. The example demonstrates that whilst some clients arrive with very clear expectations and ideas of what their event is, others have little or no idea apart from knowing that they want an event created for them. Or, perhaps more commonly, they know they want to celebrate something.

Defining events

Rather than seeking to develop another definition for events or to produce an exact meaning the aim here is to attempt to understand some of the academic views put forward to explain what events are and to draw upon those as a way of explaining what types of occasions are called events. It will also help us to understand what has been the main focus in developing our understanding of events in society and also highlight some key features of definitions.

Event management is a relatively new academic subject and so it is reasonably straightforward to trace the emergence of the concepts and definitions of events. An excellent summary of the state of play in defining events is provided by Bowdin, McPherson and Flinn (2006a) who explain events from both a US and UK perspective and highlight the key terminology that is now used to define events. They draw on the range of sources attempting to define events (Shone & Parry, 2004; Van der Wagen, 2004; Allen et al., 2005; Goldblatt, 2005; Bowdin et al., 2006b; Getz, 2006) and note that, despite this activity, there is surprisingly, a limited uniformity of accepted terms, concepts and definitions. One of the reasons for this is that events occur throughout all sections of society and across all different types of organisations and so what one individual or group might see as being special and unique (e.g. wedding), another group sees as being ordinary and regular (e.g. meeting). Often those studying events approach it from a particular viewpoint and look for a definition within the context of their own study area that explains the activity they perceive as an event. Such is the problematic nature of defining events that it may not be possible to do so:

> *it seems at times that special events are everywhere; they have become a growth industry. The field of special events is now so vast that it is impossible to provide a definition that includes all varieties and shade of events.*
>
> Bowdin et al. (2001, pp. 15–16)

Goldblatt and Getz

Nevertheless we need to have some understanding of what it is that we call 'an event'. Two of the earliest academic attempts to define events come from Donald Getz and J.J. Goldblatt in the early1990s, who identify an event as being 'special', 'one-off', 'unique' and 'beyond everyday experience', thus immediately setting them apart from other more routine activities such as work. The idea of an event being a special moment in time is a recurring feature and is used to demarcate an event from other activities in life:

> *A special event recognises an unique moment in time with ceremony and ritual to satisfy specific needs.*
>
> Goldblatt (1990)

> *Is an opportunity for leisure, social or cultural experience outside the normal range of choices or beyond everyday experience.*
>
> Getz (1991; 2005)

The significance of highlighting these two seminal ideas on events is that they establish that an event is the production and creation of 'something', that something being the unique special moment or experience. Incorporating this idea of ceremony, ritual, need and experience into the equation suggests that events also contain a physical element and a psychological element. This is expressed in the idea of events being special and that it is an occasion that is recognised as meeting a need, and subsequently creating an opportunity for some kind of experience. Appreciating that an event may also contain elements of ritual and ceremony suggests that, although each event is different, special events could have some recognisable characteristics that could be attributed to those events where there are similarities in type and reason for occurrence and in the type of experience provided, so that where these attributes occur, they can be acknowledged based on the experience from previous incarnations (of a similar event). If this was not the case then it is otherwise not viable to be able to attribute any kind of ritual or ceremony to the event since ceremonies and rituals evolve over a passage of time and therefore can never be a one-off occurrence that is not in some replicated.

Activity 1.1

1 Are all events catered for in the above definitions? If not, can you think of any events that are not?
2 Compile a list of activities and occasions that you think can be classified as an event.
3 Now compile a list of activities and occasions that cannot be classified as an event. Without a working definition of events, was it easy or difficult to compile the lists?
4 In using this approach does it then mean that there are automatically two completely different lists or will some things overlap and appear on both? What comparisons can you make between the two lists?

As an illustration of this we can see that many sports event competitions often utilise the ceremonial 'winners' podium', where the first three in competition are presented and placed on a hierarchical platform that acknowledges the winner, runner-up and third place. It is an approach adopted from local to international events in cycle racing, motor sports, athletics, rowing, amateur boxing and so on. The Olympics, Commonwealth Games and World Athletic Championships use this approach as the ceremonial conclusion to competition with the awarding of a gold, silver and bronze medal to the respective athletes. The ceremonial ritual is completed when the national flag of the three winners is hoisted high in the arena and the winners' national anthem is played.

The actual style of winners' presentations in sport per se is not rigidly defined, and there are distinctions between mass start events (running, cycling) and elimination events (boxing, tennis) as well as team (football) and individual (golf) events that influence the type of winners' ceremony but there are also similarities adopted across many sports and these aspects of the ceremony have, in some cases, been built up over several previous or similar occurrences. Some ceremonial and ritual traditions are long established reflecting the long history of the sport and they provide continuity of the event and where the winners' ceremony reflects a similar experience for the current champion that past ones had. Others are relatively new reflecting either ceremonial adjustment, structural changes to the sport or possible sponsorship changes. The now ritualistic spraying of champagne that accompanies a podium place in Formula One has only been a feature since the 1960s and its appearance is attributed to the late driver Graham Hill who spontaneously celebrated winning by spraying what was then real champagne over the crowd. So whilst such features are not identical each time they occur due in no part to change of location and personnel, they nevertheless have a resonance about them that people identify as being a part of the event and its overall experience for competitors and spectators.

The Goldblatt and Getz paradigm, that events are 'a unique moment in time', has become commonly understood and adopted. The principle of the definition is to set events aside from everyday occurrences, i.e. those things that we do that are routine and part of our regular living. This aspect of events remains prevalent in event definitions today but due to the expansion of interest and research in the subject a more expansive and inclusive definition is required. Wilkinson writes that 'a special event is a one-off happening designed to meet the specific needs at any given time. Local community events may be defined as an activity established to involve the local population in a shared experience to their mutual benefit' (Wilkinson, 1998). This definition retains the idea of special and one off but also extends the notion to include the locale in which the event is taking place and suggests that some kind of understanding of an events relationship with the community, both involvement and location, is required to fully understand what events are all about. Brown and James (2004) also note that the idea of celebration of ceremony and ritual as a reflection of culture and community is a common feature to many definitions and is included in those put forward by Van Der Wagen (2004) and Bowdin et al. (2006b). Another view looks at events from a tourism perspective and identifies that there are a set of core attributes of special events. These are: special events should attract tourists or tourism development; be of limited duration; be one-off or infrequent occurrence; raise the awareness, image or profile of a region; offer a social experience; and be out of the ordinary (Jago & Shaw, 1999). Goldblatt (2005) whilst retaining the principle definition of events he first espoused has perhaps a way of advancing our ideas on the subject with the suggestion that we move on from 'special events' and into 'event management'. If we focus our attention on the process of management as opposed to the outputs we can more readily understand events. They then become not only special in terms of the experience they give people but also special in terms of the processes used to create that experience. The question this then raises is should there be a significant level of event management activity for us to classify something as an event. To give a very basic understanding something that is regular and routine, both in terms of place and activity, is not an event as it requires regular and almost identical processes each time it takes palace. However something that is infrequent requires irregular and different processes is an event. Even then though the issue is not so straightforward, especially in attempting to explain the activities that some people engage in that they might call an event, but are in fact a routine occasion. It can be a confusing and sometime uncertain difference.

Activity 1.2

Read the following notes and answer the question with explanation:

1 Is this an event or not?
   Let's consider some conundrums for event management. If a music entrepreneur organises a one-off monthly occurrence is this an event or not? Let's say they take a venue, and make a booking to put on a dance club night. They name the club night 'World Beats, book some deejays, a sound system, hire staff, purchase beverages, produce publicity material, hire security people and so on. This instinctively seems to be an event, as it is neither regular nor routine but is a special one-off night. The evening is a success, and so they decide to do more, and in fact make the evening every month for the foreseeable future. Is this now no longer an event? At what point does this regularity cease to define the evening as an event? But we can take this problematic point further by considering those who might either attend

or feature at the evening. If the organiser regularly has 'guest' deejays 1 week, another the next, each playing different types of dance music, then they have made the evening a special event because of the infrequency of these deejays appearance at the club night. This seems to be practising the skills of event management every month, and those they are creating special nights through their selection of deejays and their choice of music. Of course though they will have regular 'attendees' who come to the club night every month, irrespective of who is the deejay. Then they will have people who only come along precisely because of the deejay and who see that particular night as a special one off. At what point is there a crossover between a routine activity and a special event?

This leaves us with a picture of the initial processes involved in event management and helps highlight that an event is not something that can just happen as a by-product of, say, facilities being available. There is no such thing as an event until someone sits down to begin the process of creating one. And then that event has to be planned, organised, managed and, of course, designed. Ultimately that event is then experienced by those involved, whether they are working on the event, watching or attending it or participating in it. Considering two perspectives, the provider and the consumer, offers another way for helping us to define events (Getz, 2005, p. 16):

> *A special event is a one-time or infrequently occurring event outside normal programmes or activities of the sponsoring or organising body. To the customer or guest, a special event is an opportunity for leisure, social or cultural experience outside the normal range of choices or beyond everyday experience.*

Non-celebratory events

This view begins to also draw in a missing element from the previous definitions and that is the lack of any perspective of events where there is no need for celebration. In other words the definition tends to be effective only for certain event types and largely ignores business or organisational type events. To redress this Shone and Parry (2004) have produced a fairly convincing definition that draws in many of the elements for previous definitions and attempt to apply to all event types. They consider events as a categorisation on the following lines that they are either leisure, personal, cultural or organisational. They identify that the nature of previous definitions may have worked for celebratory special events but was less convincing for more organisational ones. So to give all of this a meaningful definition they explain:

> *Special events are: That phenomenon arising from those non-routine occasions which have leisure, cultural, personal or organisational objectives set apart from the normal activity of daily life, whose purpose is to enlighten, celebrate, entertain or challenge the experience of a group of people. (p. 3)*

EMBOK

This seems a very constructive definition and one that can be applied to not only the many different types of events but also to the many different types of people involved in events and provides a base from which to develop our understanding of events.

A similar attempt to develop an all-inclusive approach is taken by EMBOK (Events Management Body of Knowledge) that defines an event as follows:

> *Event management is the process by which an event is planned, prepared and produced. As with any other form of management, it encompasses the assessment, definition, acquisition, allocation, direction, control and analysis of time, finances, people, products, services and other resources to achieve objectives. An event manager's job is to oversee and arrange every aspect of an event, including researching, planning, organizing, implementing, controlling and evaluating an event's design, activities and production.*
>
> Silvers (2004a) Update EMBOK structure

Silvers then develops a fuller taxonomy for the domains, although at the time of going to press this was only completed for four of the five domains, the incomplete one being design. By taking on board these definitions and reflecting on what an event is, there is a clear calling of a need to be aware of the huge construction process involved in event management. The inclusion by EMBOK of a design domain and the recognition that creativity is a core value of the event gives a focus to the role of artistic interpretation and expression and, ultimately, points the way forward for understanding events for the experiential dimensions they exhibit (Jackson, 2005).

Understanding event characteristics

One way of now beginning to identify what events are is to make a list of factors that are readily associated with them as is done in the case of tourism, leisure, sport or hospitality. Another approach that could be used is to consider what types of activities and/or occasions cannot be classified as events, this helps to think about distinctions and similarities between events and non-events. Different approaches have been taken in the study of this with some sources providing a historical chronology charting the history of events (Shone & Parry, 2004; Bowdin, McPherson & Flinn, 2006a) whilst others have then identified a number of features that make up an event by indicating the different characteristics (Bowdin et al., 2001; Shone & Parry, 2004; Allen et al., 2005; Goldblatt, 2005). Considering some of those specific events Goldblatt (2005) suggests the following: civic events; expositions; fairs and festivals; hospitality; meetings and conferences; retail events; social-life-cycles events; tourism would be applicable. One point that begins to emerge from this is a way of interpreting events by expression of types. Society as a whole tends to group things of a similar type into genres, notably in film and music. Table 1.1 list the set of event genres from the EMBOK project and is taken from Silvers (2004a) and provides a fairly solid overview of the event genre landscape.

Another way of considering events is to group them according to their size, and to a certain extent status such as (Table 1.1):

Mega-events; Hallmark Events; Major Events; Sporting Events; Cultural Events; Business Events.

Bowdin et al. (2006b)

These ideas on events provide an overall structure into which most events can be fitted. What we have is quite a wide array of event types and this gives us some idea of the scope of the industry. To exemplify this further, in an online survey conducted in 2005 *RSVP Magazine* gave another indication of the range of these activities that we now classify under events management:

After-show parties
Award ceremonies
Bespoke parties

Table 1.1   The event genre of event management.

Business and corporate events	Any event that supports business objectives, including management functions, corporate communications, training, marketing, incentives, employee relations and customer relations, scheduled alone or in conjunction with other events.
Cause-related and fund-raising events	An event created by or for a charitable or cause-related group for the purpose of attracting revenue, support and/or awareness, scheduled alone or in conjunction with other events.
Exhibitions, expositions and fairs	An event bringing buyers and sellers and interested persons together to view and/or sell products, services and other resources to a specific industry or the general public, scheduled alone or in conjunction with other events.
Entertainment and leisure events	A one-time or periodic, free or ticketed performance or exhibition event created for entertainment purposes, scheduled alone or in conjunction with other events.
Festivals	A cultural celebration, either secular or religious, created by and/or for the public, scheduled alone or in conjunction with other events. (Many festivals include bringing buyer and seller together in a festive atmosphere.)
Government and civic events	An event comprised of or created by or for political parties, communities, or municipal or national government entities, scheduled alone or in conjunction with other events.
Hallmark events	An event of such significance and/or scope that its image or stature assures national and international recognition and interest.
Marketing events	A commerce-oriented event to facilitate bringing buyer and seller together or to create awareness of a commercial product or service, scheduled alone or in conjunction with other events.
Meeting and convention events	The assembly of people for the purpose of exchanging information, debate or discussion, consensus or decisions, education, and relationship building, scheduled alone or in conjunction with other events.

(Continued)

Table 1.1 (*Continued*)

Social/life-cycle events	A private event, by invitation only, celebrating or commemorating a cultural, religious, communal, societal or life-cycle occasion, scheduled alone or in conjunction with other events.
Sports events	A spectator or participatory event involving recreational or competitive sport activities, scheduled alone or in conjunction with other events.

Brand experiences (live events)
Charity events
Christmas parties
Conferences
Corporate away days
Corporate hospitality (at pre-arranged events)
Exhibitions field marketing (product sampling)
Film premieres
Gala dinners
Incentive travel
Private parties
Product launches

It is through such a listing that we can easily see what an event is by name and when compared side by side with other events we can see, for example, that a regular screening at a cinema is not an event but a film premiere is. What appears to clearly dictate the notion of the event is the output as those attending experience it. Events therefore have a crucial differentiation to other types of occasions and such lists are invaluable for they give an insight into what named types of occasions we can call an event at least in terms of their output. The problem of course is that the lists can become never ending as new event types are added.

Stakeholders

These occasions that we now call 'events' that result from the practice of 'event management' then covers an ever-widening community of people, businesses, products, services and suppliers who are involved in events or events-related activities. To attempt to consolidate the process a little bit Goldblatt (2005) develops the 'event management professional model' as a means to help identify the processes of event management and that consists of: event management itself as a function that requires 'human assembly', the event manager as the person responsible for creating the event, the sub-field specialisations that define different events and the stakeholders, all those who have some investment in the event. Including the idea of stakeholders begins to suggest a much wider awareness of whom events are for and suggests there is further complexity to the understanding and analysis of events, particularly when we focus on the impact and experience that an event produces. Stakeholders can be any one individual or company or group who has a relationship with the event (Bowdin et al., 2001). This suggests a myriad of potential relationships and Bowdin et al. (2001) note that increased regulation 'and the growth of government involvement in events, the environment in which events are staged has become much more complex' (p. 49). Attempting to understand events in modern society requires us to understand far more about these complex layers of relationships that events have to offer. With such increased complexity, approaches to understanding and explaining events that tend to focus on a single direct output experience now need to be re-developed so we can explore more fully these relationships between stakeholders. The presence of multi-stakeholders suggests that there cannot be a singular experience in the first place. Secondly, in this multi-layered experience of several stakeholders, who is it that is thought to be having the experience of the unique moment? The organisers, the participants, the guests; the spectators; the workers; the contract service and product suppliers; the client company; the individual; the sponsor; the media. For most parts it is participants and guests that are the subject of study here but it should not be forgotten that the success of a range of events relies on other stakeholders receiving an appropriate experience. We can also consider further groupings within stakeholders where experience of the event may be determined by age, gender and (for participant events) ability. So here we have multi-stakeholders and further variables within each group of stakeholders suggesting we cannot simply treat them all the same.

Case study 1.1

Programming for different stakeholders

Focus of case study

Participant sport events have potentially many different stakeholders

Designing different entry points appeals to this range

Events, like other activities, can also have a programming schedule, e.g. award ceremony, entertainment, conference presentations, and it is important to remember this when sitting down to plan and design an event where there are different levels of stakeholder involvement. The programming schedule requires not just a sound practical knowledge but it requires a conceptual approach to understanding how an event will unfold for all stakeholders. The programme itself requires conceptualising due to the complexity and variety of stakeholders, a complexity that operates on both a symbolic level and a practical one. For non-professional or locally based events the symbolic is the familiarity of the structure that is recognised from other more prestigious events. So a common format for football events is to have a 'World Cup' format. On a practical level it is about clarity of structure but also equity of opportunity to participate.

Most preliminary sports coaching courses explain how to plan competitive events and this requires understanding of the structures of competition in tandem with the level and interest factor of stakeholders. There are several options for programming a competition such as a ladder, league or series table, knock out, mini-league, round robin and various combinations of those. Whatever the format, the programme leads to the logical end point that of a winner(s) and the event is programmed accordingly, in a chronological fashion where each stage progresses. To conceptualise this at the varying levels of stakeholders, in respect of their ability level, age, gender and competitive instinct, is to be acutely aware of the many variables and the multi-layered nature of events of this type. Thus experience of participation can be framed within a category system in relation to these factors. Popular charity participation events such as fun runs, marathons, cycle rides or walks often provide different 'routes' of participation to encourage a widespread of participants. For example the Sport Relief 2006 fund-raiser included a 'go the extra mile' option targeted at children and schools. The idea of running a mile was an attainable target for many children and so the 'programme' of potential fund-raising activities promoted by Sport Relief offered a communal school-based experience. In more regular sports competitions the opportunities to attract groupings within participant stakeholders can be shaped in many ways that are particular to the sport and the event. Take, for example, the case of a sports event such as a Mountain Bike Race. The following entry form (Figure 1.1) provides a wide range of participation entrant routes based on age, ability, distance, gender and seriousness, and covers age lower than 10 through to age over 50 years. It recognises that participant stakeholders interests are not uniformly the same and so the programme of races within the single event attempts to meet as wide a range of interest as practicable.

TICK YOUR CATEGORY	MALE Laps		FEMALE Laps		COST PER EVENT
UNDER 12 Age 10–11	1		1		£6
JUVENILE Age 12–14	2		1		£9
YOUTH Age 15–16	2		1		£9
SUPER MASTER Age 30–49	4		3		£15
MASTER Age 30–39	3				£14
VETERAN Age 40–49	3				£14
MASTER and VETERAN FEMALE Age 30+			2		£14
GRAND VETERAN Age 50+	3				£14
BEGINNER Age 12+	1		1		£8
FUN Age 17+	2		1		£13
OPEN Age 17+	3		2		£14
SPORT Age 17+	4		3		£15
EXPERT Age 17+	5		4		£16
LATE ENTRY CHARGE					£2
CATEGORY CHANGE					£2
TOTAL PAYABLE				£	

Figure 1.1 Entry form showing wide range of participation entrant routes.

Some of the earlier definitions of events tended to focus on the experience as the 'output' received only by those attending the event as a guest. So reference to stakeholders offers the possibility of understanding the event experience across a wider spectrum of interests. It has been adopted in many walks of life including government and is part of an attempt to embrace the wider community involvement in all manner of projects and to ensure that interests are not solely vested in one camp but are shared across many. As events have grown in size and scope they must now meet a plethora of other needs, and these are characterised by the following stakeholder interest (Allen et al., 2005).

Host organisation
Host community
Media
Sponsors
Co-workers
Participants and spectators

To this list Bowdin et al. (2006a) adds industry professionals; associations and federations; and educators. These headings cover just about all likely stakeholders but if they were to be broken down further into different segments for each one there would be a considerable list still of inter-linking and overlapping stakeholder interests. Whilst there will be these overlaps of requirement there will also be distinct differences within the different segments of each grouping and quite realistically different aims for the event. This makes the job of dealing with them a far more challenging proposition. The relative importance then of an event to each or anyone of these groups depends of course upon the event and its purpose but in most cases these groups are not seen as mutually exclusive to one another otherwise we would have some very bitty and disjointed events. More often than not stakeholders recognise the over-laps between their personal interests and those of other groups and accept the accommodation that comes with it. There are some cases where the host organisation may also be the sponsors and provide the participants and spectators at an event. Indeed within a sports event framework a sport organisations own list of member stakeholders, whilst not adding to the list above, adds to the complexity and suggests there are some intricate and delicate decisions to be made about how events managers relate to their stakeholders in such instances.

Case study 1.2

London Fashion Weekend

Focus of case study

This activity looks at the difficulty of meeting different stakeholder needs.

London Fashion Weekend (LFWend), London's premier designer sales event usually follows on from London Fashion Week. LFWend is an opportunity for fashion designers to sell off their older season garments, accessories or samples to the general public and for the last few years has taken place in huge marquee located just off Kings Road, London.

Consider the following Figure 1.2. It shows payment queue aisles leading up to a payment booth.

Figure 1.2 Payment queue aisles leading up to a payment booth. (photograph authors own)

The style epitomises queuing systems used at theme attractions where visitors are herded together in a series of zig-zag style pens before exiting to a pay booth (at the far left). The system uses little space and is functional.

What type of experience does it give visitors?

Is the paying system experience of any relevance to the overall experience of attending the event?

The payment system itself is the last point in a selection and purchase system adopted by the organisers of the event. The system has interesting implications for stakeholder groups at the event. It is largely in place to satisfy (a) the organisers and (b) the visitors but not (c) the designers. Shoppers to the event cannot pay the designers direct for any items, they have to pay at the booths. The system is as follows: Shopper A arrives in the morning at 10.30 a.m. visits stand 1 and selects two items of clothing to buy. Stand 1 wraps up the items and gives Shopper A a docket which they can then take to the payment booth. Once paid for, Shopper A returns to stand 1 and hands over the checked docket and in return gets their goods. However before doing that Shopper A decides to carry on shopping, for several hours or so by which time they have also selected items from stands 2, 3, 4, 5, 6 and so on. They now have a selection of dockets and, realising the amount of money/items they have selected, they decide to reject some of them and throw several dockets into a bin. They go to the pay booth and purchase goods from stands 4, 5 and 6 only. They go back to those stands, get their goods and leave. The time is 3.30 p.m. At 6 p.m. stands 1, 2 and 3 still have goods wrapped up for Shopper A who has long since left the building. They now realise this and unpack the goods and display them for the next day. The goods though have now been off display for 8 hours, when maybe someone else might have bought them. However the designers have a problem because if they tell customers they can only 'hold' items for 2 hours, this will put people off buying them. At the end of day it is not uncommon for designers to have anything between 10 and 12 items wrapped up for buyers who will not come back to collect them.

Who benefits?

The organiser, since they control the flow of purchases, an important element for them since they take a percentage (around 22%) of sales.

The shopper since they do not have to carry bags around them whilst they shop, but also they can shop with impunity and can discard items without penalty if they change their mind later.

Who doesn't benefit?

The designers as they are left hoping the shopper will return and pick up their goods.

If they don't the designers are left with several items apparently sold but are actually not, and that are also not on display for other potential shoppers either.

Question: Is there a design solution for payment that would be beneficial to all stakeholders?

Events that have a high media factor have a multitude of stakeholders (think of the Academy Awards Ceremony) and often the significance of dealing with, say the PR side of the event, is seen as a more important part of the event than the actual event function. This is because the sponsorship of the event thrives on press exposure and without it the future of the event is probably in jeopardy so ensuring that this section of the event runs perfectly is an essential factor. Freud Communications manage the press for the Orange BAFTAs and their Communications Director, Toby Burnham, feels that, to all intents and purpose, he is the public and media face of the event organisation and logistics since his team orchestrates the entire media experience. This involves designing and managing the entire media side of the event and includes the arrival and exit of celebrities, the interviews and photo ops, the red carpet area, the media access, the in-house filming and the creation of a hi-tech media zone that operates directly parallel to the award ceremony and where all those covering the event can instantly access images, quotes, etc. and feed them into their respective broadcasters in print, TV and radio. If the event fails, and despite not being the event manager as such, it is felt that Freud would be held responsible. So in thinking about stakeholders as providing multi-layered relationships within an event it is possible to begin to see a series of potential interactions occurring that any basic event management process needs to be aware. This in turn suggests that any understanding of events needs to be developed from this broad base.

Organisational overlap

What emerges from this existing research on event types is the overlap both from an organisational point of view and a delivery point of view and so it should be added that many events are not one-dimensional but are multi-layered in terms of the experiences they offer and for a multitude of stakeholders. Hence we reach a situation where events are considered to have multiple layers and consequently many overlaps between each of these. Overlap occurs in many areas of event management, which although different, have similar occasions within them. Shone and Parry (2004) suggest this occurs where personal and organisational events meet (graduation ceremony) or where leisure and cultural events meet (carnival) or where ceremonial occasions within events meet we have overlap of event characteristics and this should be seen as an important point for any such categorisation that involves frequent overlaps between personal/organisational or culture/leisure events. They conclude that:

> *Overlaps should be seen as inevitable rather than exceptional, and any attempt to categorize an event, even by analysing its objectives, its organisers or its origins, will have to take account of this*

Shone and Parry (p. 4)

In their construction of this Shone and Parry provide many useful points that can be further developed. In addition to the above they produce a typology of events that includes those of a small personal nature such as a private dinner or party right up to those of an international nature such as world fairs/expos. This fits in with their notion of overlaps and goes a long way to derive what I would regard as a multi-layered understanding of events. One of the links they also establish is the way many events share commonality of service characteristics, particularly with those services we call hospitality and/or leisure (p. 13). In pointing out these characteristics they inevitably produce more lists in an attempt to characterise the elements that make up an event. So it should be clear that there are types of events, categorisations of events and characteristics of events that can help define them. Events in themselves though are unique, special and provide a unique experience but in order to exist they require something to be planned, managed, organised and run (created, conceived, planned and executed) as there is no event until someone actually plans one and begins to think about how they can deliver it.

Summary

Like all subjects and industries that are emerging, there is a state of flux in the way they are described and understood. So we have a series of interpretations about what an event is which have been refined over a short period of time to reach point where we now have a solid platform from which to begin studying events. The single most essential point to be aware of however is that an event does not simply exist. In this introductory chapter I have given an overview of the main concepts that are used to understand and explain what an events is. What emerges is that, irrespective of the type of or genre of event, someone has to think of a reason for having an event and then someone has to organise it. In other words there has to be an event concept to begin with and from that someone has to then create an event. Even the smallest event has a degree of complexity to it in terms of what will actually occur and who will be involved and it this issue of planning and creating the event that we will look at in the next chapter.

Activity 1.3

1 One of the earlier definitions of events suggested is that they require some aspect of ceremony or ritual to them. Is this really true? What occasions would we class as an event that does not have ritual in them?

Chapter 2
Event management literature

Learning outcomes/objectives

- Be familiar with the academic texts on event management
- Understand the range of approaches to event organisation
- Appreciate that events are the result of designed environments or settings
- Develop awareness of the traditional role of design in event management
- Be aware of the limitations of event analysis
- Develop preparatory understanding of design and experience in relation to events

Introduction

In section one we established that there are various definitions of events and that it is an evolving process with a number of terms in usage although through Shone and Parry, and Silvers we seem to have something that is very close to embracing all aspects of event management. Two prominent themes in relation to these definitions emerge and these are:

• events do not simply just happen they have to be created;
• as a result of the above they provide some kind of experience for stakeholders.

In this chapter we will look at the way the majority of texts discuss event management, building upon this idea of events requiring some creative activity and delivering some type of experience. We will briefly look at the focus of general event management texts, how the impact of events is analysed and consider the extent to which design and related ideas are included in both. At this stage we will only briefly look at experiences as this is discussed in detail in Chapter 5.

Event organisation

One of the next questions to now ask is how events are organised. Many of the textbooks on event management tend to cover similar basic principles with variation in regional examples or contextual language, with the emphasis either on the UK, Australia or America. A reason for pointing this out is that event management textbooks, on the whole, tend to deal with the 'start-to-finish' of organising an event and upon which is predicated the assumption that the event itself will then be a success. This is not surprising for an emerging industry and academic subject, especially one with a strong vocational element, that the main foci of publications has been routed in practice dealing with the processes for planning, organisation and managing of the event. In broad terms this tends to look at the following: economics; planning; communication; concept; human resources; marketing; promotion; sponsorship; finance and budgets; feasibility; project management; monitoring and evaluation; safety, legal and risk; technology; logistics; evaluation; design and checklists (Getz, 1990; Watt, 1998; Masterman, 2004; Silvers, 2004a; Van der Wagen & Carlos, 2004; Allen et al., 2005; Campbell et al., 2005;

Goldblatt, 2005; Tassiopoulous, 2005; Tum et al., 2006). The general scope of these is typified by Watt who has produced a number of publications (1998; with Stayte, 1999) that are very much in the mould of manuals that provide a step-by-step work through of how to manage and organise events, as indicated by the following subtitle of one of those texts which states it is 'a comprehensive overview of event management and organisation' (1999). This highly practitioner guide offers articulate and knowledgeable sections on a 'how-to-do-it' basis, with lots of case studies and examples of forms or checklists. The balance of all the books serves both commercial and public events, and provides practical management tools to help any would be organiser. Campbell et al. (2003) covers similar territory with 'essential tips for organising conferences and events', albeit with an emphasis on conference management. There are also strong operational aspects to the work of Tum et al. (2006), Silvers (2004a) and Sonder (2004). There is similar evidence of an operational and planning application from a number of texts that attempt to expand the event management knowledge base by providing more conceptual and contextual commentary (Shone & Parry, 2004; Yeoman et al., 2004; Allen et al., 2005; Bowdin et al., 2006b) whilst 'the definitive guide to the profession. ... the logistical know-how and theoretical understanding needed to take advantage of the countless opportunities in this growing field' (Goldblatt, 2005) seeks to explain event management within both an operational and professional framework. Allen et al. (2005) 'offer students, and anyone involved in event production, an introduction to the principles associated with planning, managing and staging festivals and special events'. Shone and Parry (2004) provide the 'essential guide for anyone who needs to know how to organise special events: a festival, a celebration, a media launch or an annual fete'. There is also a developing interest in specialist areas of events which promise 'a proven framework to envision, plan, fund and produce sports events' (Supovitz, 2005) or the chance to 'experience the techniques, ideas, strategies and formulas' in entertainment Sonder (2004) and a combination of operational and cultural insight with references to festivals is provided by Yeoman et al. (2004).

This how-to-do-it approach has established a sound platform for events students and practitioners to literally pick up and organise their event by providing clear frameworks from which the practical aspects of event management are understood all supported by numerous examples and insight from around the world. The strength of the practitioner base is clear to see and the content and case studies used are not only educational and informative, they provide a wealth of material that describes events that any would be organisers can draw upon. There are, of course, differences in approaches and emphasis with several sources citing lengthy checklists and forms to illustrate how to get the job done and whilst no two publications are the same there is a feeling of repetition in some of these approaches. Each publication, however, does extend the knowledge base we have on event management and certainly the American publications are developed along slightly stronger profit motives than others. Yet the feeling remains that some, if not all, are treading over each others toes a little bit too often and that the sameness of approach has, to some extent, stifled our further understanding of event management. The pre-occupation is very much from the organisers' point of view, looking inward at what is the best way for an organiser to manage their event, and the processes required to do that. What we can establish from these sources is that events require an organisational framework and planning or management process to help deliver them.

So there is considerable information on how to do it, with guidelines on the process of management and how the implementation of this process will lead to good practice. This does not necessarily mean that the event itself will be successful or, and perhaps more importantly, that it will provide the kind of experience people are looking for. With so much focus upon how-to-do-it models this often results in a simple re-iteration of the process from one publication to the next, albeit with different cultural flavours and different events, but this repetition of form simply seems to become a functional exercise for those practising it and leaves out the more complex problem of how the event will be experienced, a fundamental part of the earlier definitions we looked at. Emerging from this practice driven approach is an analysis of events that follows an equally systematic process.

Event impact

Analysis and study of events is often done from the point of view of evaluation where the most important elements always appear to be logistics, planning and management. Detailed deconstruction of the event environment itself and examination of the relationship between design and experience remains conceptually limited in favour of more practical and pragmatic analysis of events, which often takes the form of operational evaluation. Evaluation is often linked to key performance indicators (Salem et al., 2004; Allen et al., 2005) used in conjunction with criteria based around SMART objectives (Watt, 1990). Salem et al. (2004) that provide an overview of events management and use a 'performance management model as a framework for the systematic identification and deconstruction of four major stages of event development' namely: decision; detailed planning; implementation; evaluation (Yeoman et al., 2004, p. 14). The author's do though acknowledge the role of catering as an important element in the event experience and recognises that the 'theme is an umbrella to unify the final event image' (p. 19). They also point out that the event venue or location is 'of primary significance to the overall success or failure of the event and should compliment the theme of the event' (p. 20). As a performance appraisal system it addresses many key points but has less to say in the way of how some of these elements that make up the system can be used to analyse the actual experience created. The same applies to any deeper insight into event design and its evaluation or analysis, although there is the possibility that the forms of event evaluation suggested may do this, but it is not explained how they should or could.

Other sources seek to understand the impact of events (Chernushenko, 1994; Getz, 1997; Hall, 1997; Roche, 2000; Gratton & Henry, 2001; Shibli & Gratton, 2001; Berridge, 2004; Shone & Parry, 2004; Allen et al., 2005; Bowdin et al., 2006b) and acknowledge that events have an impact upon society at both the micro and macro level and most take the view that this constitutes a shared experience, although explanations of the experience are limited. More often than not this study is broadly understood in terms of economic, political and social impacts (Bowdin et al., 2001; Shone & Parry, 2004; Allen et al., 2005; Tyrrell & Ismail, 2005) and where the events are seen as part of a regeneration strategy (Roche, 2000; Gratton & Henry, 2001; Hall, 2005). Sport has attracted attention in this respect where the direct consequences of cities bidding for and holding major games (Emery, 2001) and the legacies of sports event policy (Roche, 2000; Masterman, 2004) have been evaluated. Such impact is carried out in many ways but mostly results in factual data providing evidence of the way an event has quantitatively impacted upon an area. The normal method of assessing this is using multiplier analysis (Getz, 1997; Hall, 1997; Crompton & Lee, 2000), which converts the total expenditure in the host city to the amount of income retained. Usually this focus is on areas such as: new facilities and their legacy, sports programmes, tourist activity including visitor spend whilst the event is on, employment and hotel occupancy. What emerges from these studies of event impacts is that they tend to address the positives and negatives of events via measurable outcomes that place high importance on financial impacts (Allen et al., 2005) and by contrast provide little exploration of impacts that are less clearly measurable. The need to assess the contribution that events make in this less tangible area is recognised (Hall, 1997; Allen et al., 2005) but to develop such an analysis requires a narrative as opposed to a statistical approach (Allen et al., 2005). However, it is not at all clear what these narrative tools might be and what they might look at and it is certainly not evidenced regularly in practice or analysis of events. So it raises the question of where we might look in order to begin an attempt to develop this analysis. Limitations of narrative analysis may be a result of little uniform understanding or integration of two key areas of events: design and experience.

Events and design

In many cases the relationship between events and design is straightforward to appreciate and at first glance would apply to things such as props, décor, food, backdrop, floral arrangement, lighting and sound. These are the aspects of event design that we can readily acknowledge because most event literature categorises these elements as residing in the domain of design even if the act of design is not specifically acknowledged. A useful summary of the general consensus on design is provided in a glossary of terms by Sonder who states that design is the incorporation of a themed message along with audiovisual, entertainment, and musical elements' (Sonder, 2004, p. 411). This appears to preclude design from having any other function or role within events other than when an event is based around a theme such as Alice in Wonderland, Peter Pan, The Amazon or where entertainment is present. In reviewing how design is applied to events it is quite often viewed as an add-on, an extra ingredient that gives the event that something special as in the case with Sonder who relates design purely to theming. It is not at all uncommon for design to be seen as 'a bit of dressing', something that is added towards the end of the planning period. Even something added to brighten the place up a bit is still design, even if it is not always acknowledged as such. However, if we think about the event as the blank canvas, is this all there really is to event design a little bit of extra pazzazz, a little bit of colour, a little bit of lighting and some party food? Does this tell us that the role of design is, in fact, seen as a peripheral activity? The difficulty with this perspective is that it doesn't really help us to understand anything about event design.

It simply observes that design, of some kind, has taken place to produce some kind of display at the event. It doesn't tell us anything about design principles or techniques that may have been applied but more significantly it doesn't provide us with any framework of reference so that we can make even a cursory attempt to analyse such design features.

Is it therefore the case, ask Brown and James (2004), that the very heart and soul of events has been neglected along with the concepts of events and their design to be replaced by a top-down approach to management that sees delivery as little more than a purely logistical and organisational exercise? Within this observation lies an implicit critique that modern event management is becoming systems based, run along timeline schedules where risk management, appraisals and strategic plans are the essential factor that will deliver a successful event and as a consequence of this 'there will also be, quite possibly, a one-dimensional event that lacks the inspired something that makes an event truly great' (Brown & James, 2004, p. 63).

> *'Event management is simply, but essentially, the design and management of an event. Unfortunately the structure of the typical event management organisation, and the job description for the typical event manager, fail to include the "design" component. "Design" is excluded even from the descriptive title "event manager"'.*
>
> Brown and James (2004, p. 54)

EMBOK'S domain of design

What though is event management if it is more than simply an operational top-heavy process and to what extent does concept and design feature in its study and practice? According to Silver's updated EMBOK (Events Management Body of Knowledge) structure design should be regarded as one of the five core domains of event management alongside administration, marketing, risk and operations. The EMBOK project offers one of the strongest advocates for the inclusion of design and the domain itself consists of:

- Catering design
- Content design
- Entertainment design
- Environment design
- Production design
- Programme design
- Theme design

Design here is seen as a critical tool for event management as it relates directly to development of the event concept and experience and enables the event manager to envision and implement the event. As such event managers should see themselves as 'experiential engineers' who are able to piece together the overall picture of the event. They should regard themselves as 'packaging and managing an experience' from start to finish and imagine all aspects and details of that experience (Silvers, 2004b).

Whilst this list is more than welcome for it highlights designs importance, there is an argument that planning the event itself needs to be treated as a total designed experience since it is, in effect, a problems solving activity. There is nothing in the domain structure that suggests risk has to be designed or indeed marketing either. This though might be an unfair criticism since EMBOK is a work in progress and unlike the other four main domains, the one on design is not fully complete with a list of associated topics. It does represent though an important step in recognising the central core activity of design within event management and could be said to provide the distinctive domain that marks events out from, say, project management.

Theming

In attempting to further consider and analyse design's role within event literature the evidence suggests that it is recognised but there is no standard understanding of what it actually means or what role it should play. One of the most significant points to emerge is that there exists fairly limited insight and analysis of the designed environment in favour of more descriptive approaches of its use and application. Design is sometimes seen as a category of its own, other times as a subset of something else, often as an added extra a bit that is tagged on at the end or sometimes it is ignored. A term often used to describe an event is a 'once in a lifetime' experience. What however does this actually mean for events and how can we begin to study the aspects of an event that make it once a lifetime. Setting aside the social context, that is the chance to visit a major event that provides this experience because of say the costs of attending or the rarity of it, the term is also linked to the wow factor, that aspect of any event that makes it unique and special. Mostly we then tend to get descriptions of this content that, ergo, must result in the above being attained. A simple description whilst serving a purpose does need to be allied with a more insightful analysis of the components that make-up this special event environment and experience. One way of considering design is to think of an event as starting out with four bare walls or empty space especially if outdoors and then start to envisage how this empty space will be developed and what decisions have to be taken to achieve that. Is it reasonable to say that from this point on every decision made to fill that space and create the environment or setting is, in fact, a design-based decision since every choice made will affect the experience of the event?

Design: index references

We can examine the significance placed upon design by looking at chapter and content headings or sieving through the index sections of relevant textbooks. An index offers an alphabetical listing of names and topics along with page numbers where they are discussed. Indexes, however, are a variable in many books in terms of their comprehensiveness but they at least provide an indicator. Looking at the main core general texts on event management produces such a varied result for the inclusion of design in either chapter heading or index (Table 2.1). As we can also see from the table, experiences feature even less in the indexes although some (notably Shone & Parry, 2004; Bowdin et al., 2006b) do include event experiences as an index. We can see that in some cases both design and experience does not feature at all in either chapter heading or index. This doesn't present the whole picture however since some of those including index references have only one or two pages or discussion points, whilst those that apparently do not cover design, for example Goldblatt, do in fact discuss design at some length. One of the problems seems to be that very few really explain or analyse what design actually means or how it is applied/practiced, the tendency instead is rather to simply describe the design setting. Experiences, as suggested elsewhere in this book, are largely underconceptualised in most of the publications and get little or no meaningful discussion as a result.

As a consequence of this several terms are used under which design is included. Staging is the most commonly used term and design often features under the guise of décor. The picture, however, is confusing since several texts do not specifically discuss design, but discuss activities that will be classed as design, under different subject headings.

Such references appear in relation to conceptualising (Goldblatt, 2005); entertainment experience (Silvers, 2004b); staging (Allen et al., 2005); event design (Yeoman et al., 2004; Allen et al., 2005; Bowdin et al., 2006b);

Table 2.1 Index references design.

Author	Chapter (design related)	Index	
		Design	Experience
Allen et al.	Staging: Theming and design	Yes	No
Yeoman et al.	Event design	Yes	No
Van der Wagen	Concept and design staging	Yes	No
Bowdin	Staging	Yes	Yes
Watt	No	No	No
Goldblatt	No	No	No
Shone	No	No	Yes
Silvers	Staging experience	Yes (Décor)	No
Specialist texts			
Campbell (conferences)	No	No	No
Masterman (sports)	No	No	No
Malouf (design)	Yes	Yes	No
Monroe (design)	Yes	Yes	No

ambience (Shone & Parry, 2004); creativity (Sonder, 2004); theming and event design (Allen et al., 2005); designing and decorating (Monroe, 2006); props and design (Malouf, 1999); co-ordinating the environment (Silvers, 2004a). As we can see from the list there is quite a range of topics under which design can be attributed. This uneven approach is also reflected in descriptions of how it influences events. In terms of what we might regard as design-based activity Van der Wagen (2004) writes that 'there are numerous elements that need to be considered in developing an event concept. They include the purpose of the event, the event theme, the venue, the audience, available resources, the timing of the event and the skills of the team' (p. 20). Design is implicit in the characteristics of such as ambience, service and personal interactions that help form a part of the event, and programming the environment often holds the key to successful event outcomes (Shone & Parry, 2004). Ambience and service 'is one of the most important to the outcome. An event with the right ambience can be a huge success. An event with the wrong ambience can be a huge failure' (Shone & Parry, p. 15). The question of how the right ambience is designed appears less easy to answer and is not given any great degree of attention. What is apparent though is that in differentiating one event from another it is possible to see features such as ambience and interaction as some of the key distinctions between one event and another and indeed between events and other activities. The practicalities of creating ambient settings is discussed by several sources, all of whom look at it from a design specific approach or, as in the case of Silvers, place it as the central core of event management practice (Malouf, 1999; Brown & James, 2004; Sonder, 2004; Monroe, 2006; Silvers, 2004b).

So briefly here, to illustrate, we will look Goldblatt (2005) who confusingly has neither chapter nor index on design, but who advocates a design blueprint as one of the keys for success and stresses at the outset the importance of creating the environment:

> 'When creating the environment the special events professional must again return to the basic needs of the guests. The final design must satisfy these needs to become successful. Lighting, space, movement, décor, acoustics and even the seemingly mundane concerns as rest rooms all affect the comfort of the guest and so play vital roles on creating a successful environment'.
>
> Goldblatt (2005, p. 65)

This amounts to a reasonable listing of points that need to be considered when creating event environments. It suggests that the decisions made about what will fill the event space should be design led and that the creation of what might be called the active space is absolutely crucial to the success of any event and that the range of factors in need of consideration in this space requires comprehensive attention to detail. Such detail is what ultimately creates the environment, and it is from that environment that the experience of the event emerges. The decisions that are made about how a particular space will be used manifests directly into the kind of experience anyone attending the event will get. It indicates an emphasis upon event guests and suggests that any environment is for them and them alone. If you are not a guest at an event then what are you? That is where the discussion on stakeholders and the multi-layered nature of the event experience begins. Goldblatt is one of the most consistent advocates of the need to 'create an environment', stemming in no part from his original assertion that event managers are 'merchants of dream'. He devotes several pages to 'design; blueprint for success', drawing our attention to mind mapping, flow and tempo and raises, however briefly the idea of psychographics aiding our understanding of consumers requirements. There is also a pertinent section on audiovisual effects that offers a strong list of equipment and materials that can create special effects. He further recognises that the way any environment is created does provide for the unique settings that are attributed to different events and in doing so raises the awareness about the type of decisions that are made in constructing this environment. He identifies a number of key elements that need consideration in this process:

- Soundscaping
- Visual cues
- Smell
- Taste
- Blending
- Amenities
- Reception areas
- Function areas
- Innovative sites
- Edible displays
- Decoration
- Interactive décor
- Parades and float design
- Themes
- Environmental sensitivity
- Timeline
- Security

Oddly these are not always aligned with detailed examples of their use, or any further explorations of the types of experiences that might be subsequently created. This is a common characteristic of academic study of events in general, to produce checklists of what could be included without necessarily any accompanying explanation of how they should be used or what they will produce. There are similar lists provided by several of the event texts previously mentioned, some of which relate in some way to design. Despite the recognition however there remains minimal conceptual insight into the environments, interactions, occasions and settings that are being created. In a way we might expect this to be the case since the scope of most work is general event management and there is a large body of material to cover. But considering that most texts are underpinned by a definition that views events as something created and unique, we can surely expect more of an exploration of how creation of the environment is linked to, firstly, the understanding of event interaction based on the symbols and artefacts of design in use and, secondly, the meaning they provide for those interactions.

Case study 2.1

Star Trek Exhibition

Science Museum, London

Focus of case study

This is an introductory case study and includes some terms and references that are more fully explained in later chapters. It's purpose here is to present an initial illustration of how some aspects of design create experiential occasions, both good and bad.

The Star Trek experience was communicated as an event that connected science with popular culture. It was presented as a cultural event, significant because it was the first time that official Star Trek memorabilia had been on display outside of the USA. Local press and media carried arresting stories of how this truly was a 'special event', that no expense had been spared to relate the science fiction of the series to science fact, hence its appearance at the Science Museum. In amongst the TV show artefacts and memorabilia serious questions were raised and scientifically answered such as 'is it really possible to be beamed from one location to another?' The answer by the way is no. The London Evening Standard newspaper carried a report on the search for 'trekkies', people who knew so much about Star Trek that they would be employed as event assistants to help out the public during their visits. They would be animators, guiding and interacting with visitors, helping them understand some of the science on display and, above all else, answering questions on Star Trek. The message being transmitted here was that this was going to be a truly spectacular knowledge experience, a 'once in a lifetime' chance to see actual Star Trek artefacts. Another important aspect in this process was that there was an admission fee, in this case enhancing the special qualities and placing value on the display since entry to the Science Museum itself was actually free of charge. Located in the South West wing of the museum, it was clearly cordoned off from the rest of the free exhibition spaces indicating this was a section where a special display was being held.

The net effect of this as one researcher observed on a feedback sheet was that 'it made me feel special as I rode the lift up to the paying booth and entered the exhibition through a Perspex portal. I felt like I was entering the final frontier'. For this visitor the initial experience on arrival was a fantasy based positive one. After this point though that began to wither in ever increasing amounts. Test questions posed to the 'expert assistants' repeatedly failed to get answers, and the chronology of the exhibition (its timeline) was very haphazard. One of the most annoying features of the design was the seemingly unconcerned notion that sound and vision from several different sources carrying totally different material could be somehow 'connected' almost like a super road junction. Another researcher reported:

> *At one point it was possible to stand and watch the screen on Enterprises' space journeys whilst at the same time have the voiceovers from two other parts of the exhibition interfere with the sound. If that wasn't enough then strobe lights cut right across the main screen. It was impossible to either see or hear what was happening.*

This inability to separate different sections of the exhibition was really quite appalling but there were two further problems. The ultimate iconic image of any Star Trek is the 'bridge', the place where past Star Trek Captains have sat and exchanged pleasantries with aliens from around the galaxy or set in motion a warp speed jump to a far-flung destination. Resplendent in all its glory was a fairly detailed mock up of the original Star Trek Series Bridge. Now this, to many visitors, was the focal point of the whole experience. This was a chance to 'interact' with the event, a rare opportunity to feel as if you were somehow involved in the whole process. All visitors entering this section probably wanted to do the same thing. That was to walk up to the captains' chair, sit in it and say whatever immortal words they felt were appropriate such as 'engage', 'Scotty, can we get more power' or 'activate shields'. And of course have their friend or colleague take their picture. It was a pivotal symbolic moment within the experience.

However, the chance to interact in this way was denied. Guarding the 'bridge' were two burly 'assistants' (probably a better description is security personnel) and a very strong cable that cordoned off the whole area, especially around the captain's chair.

Any attempt to enter the bridge was denied sometimes quite vigorously and the disappointment on each visitors face was clear to see as this rare chance to physically sit in the chair and pretend was prevented. It was clear from the layout of the environment that the bridge occupied a central locational point in the experience.

On top of this the 'marshalling' of this section, and indeed other sections, was one of interjection to encourage visitors to 'move along quickly'. It was not about enlightenment as previously suggested. Whilst events of this kind often have their order of procession it is perfectly rational to want to back track on oneself and spend a few more minutes looking over a particular artefact or information point. Especially so where science and technology are being discussed. This though was deemed out of order and visitors were actively prevented from revisiting a section they had previously been through. This one-way traffic system meant exactly that, even if you were walking. In fact, opportunities to pause for reflection were few and the assistants were very keen to speed visitors through to the end. This rush to the finish had a purpose and it lay with, the merchandising opportunity.

'It seemed as if the whole purpose of this (event) was to get us through as quickly as possible into the shop, where of course we could spend as much time as possible choosing what to buy'.

Here were the wonders of modern commercialism in the form of cards, mugs, pens, games, lights, model toys and replica federation outfits including Vulcan ears. On every shelf was a sign 'never previously available outside of the USA'. Oh what joy for the prospective shopper, the chance to buy something exclusive, rare and not available to anyone in the UK who hadn't been to the exhibition? The general impression of these signs was exclusivity and rarity, but also they were placed in such a way as to give the impression that all of the goods here were on sale for the first time in this country. That would have been fine, if it were true but the simple fact was that a lot of items could be bought in the UK.

It is disappointing that many sources seem themselves to take up the idea of the wow factor as being impossible to quantify or describe. For it rather begs the question about how we know or learn about event design if we are unable to make any sense of it. In order to shed some light at the very least on the implications of event design, there must be some attempt made to not only describe the setting and environment, but also to analyse and explain, and finally make some judgement on it. At the end of it all we need to know whether the event experience worked or not but we need to know how it worked as well, and this requires more than a simple description of the setting. In order to progress our understanding of events and about what takes place within the event environment we require a more structured study of it, to understand, explain and analyse the event as it happens, as it unfolds, as it occurs and the experience it produces.

At present we are in a situation where very few analyses of events attempt to deconstruct the event in this way and explore its meaning or impact via either a design or experiential agenda. There is the vague association of the 'shared experience' as a factor in social and cultural impact as suggested previously, but this is not consistently explored. What remains are a number of descriptions of events where both design and experience appear to be fundamental to the analysis but where, in fact, the analysis undertaken is limited. In order to achieve this analysis means considering the many features that are incorporated into the event to produce the environment and it also means that there should be a way of being able to reflect upon how that environment has then performed. In this way we could regard this in the theatrical sense by seeing the event as a play unfolding before us and judging the success it has in telling the (event) story. The creation and design of the setting then provides the contextual (theatrical) backdrop for the performance. The question of performance is not meant to indicate a measurement via performance indicators that traditionally would draw in financial indicators. It is meant to suggest that, as with any created setting or structure, it needs to perform in the way it was planned and the experience it provides needs to be understood. To successfully analyse the performance of a setting requires an analysis of the event concept as a minimum starting point. This does not mean though that we have to always 'know' the exact concept underpinning the event. Whilst there is no doubt having insight into the rationale and event planning concept and design would help, we can reflect on these simply as observers or guests, since that is what most of those in attendance as guests are likely to do.

Summary

The main focus of existing event management texts is systems management led resulting in a highly functional approach to event planning and management. Despite the definitions of events indicating that designed environments and experience outcomes are important features, very few studies grapple with these in a conceptual way, with experience being the most under studied element of an event. Design is more widely recognised, but is grouped under various headings and categories so that its status within event management is not uniform (unlike say risk assessment) and as a result is under conceptualised. In some cases design warrants little or no mention whilst experience is barely acknowledged. Event analysis tends to be more concerned with measurable indicators as the default way of evidencing an events success. This however limits our understanding of events to a one-dimensional outlook and fails to consider the role design plays in creating event environments and the event experiences. Many 'analyses' tend to be little more than descriptions of events and consequently fail to establish the role of the minutiae of factors that go into events.

To begin to understand more about what occurs within events requires consideration of the following aspects of event management that are framed by what I would call the experiential occasions within an event. Firstly, there needs to be a real insight into the whole design decisions made for any event and this includes initial communication strategies and the range of features used to create an environment; secondly we need to be able to study events not only at the macro (impact) level but at a micro level and to look at individual elements and segments within the event so that we can explain what decisions result in the actual experience of the event.

Activity 2.1

Use the design headings below from EMBOK and explain how each element is integral for any specific event:

- Catering design
- Content design
- Entertainment design
- Environment design
- Production design
- Programme design
- Theme design

Chapter 3
Events industry

Learning outcomes/objectives

- Appreciate the wide range of activities that is the 'events industry'
- Understand the impetus/interest in events simulated by global events and celebrations
- Be aware of some of the market facts on different event types
- Be aware of the size and scale of certain events types via market and commercial data

Introduction

The considerable body of academic material presenting an overview of the events industry is on the increase and such activity points to the emergence of an industry attracting not only academic and educational interest but renewed business and commercial interest as well. In the previous sections I have outlined some of the main ideas on defining and explaining events and the organisational processes that are used in planning and managing events. In this chapter I will briefly draw attention to what I see as the main focus of these texts simply to illustrate what are the general areas of interest in event management and to demonstrate the range of activities that encompass the events industry.

The industry

Readers seeking a more comprehensive account of events should look to the following publications. The range and variety of activities that are classified as events is well covered (Watt, 1999; Bowdin et al., 2001, 2006b; Shone & Parry, 2004; Allen et al., 2002, 2005; Goldblatt, 2005 (2002)). These authors explore not only the types of occasions that are defined as events but also the categories, typologies, characteristics and contexts that can be used to understand events. They also typify events through size and scale to present a set of common categories for understanding them. Shone and Parry (2004) refer to the differences in event complexity and uncertainty to produce a typology of all types of events. Allen et al. (2002, 2005) looking at festival and special event management point out events being characterised as, but not exclusively, either mega-events (Olympic Games), hallmark-events (Rio Carnival) and major-events (Australian Open Tennis) whilst Bowdin et al. (2001) adds a range of event types to include sport, cultural and business events. The significance of events in society and the emergence of an events industry and an events profession are featured in (Bowdin et al., 2001; Goldblatt, 2005). Elsewhere other interest focuses on the role and purpose of events in society as explored through event impact and the role events play in economic regeneration (Gratton & Henry, 2001) and the market demand for events (Shone & Parry, 2004). Attention has also been turned to the specific sectors of the industry such as conferences and conventions (Rogers, 2003), festivals (Yeoman et al., 2004), sports (Masterman, 2004) and meetings (Allen et al., 2005). Finally, events have become a subject for understanding in the context of culture, globalisation and modernity in which events such as the Olympics are highly visible as part of dense social calendar of public events (Roche, 2000). Ultimately we are presented with a picture of an expanding interest in events as a subject of study, a maturing profession and as a developing industry sector in society.

The 'events industry' is a growing global business as the role and impact of events in society is becoming more recognised than ever (Shone & Parry, 2004; Allen et al., 2005; Bowdin et al., 2006b), as an academic subject area, as a tool for promoting business, as a leisure time activity, as an income generator, as source for urban regeneration, as a feature of tourist destinations, and as a career path. Its emergence over the past decade has been described as 'vibrant', as events have grown in terms of their number, diversity and popularity (Arcodia & Reid, 2004). As Allen et al. (2005) state 'today, events are central to our culture as perhaps never before'. The central importance of events has been stimulated by numerous social, political and cultural developments that have given impetus to the emergence of events as an industry, career, academic subject and a leisure and business activity. One of the most identifiable milestones propelling the event industry forward has been the Millennium Celebrations. A true universal celebration, the millennium showcased the skills of event management in every country in the world from small islands in Polynesia to the great urban metropolises of London, Beijing and Paris. It also led to many amateurs as well as professionals organising their own brand of millennium razzmatazz. In expectation of this combined funding from the Department of Culture, Media and Sport, The Millennium Commission, London Arts Board and London Borough Grants resulted in the production of a 'Millenniums Celebrations Toolkit', almost like an idiots guide to how events should be organised. An outstanding success the toolkit was given away free to thousands of Londoners who felt it necessary to 'put on something' for the millennium. Formal, informal, large, small, free, paying, indoors, outdoors, friends, relatives no matter what the size or scope of the event this was a landmark celebration for just about everyone the world over to ensure that this unique moment in time was memorable for all concerned.

The millennium

These series of events in different cultures worldwide also highlighted the particular ways in which each cultures or nation chose to celebrate its millennium, bringing to the fore design attributes and symbols of nations that would mark out the millennium experience for a nation.

In London a square mile of the city was closed off to traffic from mid-afternoon until mid-morning the following day and the great historic bridges spanning the Thames served as a backdrop to the inevitable fireworks display. Viewers tuning to CNN would have witnessed spectacular celebrations across the world as each timeline left the old millenium behind and entered the new one.

These worldwide celebrations at the end (or beginning) of the millennium which turned into, via television, a global unity festival, traversing timelines and cultures in a way no previous celebration had managed and to which every country was invited and attended showcased the skills of event management. The fever of celebration spread downwards (or upwards depending on your social viewpoint) as public money counted in $ millions was pumped into preparing a spectacular socio-cultural event that every nations citizens received an invitation to. The build-up to the millennium was unique, as it demonstrated, probably for the first time at least on a global scale, the support governments in general were now giving to events on both a national and local scale. In the UK funding for community projects dwarfed previous aid of this kind and £100 million from the National Lottery Millennium Commission was gifted to the Millennium Festival that included an estimated 2000 events across the UK (Bowdin et al., 2006b). Millennium funding attracted bids from and for countless diverse projects and groups as well as individuals.

'One of the largest events was the Beacon Millennium Project, where 1400 beacons were lit across the UK on 31 December 1999, providing the focus for community celebrations. Further initiatives included investment of over £1.3 billion in around 200 new buildings, environmental projects, visitor attractions and a total of £200 million provided as 40,000 grants, or 'Millennium Awards' for individuals to put their ideas into action for their communities'.

Bowdin, McPherson and Flinn (2006a)

The millennium bore witness to Roche's sense of events becoming a part of the global community and acting as 'important elements in the orientation of national societies to international or global society' (2000, p. 7). Was there competition between nations for the biggest, best, most funded, most daring, most articulate, most attended, most egregious support for millennium events and projects? If that was the case, the UK was not going to be left behind and the much maligned 'Millennium Dome' cost in the region of £900 million simply to exist for one calendar year and was as one of Britain's ways of celebrating the millennium attracting over 10 million visitors, far more than any other UK attraction, or indeed event in 2000. In turn a further 2 million people memorably took to the closed streets of central London to ring in the dawn of the new century. In terms of celebration the size, scale and cultural impact offered both national and international publics an experience of something that was unique. The same could also be said for Sydney, Paris, Beijing, New York, Tokyo, Berlin, Kuala Lumpur and many other major cities around the world. News bulletins around the globe devoted hours of coverage to the emerging millennium as the international timeline heralded in successive celebrations.

> *'From a sprinkle of South Pacific islands to the skyscrapers of the Americas, across the pyramids, the Parthenon and the temples of Angkor Wat, humanity stood on the threshold of a new millennium Friday, linked by satellite technology for the most closely watched midnight in history. The world celebration was tempered, however, by unease over Earth's vulnerability to terrorism and its dependence on computer technology, but by morning, the parties ended, and the dawning of 2000 brought relief that the world was spared acts of terrorism and saw only very minor, and very few, Y2K computer glitches. The celebrations had been large and small, from New York's Times Square, where the official attendance estimate was some 2 million, to the 100 climbers who toasted atop Mount Kilimanjaro in Africa (www.wndu.com)'.*

It is through these and other such spectacular occasions that the presence, interest and impact of events has been generated at international, national and local level.

The Olympics

If the millennium itself were not enough, the year 2000 then hosted what is now regarded as the most impressive Olympics to date, those held in Sydney, Australia. Perhaps the most feel good games of all, Sydney hosted an event of breathtaking scale from the opening ceremony in Sydney harbour to the final closing speeches (White, 2006). Generating in excess of A$7 billion increase to Australia's economy the Olympics was seen by almost 85% of the world's population. More significantly the Olympics, as Roche (2000) has pointed out are in essence localised events with the capacity to carry and project global cultural meanings through their character as tourist and media events. In other words, to simplify what is a quite complex discussion, the meaning and images associated with the Olympics are diffused via tourism and the media, presenting the opportunity for a host city and nation to present itself to a global market and in turn generate both short- and long-term economic benefits of an event via the flow of tourists. Events like this have a cultural value and can take a cultural form, a point that is discussed in some length and which in turn contributes to popular culture (Roche, 2000). The success of the Olympics in achieving this has not always been evident as can be seen by not only the negative financial impacts of past games (most notably Montreal in 1976) but also by the stature and number of candidate cities bidding to host the games. Between 1964 and 1998 no more than four candidates bid each time for the games, and in 1980 and 1984 the numbers were one and two, respectively. For the 2004 games, hosted by Athens, there were 11 candidates that included Rio, Rome, Istanbul, Buenos Aires and Stockholm. For the recently awarded 2012 games the candidate list was impressive in number (11) and in quality with the final selection being made from London, Paris, Moscow, New York and Madrid. In a UK context the bid itself raised the profile of events more than ever and raised awareness of events skills as the bid committee attempted to show the country and the world that it had the support, infrastructure and personnel to deliver the largest event in the world. The skills debate alone featured regularly in industry publications such as Event Magazine, but the media in general helped create a higher profile with their coverage of the plans for the Olympic sites.

The importance of the Olympics was underlined by the International Olympic Committee's (IOC) report on viewing figures for the 2004 Athens Games. Speaking at the 15th edition of Sportel, the International Sports Television Convention, the President of the IOC, Jacques Rogge, announced that the Athens 2004 Olympic Games global broadcast broke all records. Rogge confirmed that with over 300 channels broadcasting the Olympic Games to 220 countries and territories, 35,000 hours of dedicated coverage (2000 per day), an increased number of 3.9 billion people (unduplicated) accessing the images of the Games, and a dramatic increase in live and prime-time coverage, this was the strongest Olympic broadcast ever. This represented a staggering increase in viewing hours of 50% compared to Sydney 2000, with each European watching in average 14 hours of the Athens Games. On top of that the social impact of the Olympics was at the forefront of discussions, amidst concerns that any legacy left would leave a beneficial not detrimental imprint for the host. The plans and designs that have been put forward showing how the 2012 Olympics will look and feel, are a concerted attempt to project the type of experience participants and visitors will get when they visit. For example, London made a big feature out of the fact it intended to locate the athlete's village within the Olympic Park itself, a novel approach not seen in previous Olympics.

Conferences and exhibitions

One part of the events industry in full bloom is the conference and exhibition sector which has seen a significant list of new venues being built to cater for the 'global conference market' and which demonstrates a significant amount of financial investment. Rogers (2003) states that 'since the 1960s there has been a steadily increasing investment in the whole infrastructure that supports conferences, meetings and related events, an investment which accelerated into rapid growth during the 1990s' (p. 4). Fuelling this emergence of an industry even further was the activities of consultant Grant Thornton and the formation of a Mayoral Commission who reported on the feasibility of a proposed multi-million pound state-of-the-art International Convention Centre (ICC) in London. Initial findings from their research suggested that up to £27 million of work is turned away each year because London does not have a 3–5000 capacity convention centre. Most operators within the industry believe it is not a question of if the centre is going to be built, just a question of when, where and how much it will cost. The argument of market viability, that there was sufficient enough events business to make the centre worthwhile, has long since been accepted despite the plethora of medium-sized venues that exist both through multi-purpose venues such as Excel, hotels (Novotel) and sports venues (Twickenham). The lack of a major facility in the capital is in stark contrast to the situation not only in the rest of the world but also in the rest of UK where new conference and convention facilities have been built. Over £200 million has been invested in the past decade in Plymouth, Sheffield, Manchester, Newcastle and Belfast. In Australia five new centres have been built since 1999 and major investments have taken place in North America, Asia, the Pacific rim and in East European countries (Rogers, 2003). Conference tourism is now accepted as a global industry as evidenced by one of its major trade shows, The European Incentive and Business Travel and Meetings Exhibition (EIBTM), which between 1988 and 2002 witnessed a rise in countries exhibiting from 54 to 100 and saw its visitor numbers almost double (Rogers, 2003). Indeed a Keynote Report into the Conferences and Exhibitions Market (2004), identified as much the market and trend for events in this area:

'Reed Exhibitions Ltd, the market leader in the exhibitions industry, provides the most succinct summary of the exhibitions industry: "Exhibitions are a major contributor to local and national economies and play a key role in industrial and commercial development, particularly in emerging markets. They provide a shop window for regional

*and national industry, stimulate foreign investment in industry and infrastructure,
and facilitate technology transfer. They also create employment and generate direct
spending on hotels, restaurants, transport and local business"'.*

Keynote (2004)

It seems like the market for events and event-related activity is indeed buoyant. Along side this there has been the continued growth and development of organisations and associations who represent the interests of events people and companies. These cover almost everything to do with events from conferences and meetings to suppliers and there are now organisations the world over representing the interests of individuals and groups involved in event management. For example, in the USA the relatively newly created Convention Industry Council has 31 member organisations who represent more than 98,000 individuals as well as 15,000 firms and properties involved in the meetings, conventions and exhibitions industry. Smaller societies are also showing an increase in memberships with International Special Events Society (ISES) UK attracting its 200th member in 2006.

On the back of this there is now evidence of a foundation for a bonafide industry that represents a shift in emphasis for events that in the past would have otherwise been seen as part of more established sectors such as hospitality and tourism. It is though difficult to actually pin down the size of this industry simply because events do form a part of so many other sectors and people working on events may not classify their selves as being in the event industry. Here, I am thinking of people who might work for charities, PR companies, large corporations, design consultants, staffing or security firms whose companies main area of work may not be events. By its very nature event organisation itself is complex and there are likely to be lots of crossover between people working in different sectors but applying their skills to events. The education sector, as we shall see below, is growing but there is not a history of academic qualifications for events and so the vast majority of employers and employees currently working in events who have academic qualifications have entered the industry from diverse subject areas such as business, law, marketing, PR, accountancy, hospitality, tourism, leisure and design. A big challenge faced by the industry is that, irrespective of what is defined and written about events by academics and practitioners, unless this is reflected in conventions for classifying data, then the data on events will not be collected in a recognisable form (Bowdin, McPherson & Flinn, 2006a). Consequently hard data on the overall size and scale of the industry is difficult to obtain because of this and because of the variety of sectors in the event industry. What information is available is usually a result of research into other specific industries such as sport, marketing, hospitality, tourism and that, often indirectly provides data on events.

Importance of events

The importance of events as a vehicle for tourism was exemplified by Visit London co-ordinating 100 free events in the summer/autumn of 2005 designed specifically to boost the visitor economy in London (Fletcher, 2005). One sector of the industry seeing considerable development is the exhibitions sector. An IRN surrey showed that between 2001 and 2003 overseas visitors to the UK in this market increased by 60% (Event Magazine, 2004). This appears to have continued since then as demonstrated through research conducted by KPMG for the Association of Exhibition Organisers and the Association of Event Venues that reported the industry was worth £9.3 billion with direct employment of almost 56,000 people, with indirect employment estimated to be 136,000. With more than 1800 exhibitions taking place each year the attraction to visitors is great and boosts the industry's image to the extent that UK shows bring in 17 million people each year and in the region of 270,000 different exhibiting companies. Accruing from such visits is expenditure over £750 million on hotel rooms, travel and food and drink (Fletcher, 2005). Such activity is not though confined to the UK, Europe has a whole now has over 15,000,000 m^2 of exhibition space and a market share of 57%. According to the Association of German Trade Fairs Industry (AUMA), following a slump in 2001 that reflected a decline in general in the German economy, international exhibitors has risen by 2.5% from 2004 with over 2.2 million visitors, an all time high, registering for 154 events (Bond, 2005). France too is in the grip of event growth with the number of visitors to consumer shows increasing by 2.4% from 2003 to 2004 and with the Port De Versailles boasting 220,000 m^2 of space it is one of the largest in Europe and provides France with some of its biggest trade shows with The World Car Show, attracting a staggering 1,447,753 visitors on its last run in 2004. There is also clear sign of the globalised product becoming stronger as overseas exhibitors to UK trade shows continues to rise at both International CONFEX and the business exhibition Spring Fair. The latter attracted almost 4000 exhibitors, 8000 overseas buyers and the largest contingent of exhibitors from North America to date

(Fletcher, March 2006). The scale of some events demonstrates their value as economic contributors, providing employment across numerous related industries. Catering is one area that benefits greatly since food is a component of the majority of events. The internationally renowned Chelsea Flower Show requires food for over 20,000 people per day from a daily attendance of 40,000 whilst Sodexho Prestige, who won Events Magazine's caterer of the year award 2004, provide catering services at Royal Ascot through the employment of 4500 temporary staff, 150 managers, 170 chefs serving 115,000 covers per day. The Ultimate Experience, a corporate event management company with 19 staff organising summer and Xmas parties, conferences, team building events and venue management worked on 323 events in 2004 and entertained around 9000 guests from a client list of 450 companies. Whilst these examples barely scratch the surface of event activity they do provide an illustration of the how important the industry has now become to society.

Brand experiences

To add to this is the emergence and growth of event product launches or live brand experiences as they are coming to be known. The increase in spending on product launches represents a cultural shift for events that may be quite seismic and has heralded the arrival of the live brand experience. In the past events have not featured heavily on marketing budgets but now there is strong evidence to suggest that events have become one of the main areas for developments in marketing. In 2004 a new association The Live Brand Experience launched, adding yet another rung to the number of industry associations, and whose aim is to see live brand experiences develop as a mainstream medium. Is this a significant development? The answer is most likely yes since it dovetails with observations made about the emergence of experiences in society (O'Sullivan & Spangler, 1999; Pine & Gilmore, 1999; Jackson, 2005). One of the biggest spenders on marketing, Unilever, who have a $4 billion budget have officially incorporated live brand event experiences into their strategy and, consequently, allocated a sizeable budget to deliver those events. This is very much in line with Event Magazine's 2005 industry survey indication that 85% of event companies would increase their spending budgets by over 30% from the previous year and that spending per head on an event was on the increase, with product launches leading the way with a £102 spend per head. There is a similar situation found in other parts of the world, particularly America, with 96% of corporate marketing executives utilising events in their marketing strategies whilst 93% view the importance of event marketing to be a constant or increasing factor. Additionally, Event View 2005/2006, the fourth annual study of face-to-face marketing trends points out that more than 50% of survey respondents report the role of event marketing as a 'lead tactic' or a 'vital component' of the marketing mix. The survey, previously called Global Event Trends Survey is conducted with 700 key executives with decision-making responsibilities in marketing and personnel in North American, European and Asia Pacific corporations with sales exceeding $250 million. Respondents are drawn from a range of industries including automotive, technology, healthcare, financial services, consumer, manufacturing and associations. The survey possibly represents a catalytic point in the event profession as it rises to the very top of executives' strategies for future initiatives in product and brand awareness.

> 'For the first time, "enhancing the customer relationship" rose to the top as event marketing's predominant criteria for success, compared with brand preference, awareness, product knowledge and leads indicated in previous years. When asked to rate on a scale of one ("not at all important") to five ("very important") the importance of customer or employee satisfaction to the success of an event, respondents reported a mean score of 4.2'. (Press release)

Event marketing was seen as the top marketing tactic for return on investment (ROI), globally, with respondents indicating that more than a quarter of total marketing communication budgets are now allocated for event marketing programs and more than a third of all respondents anticipate their event marketing budgets increasing in the future. Events' growing importance cannot be underestimated and it is not likely to be a passing fad as 49% (an increase of 7% from 2003) of North American respondents reported that event marketing will continue to grow in importance. A similar figure of 52% and 7% increase characterised European responses. One reason for this is the perceived ROI that events produce, a return that is regarded as being greater than other communication strategies. Events have a real role to play here simply because other forms of communicating are now becoming so saturated that, strategically, events can offer a more direct and experential relationship between brand and consumer. Previously business and industry have relied on traditional communication approaches to sell and promote their products. Now they are beginning to look at how brand event experiences can be used to do the job by giving them a more emotive quality. The survey helps strengthen the argument that events are playing an ever more important role in industry per se and, it logically follows, that the event industry itself and the skills associated with it are becoming more valued and recognised than ever before. The discipline of event management is expanding significantly from it's cultural and celebratory origins to one where the role of events in business is developing as it's effectiveness in brand marketing is more clearly understood and the levels of investment increase as a result.

Longevity (UK)

A high number of events are now firmly established as annual fixtures. The Clothes Show Live, an event spawned from an old BBC programme that last ran in 1996, is now entering its 17th year and is owned and organised by Haymarket Exhibitions. Now spread over 6 days the event attracted over 180,000 visitors in 2004 and included a Fashion Theatre seating 5500. A mix of a shopping experience and a fashion show, exhibitor sales for 2003 totalled approximately £19 million.

We have, of course, the large tract of recurring hallmark, cultural and sporting events that are firmly established on any nations events calendar but other event types are also becoming established as annual events. In the UK New Designers, a unique event created for 'showcasing the work, talent and energy of Britain's leading graduate designers' celebrated it's 21st anniversary in 2006 and claims to be the largest and most celebrated event of its kind in Europe. The event boasts over 40 industry awards and prizes for the work on display during its run in July and has both a consumer and trade audience of over 14,000. Events of this type will only flourish if supported and recognised by industry and consumers alike and after 21 years, I think we can safely say that is the case.

Visible events

Events have become ever more prominent with mega and hallmark events such as the Fédération Internationale de Football Association (FIFA) World Cup, Glastonbury and the Notting Hill carnival leading the way. These events have been credited with bringing considerable positive impacts to a host location as seen in the areas of social and cultural, physical and environmental, political and tourism and economic benefits (Allen et al., 2002, 2005). Their strategic business and socio-cultural importance lies at the root of Salt Lake City's recently exposed (but successful) sweeteners to persuade IOC members to vote for it to hold the 2002 Winter Olympics. Beijing's investment in facilities and infrastructure for the 2008 games is not just about enabling sport to perform in ideal situations, it is about China showcasing itself to a modern commercial world and the long-term benefits it perceives will accrue from that. But it is not all about the mega-events even if they do provide an important central hub from which events can further develop. There are now any number of status entertainment and award events attracting more press coverage and media exposure than ever before and showcasing to the world the appeal of the modern event: BAFTAS; BRITS; MOBO Awards; Oscars; EMMYS; MTV European Music Awards. Such events are the partial feeding ground for the enormous rise of celebrity publications and celebrity features in magazines such as Hello; OK; Now; Glamour. For example, the media fallout from the Academy Awards can be felt some months after with mini-features on the stars' image and their outfits (both good and bad) plus the slow release of the après Oscars party stories where Elton John's hosting of a party attracts almost as much attention as the ceremony itself. The bubble of uniqueness and special is created by the exclusivity of some of these events. As income generators events are getting a lot of attention and the early part of 2005 was witness to a potentially eruptive storm gathering over Formula 1 as a large portion of owners played along with the idea of re-organising the championship outside of the Federation Internationale de Automobile (FIA) and via a new organising body. At stake was an argument over what percentage share of $800 million each owner should be entitled. The value of a Formula 1 race to an area was never more starkly felt when the annual Grand Prix at Silverstone was put under threat. The economic ramifications for the immediate area around the circuit were spelt out for all with a potential revenue loss of £20 million per year, putting a lot of businesses at risk. Employment during the weekend and period leading up to the Grand Prix is estimated at 1150 full-time jobs in the UK (Allen et al., 2005).

Summary

The events industry is, at the moment, blossoming. It is now widely recognised as an industry sector and, politically, is seen as a major potential source of revenue and employment. It is important to tourism, hospitality and sport and events frequently form the foundation for a regions' regeneration strategy. It is part of a global industry providing business opportunities for companies to showcase their expertise. As events develop then so does the commercial activity around them as suppliers of infrastructure, services and goods begin to see more opportunities to provide support. This stimulation, inevitably, leads to more job creation and with that comes more recognition of the skills need to plan, organise and manage events.

Activity 3.1

1 Select three or four segments of the events industry and collect data on growth or decline over the past 3 years. What evidence is available that the industry is booming?
2 Conduct research on televised events and draw up a list of the ones with the largest global or continental viewing audience. Compare this, where possible, with data for the live viewing audience.
3 Compare the ratios for each event for live: television, and then rank the events that have the highest or lowest ratios. What does this suggest about the nature of the industry.

Chapter 4
UK events education

Learning outcomes/objectives

- Identify the key players in events education
- Acknowledge the emergence of events as an undergraduate subject area

Introduction

In the UK there has been a huge leap of interest in events management as an academic subject area at undergraduate level as more and more universities either run specialist events courses or include events as part of their curriculum. Is this, as Bowdin (2003) asks, likely to come 'as a surprise for some that the study of events, or events management, is being considered, while others may question whether events management is emerging or indeed niche'? Emerging or niche, what is abundantly clear is that there is a momentum to the academic development of events management and there is now an understanding, if not a total acceptance, that there are a set of knowledge and skills that comprise 'event management'.

Emerging education

Leading professional associations such as CHME (Council for Hospitality Management Education) and ATHE (Association for Tourism in Higher Education) have started to incorporate events in to their list of activities and both are involved in the development of a standard practice for event work experience through the PATH (Placement Advisors for Tourism and Hospitality) network. The HEA (Higher Education Academy) subject area for HLST (Hospitality Leisure Sport & Tourism) has also produced a Networks' Resource Guide on Events Management (Bowdin, 2003) that follows similar ones in hospitality, tourism, leisure and sport. In the latest round (2006) for developing QAA (Quality Assurance Agency) benchmark statements the Association for Events Management Education (AEME) is accepted as the body to represent the views of event management education the result of which is likely to see event subject benchmarks included for the first time as a separate section under Hospitality Leisure Sport and Tourism. Further awareness of the skills element of events has penetrated government via People 1st, the Sector Skills Council for the Hospitality, Leisure, Travel and Tourism industries, which exists to ensure that the skills employers need are the skills they get. Events is now a part of the 14 skill industries that make up People 1st and in 2005 commissioned the AEME to conduct a literature review of existing research in order to help understand the scope and size of the events industry. The output from that research will inform the way People 1st goes forward in measuring the skills and labour needs of this important industry. The developing of a set of generic management skills specific to event management (Getz & Wicks, 1994) will provide the impetus for its development and emergence. Allen et al. (2005) point out the factors influencing the emergence of events as a discreet discipline in Australia and explain that the 'the use of events by government and industry has grown, event budgets have increased, and the logistics of events have become more complex, the need has emerged for skilled event professionals who can meet the industry's specific requirements (p. 19).

Richard Beggs, Managing Director of Moving Venue Management, Honorary Fellow For Event Management at Thames Valley University and former Director for Education with the International Special Events Society (ISES) (UK) in a speech to the ISES European Education Conference 2005 acknowledged that institutions are likely to develop courses in the area, stating that 'event management is such a new discipline and it needs to be looked at academically. Its not just about theming, it's about understanding how to use database management tools, setting objectives for events, measuring return on investment – these are all business tools that can be learnt in an academic environment'. There is here an awareness that as the event industry matures then the qualification level of employees who enter it needs to be established in order to provide a framework for an academic entry as well as the traditional work based one. It is not only in the UK though where development is growing rapidly, a similar picture is found in Australia and America. Likewise in Europe notably Ireland, France and the Netherlands have seen new courses appear or events have become a component of existing courses (Bowdin, 2003). As with most professional and academic developments the emergence of association and groupings is never too far away as the need to legitimise and recognise the core principles of knowledge in the subject are sought. In the summer of 2005 the EMBOK (Events Management Body of Knowledge) Conference took place in Johannesburg drawing together some 300 or so academics and institutions to reflect on an event management body of knowledge that could be applied to all courses using the term to define their content. Such gatherings are not simply undertaken for the sake of it and represent a growing awareness of the need to develop a discipline recognised by its own set of characteristics.

Non-academic workforce

Event companies, associations and the industry generally are now themselves waking up to the fact that a trained workforce could be a bonus to them and that it is possible to develop event skills through education and, of course, training. The profile of education in industry makes for interesting reading with 50% of staff highly qualified compared to only 30% of employers. Significantly only 1% of those had a degree in event management (Wills, 2005). One of the foremost suppliers of events personnel, Esprit, has begun a process to try and develop competence recognition within its organisation. The principle behind it is that as staff mature and progress, then new entries into the workplace can be both recognised and developed in line with the key competencies of the employer's main job roles. In the past these have been loosely defined through senior staff experience and past down to junior staff in an ad hoc manner. In this respect the position is not dissimilar to that of leisure management some 30 years ago where there was largely an absence of a specific degree educated workforce and where entry to the profession was through a disparate set of qualifications such as coaching badges, life-saving certificates and voluntary involvement and where subsequent advancement was based on experience rather than educational attainment. To meet the need of this growing and emerging profession, not only did the traditional organisations in the area, ILAM and ISRM begin to develop their own professional training and qualifications, but the education sector did so as well from further through to postgraduate education. The evidence of that today is clear, as it is possible to chart a development line from post 16 through to Masters level education for leisure management. Leisure has developed as a subject in its own right but is also linked with many other subject areas such as hospitality, tourism, business, sport, media and recreation. The UCAS website for 2007 entries produced 475 courses for 'leisure' (www.ucas.co.uk). Alongside such development, of course, has been a series of new publications, journals, conferences and associations established to further the study of leisure. It is not unreasonable to argue that event management finds itself in a similar position to day and as it seeks to establish itself as a credible source for academic qualifications.

Event degrees

So it is possible that by looking at the development of a subject area in this way we can begin to see the evidence of the emergence of an academic discipline in areas of new courses, research, associations and publications. There is a very similar parallel emerging with events management in education, which is often seen as complementing the wider industry where it is recognised as a force within the occupational ladder as well as the social, political and business one. Events Management in the UK has burst into Higher Education almost overnight to the extent that where as in the late 1990s very few were offering courses in events, a search through UCAS for the word events results in 211 events courses scheduled for 2007 (UCAS, 2006). If that were not a strong enough claim the increase in numbers for student intake in 2005, taken anecdotally from conversations with course leaders, shows percentage increases from 2004 in the range of 50–80%, with some even doubling their cohort. As such figures have emerged so too has the resultant increase in activity and interest from industry as the opportunity to directly target a specific workforce has been identified. This is especially so as many, if not all, events courses have a strong vocational element to them and many require either a period of work in events, for example 400 hours, or a sandwich placement (9 months). Consequently the request for such staff from employers has massively increased in the last few years, up by some 40% in some cases (TVU, 2006) with viable contacts in the event industry offering a combination of seasonal work, permanent part-time work, on the day work, office positions and full-time positions as well as placement work.

Industry and academia

The emergence of an academic option has undoubtedly helped the profession itself become more recognised as a legitimate and identifiable working practice and in turn it, the profession, has begun to recognise there is a need to play a role in assisting and developing education and training. Established associations such as MPI (Meetings Professional International) have, since 1984, via the MPI Foundation, invested more than $10 million in visionary research and education to shape an industry that is, globally, worth $102.3. It is the world's largest association for the meetings profession, with more than 20,000 members in 60 countries and MPI's strategic plan drives both education and the need to create and provide career pathways for future meetings professionals. As a consequence of this MPI UK is looking at working in partnership with a number of universities to associate or directly sponsor a meetings and conference-based module that what would be a landmark relationship between event education and industry. Similarly ISES UK, having directly involved students from Thames Valley University in the running of their European Conference, are investigating the ways and means of introducing internships for event students at their member organisations and considering setting up an ISES Education Board to develop this idea. Furthermore, and to acknowledge the growing numbers of event courses and educationalists specialising in the area, a new organisation was set up in the UK in 2004 called the AEME whose purpose for existence is to help make people more aware of the skills and knowledge required to be an event manager and planner. It is on the back of such initiatives that new textbooks have also begun to appear covering both general events management and sub-fields, whilst major conferences such as the Leisure Studies Association devoted their 2005 conference theme to the subject of events and attracted a global delegation of presenters and audience.

As academics begin to direct their attention to the subject then the wealth of material for study will inevitably become more apparent. Much of this research and study is likely to be the result of a more focussed specialism in event practices developing away from more generic field of 'events' and toward event management practice within the context of PR, sport, leisure, tourism, social science, hospitality, law, health and safety, technology, culture and so forth. This can be seen already in the appearance of event-based teaching in courses covering PR, media management, creative and technology, and as well as the growth in textbooks, there are dedicated research journals such as Events Management, Journal of Convention and Exhibition Management and Journal of Event Management Research. How coincidental though, especially in the UK, that this should all happen at roughly the same time. The increase in courses offered is quite staggering over the last few years and where once we might have had say leisure management it seems we now have events management. But why events, what has propelled an industry with a fledgling academic history into a major player/subject in Universities up and down the country. Events from small internal business meetings to global impact ones like the Olympics have captured people's interest and imagination, for the time being at least.

Summary

As previously stated the 'imperative' need to mark and celebrate the millennium has drawn in government and the public consciousness around the idea of celebration and has left us with a situation where mega-events have high-political profile on a par with the kind of high political and cultural profile they had in 1900 (Roche, 2000). It seems that everywhere we look events form a significant part of our cultural landscape.

Activity 4.1

Although academic courses are growing it is not clear how much uniformity there is between them:

1 Using UCAS as a reference, University websites, Prospectuses and any other available information research the content of event management courses to see where synergy occurs.
2 To what extent are there common sets of event skills being taught?
3 Focus specifically on the domain of 'design' and list the number of courses that offer modules or study options in event design.

Part Two

Ideas of Experience and Design for Events

Chapter 5
Understanding experiences

Learning outcomes/objectives

- Be familiar with experience within the context of leisure and tourism
- Understand what is meant by the term 'experience'
- Understand how experiences are formed and framed
- Establish preliminary links between event, experience and design

Introduction

This chapter builds upon the discussion earlier on creating and designing event environments to produce an experience. The idea of experience playing a central role in our purchase of goods and services is a key feature of modern society's choice of goods and services (Henley Centre, 1996; Pine & Gilmore, 1998; O' Sullivan & Spangler, 1999; Warehouse, 2000; Ransley & Ingram, 2004). This suggests that by enhancing the discussion and study of provision away from the more traditional approach that focuses on the process of management, provision and programming of facilities (Farrell & Lundegren, 1991; Badmin, 1992; Grainger-Jones, 1999), towards one that adopts a deeper understanding of the way in which the elements of provision are envisioned, delivered and experienced, we will further our knowledge of how providers of experiences construct the experience they offer and in return we can begin to develop a way to deconstruct how participants then interpret those elements of the experience they receive. Such an approach also enables a further understanding of the meaning experiences have for both participants and providers (Bitner, 1990; Wakefield & Blodgett, 1996; Mannell, 2000).

If we refer back to Table 2.1 it includes notes on the extent to which experience features in events literature. As we can see and as Jackson (2005) argues, event experience, the product of the design, is almost totally absent from chapters or headings that purport to discuss event management suggesting that it too, like design, is under conceptualised and under studied as a result. In turn there is little or no meaningful consideration given to any relationship between design and experience that would enable us to learn more about how event experiences can be studied. Experiences however have been applied to other areas as a method for understanding more about what it is that take place when we attend or engage in certain activities.

Leisure experiences

The study of leisure and leisure management is now covered by a wealth of material that seeks to understand and explain the nature of leisure provision and participation that reflects either a leisure study or leisure management focus (Roberts, 1970; Kaplan, 1975; Neulinger, 1981; Haywood et al., 1995; Torkildsen, 2004). Generic leisure management sources focussing on the operational and management aspects of facilities and services (Badmin, 1992; Collins & Cooper, 1998; Grainger-Jones, 1999; Wolsey & Abrams, 2001) seek to explore the processes of leisure with an operations management context which describes the systems used in the delivery of leisure services. Less operational but equally generic approaches centre upon the range and make-up of leisure activities or the characteristics that make up leisure with an emphasis placed upon the patterns of leisure activity and the role of leisure in society (Neulinger, 1981; Kelly, 1994; Haywood et al., 1995; Torkildsen, 2005). Established bodies like the Leisure Studies Association have a publications back catalogue with over 75 volumes published since 1975 covering just about every aspect of leisure, for example in relation to community (Haworth & Veal, 1977), popular culture (Tomlinson, 1983), tourism (Stabler, 1989), participation (Botterill, 1989), image and lifestyle (Breckenridge, 1993), gender (Aitchison & Jordan, 1998; Anderson & Lawrence, 2001), volunteers (Nichols, 2003), partnerships (Berridge & McFee, 2002) and planning (Collins, 2000). Snape (2004) provides a very useful resource base for the study of leisure in society that also notes these key areas of interest, and Robinson (2005) provides the same for leisure and sport management. Such studies provide a base of material that has helped us to understand, in considerable detail, the role leisure plays in people's lives and, perhaps more importantly, the factors that influence both provision and planning of leisure and the opportunities and constraints on leisure participation. There are also those which embrace the generic subject but do so from a particular perspective such as an emphasis on either sociology (Critcher et al., 1995) or psychology (Argyle, 1996). Some of these social and psychological studies in the area (Dumazedier, 1974; Mannell & Kleiber, 1997) attempt to unravel the significances of leisure participation by addressing motivational needs and satisfactions. These theories of leisure that form a psychological & sociological perspective tend to be where the discussion of experience of leisure is most informed. Kelly and Godbey (1992) in looking to identify the specific qualities that make up leisure conclude, that if such qualities exist they must be found in the experience that is designated as leisure.

Experience from participation can be immediate and can be studied to show what levels of satisfaction people are getting at particular moments (Mannell, 1999). One tool utilised is that of self-expression theory whereby the emphasis is on the physical environment as a key factor in the need for leisure. Further research on how leisure is experienced and the meaning that it has for us as individuals and society has looked at it the context of need satisfaction (Tinsley, 1997), motivation and outcome (Iso-Ahola, 1982), psychological foundation (Iso-Ahola, 1980), gender (Deem, 1986; Hargreaves, 1994; Shaw, 1994), optimal stimulation and lifestyle (Wahlers et al., 1985), culture (Urry, 1995; Gale, 1996). These attempts to understand leisure view experiences in a more conceptual way that offers a different view of leisure service delivery from purely management-based studies that tend to look at the operations of facilities and how they are programmed, resourced, operated and financed. In these latter approaches it is very much about fitting programmes into schedules and facilities and the study of the practical tools needed to achieve that rather than the experience that such programming might produce.

Where recognition of the experience forms a part of the understanding of leisure, it is often framed within a passive and active model. The beginnings of a more complete understanding of leisure recognise that leisure activities and experiences cannot be fully understood as a self-contained sphere of life. In constructing any typology of activities through the formal and contextual dimension they (activities) exhibit, it is pointed out that in the active process itself, there is involvement in the actual production of the experience, of the skills, of the artefacts or objects, and lastly, of the performance itself . In the passive process 'participants are involved in the consumption of experiences, knowledge, artefacts, performances and goods produced for them by others (Haywood et al., 1995). This approach of typologies of activities helps us to understand 'similarities, differences and relationships between "types" of leisure activity' by breaking each one down into a band or category of key features and attributes that are easily identified. As a means of understanding leisure activity it assists us to identify with settings where creation of types of activities normally takes place. At an event we are, in the same way, either active or passive but have a further element in that we are either visiting the event or are part of its content. These settings for leisure contain a number of elements that pertain to the provision of an activity such as location, obviously, but also who the provider is and the process of production. This systematic model has the strength of uniformity in its application and makes for a relatively easy and comparable reading of types of activities and the way in which they are provided and clearly marks out the settings, and therefore the environments, in which types of activities take place. Immediately we can see how such an approach might be applied to the craft of event management, since as

I stated previously, the event itself does not exist until it is created by someone.

As the study of leisure has matured so too as the understanding of it, naturally, and in particularly there has been a much deeper rooted analysis of the motivations and satisfactions we get from these different types of activities (Argyle, 1994; Mannell, 2000) as well as the emotions, experience, image and interpretation of participation (Crouch et al., 2003). As the over-riding sense of 'freedom' inhabits nearly all views of what makes for satisfying leisure it is with this understanding that there has emerged more interest into what actually occurs (physically and mentally) whilst people are at leisure, in other words what are the very real experiences of their participation and involvement. As demonstrated by Mannell (2000) we can study this through three phases of participation namely before, during and after or pre, actual and post. This three-tiered approach suggests that one decision-making route is triggered by, first of all, promotion and marketing of the opportunity, and that this enables us to develop the initial level of interest. We then engage in the opportunity, provided through the operation and management of the service and, lastly, we reflect on the type of experience we have had, considering the level of satisfaction we have had from it based on a number of indicators. As the recognition of the central role of experience has become of interest (Berridge, 1996) and we have become more interested in participating in experiences rather than simply purchasing goods (Waterhouse, 2000) so there has emerged a necessary need to understand more about how such experiences are constructed and interpreted.

Service encounter

At the core of this understanding of leisure management is the service encounter and how it is managed. There are different views of how to study this from those interested in the social encounter to those that consider a much wider view of service operation that includes systems, procedures and information (Buswell, 2004).

"The service encounter can involve outcomes and therefore satisfaction and dissatisfaction with service performance of the organisation but a central thrust … is that the level of satisfaction with the service or transaction is affected by the experiential properties of the product or service and how they are understood and managed by the organisation." Buswell (2004, p. 3).

It is the management of experiences that requires a carefully constructed approach to the provision of services, activities and programmes and managers of such experiences need assistance in order to be able to articulate and provide them (Lentell, 1995). Experiences remain extremely challenging occasions to envision. Hull et al. (1992) has highlighted the spread of experiences gained over the course of a day by hikers where 7 experiences were studied at 12 moments with the results suggesting that the influence of management of the site clearly affects the experience, in other words the design of the programme impacts the users' experience in clear ways that are not always understood by programmers. Consequently those providing such activity need to understand that this dissection of experience occurs, making it all the more difficult to forecast how to manage such a process.

> 'In looking to understand the service encounter attention has been consequently drawn towards a deeper analysis of how that encounter unfolds and, as a result, towards the recognition of the experience individuals get through that encounter. The service encounter can involve outcomes and therefore satisfaction and dissatisfaction with the service performance of the organisation but a central thrust ... is that level of satisfaction with the service or transaction is affected by the experiential properties of the product or service and how they are understood and managed by the organisation.'
>
> Buswell (2004, p. 3)

If in the past the study of leisure treated experience either indifferently or as a singular continuous outcome, this can no longer be the case. As a society we are now more acutely aware, in an age where the range of choices is staggering, that people will make informed decisions about what type of leisure to pursue based, for example, on the information they have about the activity via marketing and their lifestyle perception of it (O'Sullivan & Spangler, 1999; Jensen, 1999). As organisations have developed different ways of providing for leisure beyond that of place, service and products they have moved into offering dreams and emotions where it seems the only thing that limits us is our imagination. Precisely because of the issues now surrounding choice in this experience context we can see that greater appreciation of the experience obtained from choice is also needed so that there is a deeper understanding of how the components of the provision are given meaning. Such leisure experiences are a product of designed experiences (Rossman, 2004) and the way in which it unravels requires further study.

But what part should be studied, what aspects of the features that make the experience should be the focus of attention and how should we begin to study and ultimately analyse it? The answer may be that we need to study every aspect of the process that leads to an experiential outcome, since only by doing this can we consider and ultimately analyse those decisions and the experience outcomes they produce. Operations and services management texts would no doubt argue that they provide the tool for doing that. However in many such texts the twin consideration of design and experiences is not always evident and analysis of the constructed provision is not afforded any analytical or conceptual evaluation in terms of meaning for participation.

There are some studies of experience within a general leisure management context and where it is seen as a fundamental part of the leisure service delivery (Johnston & Clark, 2001; Buswell, 2004; Riordan, 2004; Rossman, 2004; Torkildsen, 2005). In turn this produces an attempt to understand leisure as an experiential encounter. To understand experience we need to understand something about the associations that we make through an experience so that we can link it to both meaning and imagination because a pre-requisite of experience is imagination.

> *'If it is experience that counts, this has profound implications for leisure managers and their leisure services: what people experience is more important than, for example, product and place or event price. Marketing gurus remind us that people want to buy dreams.'*
>
> Torkildsen (2005, p. 109)

Interaction

A suggested way of achieving this is to develop a pattern of 'leisure experience in which consumer motives are translated into outcomes or benefits through a consumer process involving interaction between three key factors to time, flow and expression' Buswell (2004, p. 3). Time provides us with a chronological order, it is socially constructed, but it also provides us with a period in which we are engaging in feely chosen activities. It influences our experience by limiting the availability of time or providing a limitless period of time. Flow is associated with the feelings people have at different stages within any experience, the goal being that the best experience (the most satisfying) is achieved when a state of optimal flow is reached. Satisfaction is reached through interactive engagement, but there is not a list of attributes that we can automatically put into

an activity to ensure this will happen. This is because of the personal interpretation of satisfaction and because different types of activities equally
produce optimal experiences (Csikszentmihalyi, 1991). This occurs as a
result of our perception of any given situation, a perception that is constructed through interaction in a social occasion (Rossman, 2003). Thus
there is potential for many different levels of experience within any single
occasion as a result of the different experiences we have had previously. In
other words the level of our 'experience' via past encounters, personal
relationships, social skills, technical skills and so on will be a factor in our
level of satisfaction. Here we might think of a first time or newcomer to
the experience compared to the person who has a longer association and
reflect that they can both attain highly satisfactory experiences within the
same occasion but do so via different routes. No matter what the route, in
order to experience an event we have to engage with and interpret it
(Rossman, 2003). This means not just the physical engagement but also
the act of mentally responding to what is placed before us. In this act of
response we focus our attention on the event or activity and begin to
assess the information provided about. This in turn leads onto our interpretation of it, where we make meaning out of the information and lastly
we decide what action to take and make a decision (Kelly, 1999). This act
of denotative processing and subsequent ordering of information is a vital
aspect of experience formation (Csikszentmihalyi, 1991).

Experience meaning

There are key questions to be considered here so that we can begin to
not only conceptualise how experiences are created but also how both
providers and participants give them meaning. To understand experience further we need to be able to identify that there are meanings waiting for interpretation and in this search for the sign (meaning) people
interpret experience differently. Such a situation would explain why
some people use experiential choice as an 'attempt to construct social
position' and this forms part of an investigation into how facilities are
used by residents to construct social position and lifestyle (Wynne,
1998). This points towards experience choice being not only the result of
communication but re-affirms that it is also a result of interpretation in
relation to other social factors that will influence whether we accept the
experience or not. We know, for instance, that experiences are created
for us through the planning and programming of leisure services and
that by our attendance at and within them we have indicated choice,

but the question of how we might interpret and study the actual experiences themselves requires understanding of how we make meaning out of the information in the first place. To begin with we need to explore the experiential properties of what we are offered (Pine & Gilmore, 1999; Gummeson, 2002; Buswell, 2005).

Experiential properties

In discussing the experiential properties of a particular engagement, Tomlinson (1990) observed 'in York you experience the city's Viking history now, rather than just looking in on it via dead relics of the past'. There is a realisation here that the experience derived from any programmed service (e.g. activity, event, production) is the essential component that influences our level of satisfaction, and that the factors that control that experience are very much bound up in the way the experience has been designed (e.g. qualitatively, sequentially, visually, ergonomically). The choices made in each of these areas, for instance, has a direct impact upon the type of experience we have. The experience itself is the by-product of a consciously designed environment where clear decisions have been made. Buswell writes that 'service encounters cannot be left to chance and are planned and managed most effectively when the characteristics of the service process and the psychology of the consumer process are fully understood' (2005, p. 4). The meaning that managed contexts have for participants is not straightforward since, as individuals, we perceive experiences in different ways. But the constructs and the experiences are not necessarily static, in fact in many leisure occasions they are dynamic and likely to change throughout the course of the experience. Our perception and interpretation is a complex response on our part, formed as a result of constructs developed from a multiple array of possibilities. Clawson (1963) in the development of the 'multi-phased nature' of experience suggests there are five key stages and each produce a different experience. The five stages cited are: (a) anticipation, (b) travel to site, (c) on-site activity, (d) return travel, (e) recollection. The meaning we place on these managed contexts is therefore prone to fluctuation and variation during the course of the experience, a situation that results in it being regarded as multi-phasic or multi-dimensional (Lee et al., 1994; Hull et al., 1996). In drawing attention to this multi-dimensional nature of experience, Kelly (1990) points out that these can be classed as either pleasant and/or unpleasant, positive and/or negative and that they can be identified as transitory taking place in short, interrupted episodes rather than for extended periods. This indicates that experiences are multi-dimensional in nature.

> *So as we encounter an experience it is not static from beginning to end but rather it is 'shaped by myriad complex perceptual constructs and this explains why it is regarded as a multi-dimensional phenomenon'.*
>
> Buswell (2004, p. 5)

There is a recurring theme emerging about the way experiences are formulated that points out that they occur in managed contexts and therefore constructed environments. Variation to that occurs in natural experiences where we as individuals have taken our own path and are reliant on no other programmed factor enabling us to gain the experience. If though our experience in this context has been obtained as part of a packaged or programmed encounter then we can suggest also that it is managed for us as well, even if the experience we are seeking is a result of the natural environment. This leaves us with purposefully constructed encounters where decisions have been made and where the 'managers' skill lies in their ability to analyse and interpret the meaning attached by people to the events and phenomena taking place' (Buswell, 2004, p. 5) and subsequently providing for this. In managing to achieve this successfully they are then able to construct a programme that either affirms the experience or establishes a new one. The contexts that are created are therefore the result of pre-determined foresight, where perceptual constructs and relationships are identified and predicted in order for the experience to unfold as intended. The delivery of this experience through the service provision is the function of those who serve to act as professionals in the field of leisure. Rossman (2004) writes that:

> *'Designing and delivering recreation and leisure services is the major function of the leisure service profession. Leisure experiences are the basic units of service that the leisure service profession provides. This engaged experience is the vehicle through which other outcomes are accomplished'*
>
> (ibid., p. ix)

In leisure programming literature this approach, according to Rossman (2004) is under theorised and books published on the subject (Badmin, 1993; Carpenter and Howe, 1995; DeGraaf et al., 1999; Torkildsen, 2005) have a tendency to be a result of accepted practice rather than as a result of a theorised process. For practical purposes this is usually expressed as a result of the planning, development and programming of leisure facilities and activities through which the service itself is provided. Designing facilities and the activities delivered in them is often expressed in terms of planning, that is structural and service planning as opposed to planning for leisure where the issue is demand (Veal, 2002). In defining specifications clearly in advance and by conceptualising, for example, space and operations we can begin to understand more about what will take place in the facility once it is built. This can be done though whilst it is being planned so that we know more about how the facility will operate. By using flow charts and diagrams superimposed over a space plan it is possible to envisage how users of the area interact with the space they are in (Parry, 2004). Understanding the speed and direction of movement enables design decisions to be made that will enable planners to construct the type of environment they want customers to emerge into and also allow for the use of any specific materials, objects or directional pointers that are felt important for them to interact with. In this way the reception becomes a designed environment where it is hoped the experience envisaged in the planning will be reflected in practice.

Servicescape

That experience is then a product of the particular servicescape that revolves around the physical nature of the objects in reception and the service delivery itself. Service delivery has been a popular topic for study in the leisure industry as it attempts to grapple with the meaning of quality service. In this search for quality, which is a difficult thing to define, providers have turned to the processes of quality for help and investigated the adoption of standards based around ideas such as Total Quality Management (TQM) and Investors in People. Here the driving force is more often than not that there is a systematic management process lying behind the orchestration of any service programme. In this service quality remit, the attention is directed towards these processes of delivery. Whilst Torkildsen (1995) also offers an insight into the reception layout of a leisure centre, there is very little space given in other leisure service quality publications to the design of settings from which the experience will be developed. It is almost as if a designed environment is an irrelevance in such studies of leisure time activity. Torkildsen concludes that 'the leisure experience always requires the active participation of the participant in constructing the experience. At a minimum the participant must take in and interpret the meaning of the sensory stimuli provided'. The interpretation of this stimuli is the key to understanding the experience for individuals but it is also essential that we know something about the origin of the stimuli itself and the rationale for choosing certain types of stimuli that have been provided for us. In the same way that Rossman (2004) examines leisure experiences, to which we know a large proportion of events belong, we can examine all event experiences, whether they be leisure or business. Recognising and understanding more about how experiences are constructed and interpreted, and the way they unfold in the course of an activity for participants, will enables us to be more aware of how to think about creating them.

In most theory there is a high concentration on the value and outcome with little attention being paid to the experience itself (Torkildsen, 2004). He asks about the opportunities that are needed 'to experience the satisfactions that leisure hold' and notes that 'providers should be concerned with the quality of experience for the individual and not just with the quantity of the facilities and the numbers attending'. He comments that 'very little is known about the experience, what it is and what it does for people. Furthermore planners and providers have come far in the development of recreation facilities, programmes and services with so little understanding of the result that they are trying to produce'. The significance, therefore, of the experience in leisure should not be underestimated if it is a major feature of our total life experience. Its importance in leisure is central, therefore it is important to recognise that experiences must be designed to confirm, challenge or enhance expectations and perceptions. Where there does exist a body of work is in the participant approach to experience, where individual recollections and accounts are analysed. In this respect there are a number of ideas that can be used to understand more about the subject as I suggested earlier.

This point can be further highlighted by looking at, for instance gendered approaches to the study of leisure where it is clear from the experiences of many women that the experiential nature of leisure provision is a contested one that does not reflect their motivations and satisfactions (Aitchison, 2003). It has been observed, for example, that women often service men's leisure, that they are in, some cases, barred from sites where men's leisure takes place or those sites are made unpleasant and unappealing for them (Deem, 1986). Even when they are allowed entry it is done so entirely on male terms. These terms are not just based around social relations but they appear to be devoid of a realisation of how women may experience such environments (Green et al., 1990).

Tourism experiences

There is a crossover of study between leisure and tourism in many areas that is born out of the similarity of service type and delivery. Tourism often occurs as a result of a period of time we have set aside that is defined as leisure, whilst leisure activities are often undertaken as a result of tourism that is when we are on holiday. As with leisure people take part in tourism with sense of choice and freedom. Thus some of the earlier discussions on leisure experience have also been conducted within a tourism frame of reference (Hull et al., 1992) and some of the discussion and arguments can be applied equally to tourism. One of the attributes of leisure, that it is required to be psychologically rewarding and should be optimally arousing (Iso-Ahola, 1999), could, it seems, be applied to tourism. As with leisure, tourist typologies have been developed to aid our understanding of the role of tourism (Pearce, 1985; Yiannakis & Gibson, 1992), and the characteristics of tourist type activities (Smith, 1989; Ryan, 2002; Wickens, 2002).

Motivation

Tourist behaviour is understood and explained within a number of different contexts but a key factor in developing an understanding is the nature and type of the experiences tourists get. Tourist motivations for choosing such experiences are predicated on the same underlying basic needs that have been used to explain leisure, sport and tourism namely needs theory of personality, hierarchical theory of needs and the concept of optimal level of stimulation (Gibson, 2005). The experience choices made are then often related to the level of stimulation within individuals (Wahlers & Etzek, 1985) with some particular experiences being avoided (Lepp & Gibson, 2003). The subsequent experience from this choice has been conceptualised to aid in our understanding of how tourism provides the activity or environment (Crompton, 1979; Goeldner & Ritchie, 2003). Studying the consumption of this experience of tourism has produced not only a deep understanding of what experiences are sought but also what key components are required for certain tourism activities to be successful. Matching the motivations of individuals with the attributes of a destination is seen as a particular important part of vacation satisfaction. Tourist planning provides models for constructing new resorts (Lawson & Bovey-Baud, 1999) and the development of such experiences is often characterised with particular elements that are key to the experience (Gale, 1996).

Gaze and experience

Urry (1995) offers further insights into how tourism is produced and consumed through the idea of the 'tourist gaze' as a means for deconstructing the experience gained from visiting tourist sites and Ryan (1997) seeks to understand the 'meaning of experiences' and apply it more fully within a tourism context (that also includes special events). Ryan further illustrates how experiences can be understood stating that it:

'is accepted that experience is, by definition, a subjective process ...
It would be argued that experiences can be manipulated by both planned and
unplanned environments'

(ibid., p. x)

Ryan's book (1997), with contributions from several authors in the field notably Getz and Page explores attitudes, motivations and interactions in tourisms and explores how they affect the quality of the experience. In reflecting on the tourist gaze and how images of tourism (e.g. in brochures) are viewed, he suggests that 'each (person) can impose their own meaning upon the picture establishing a context from their own individual circumstances' (ibid., p. 5). Page in his analysis of urban tourism attempts to understand the deeper relationships involved in the construction of experiences, including the means by which tourist react to new environments and how they interact and acquire information about that environment. He identifies that social psychology, in similar way for leisure, tends to focus on the motivations for tourist choices. Typically these constructs result in service quality ratings as the defining component of the experience. As a reflection of more competition and the increase in marketing and promotion he draws the attention to the importance of gap analysis in examining the difference between the image promised in place marketing and the reality. Experiences derived are implicated by the gap between their perceptions and the 'bundle of products they consume' (ibid., p. 132). He concludes that to avoid such gaps the 'managing the different elements of this experience in a realistic manners is requiring more attention'. His suggestion is that only through an experience quality remit can this be achieved. In a chapter in the same publication, Getz and Cheyne discuss more specifically tourism in relation to special events (or event related tourism) and state the importance of the experience:

> *'Special events, from the visitor's perspective, provide opportunities for leisure, social or cultural experiences outside the normal range of choices or beyond everyday experience (Getz, 1991). By implication, travel motivated by events, when compared with other tourist attractions should be centred on unique benefits and involves unusual behaviour (p. 136).'*

They conclude that only through having a better knowledge of the event experience, and especially the ways in which customers buy or develop packages, will we be able to ultimately develop and increase the process of event production and marketing.

Summary

The study of leisure and tourism provides us with a platform from which to develop the study of event experiences. In this discussion there is the emergence of an events perspective, in this case within a leisure/tourism framework, where it is understood that experience is central to the type of leisure and tourism activities we engage in. By having a deeper knowledge of how that experience is interpreted we will be able to influence the way it is produced. From a tourism perspective there is exploration of a range of ideas including postmodernist de-constructivism and the types of experience that tourists seek, whilst from a leisure perspective it is expressed that we need to conceptualise the experience of users in terms of design and programming so that we can provide fulfilling experiences.

Activity 5.1

Pick three or four leisure or tourist activities you have participated in or are about to. Break each one down in terms of time allocation and, if relevant, in terms of section and/or activities (e.g. 4 hours, broken down into 15 minute segments, 2 sections/activities).

Try and think about what terms would be used to describe your experience at each time point and at what aspect of the experience your response is/was directed at, starting from the moment you arrived. You can use some of the following terms to help you:

- Excitement
- Bliss
- Annoyance
- Irritation
- Happiness
- Morale
- Bored

Chapter 6
Understanding design

Learning outcomes/objectives

- Understand what is meant by the term 'design'
- Appreciate the broad range of applications that relate to design
- Understand how design fits within the events framework
- Understand the purpose of creativity in events management
- Be aware of how creative pitches are developed
- Be familiar with a creative process for event design

Introduction

Design is essential to an event's success because it leads to improvement of the event on every level.

Brown and James (2004)

As the above quote suggests, in the context of event management it is important to see design as an integral element of the whole event process, as was briefly discussed in Chapter 2, and not as some abstract or separate or indeed purely specialist activity undertaken only by those either fulfilling the professional requirements of design or who are employed in a design capacity. This is important because whilst events themselves are experienced on many different levels, the use of design concepts and ideas is also utilised with different levels of input and application. The role of design in events does have a function that is applied with greater levels of creativity for certain aspects of the event than others (Malouf, 1999; Silvers, 2004a; Monroe, 2006) and that design layout of larger events is also recognised in terms of site (Velarde, 2001), but it is not always apparent that design considerations are being applied to all other aspects of the event process as part of an overall event design agenda. In order to fully understand the relationship between design and events it is appropriate at this point to discuss what we mean by design.

What is design?

In enterprise, creativity is the key to success … creativity is the essential defining branding strategy, in devising visual identities to accentuate recognition.

R Van Wezel. Foreword – British Design (2003)

A common view of design is that it is a skilled, creative endeavour that produces some element of artistic interpretation for anything from clothes to cars (Byars, 2004). Understanding and interpreting the meaning of design is, for most of us, not always the easiest of tasks since the difficulty lies in analysing or extracting meaning from the design. When we talk about design we can usually describe something that has been designed and mostly we can refer to design as being creative (Newark, 2006). Research on creativity sources will yield copious amounts of technical explanations and applications for design (Ulrich & Eppinger, 2004). These are the guides that explain how to design, the application of ideas and technical skills that lead a person to be called a designer. However the purpose of this study is not to teach people how to undertake design but to understand the role of design, have awareness of some of the creative frameworks for design and to provide an analysis of design as it influences events. The first thing we need to do in order to begin thinking about what design actually means for events is to be able to understand what is design?

An important point to accept is that there are numerous dictionary and intellectual versions that explain design and that design is applied to a whole host of activities and in host of different context such as product design, consumer design, interior design, graphic design and industrial design (Bayley, 1985). The most commonly recurring definition of design is to classify it as being a purposeful activity (Markus, 2002). In other words it is something carried out with a predefined idea of what should occur as a result of the activity of design (Ulrich & Eppinger, 2004). A dictionary definition explains design as being 'to mark out; to plan, purpose, intend' and is a 'plan conceived in the mind, of something to be done' (shorter Oxford English Dictionary). It can be viewed as the form of something, and the way it is arranged, suggesting that we should have a more expansive version of design where every human is a designer. In this view all fields have the potential for design especially where it requires careful consideration of a concept of action, a mechanism for carrying that out and a reflection or estimation of the effect that has (Potter, 2002). This seems to be a very inclusive and wide ranging understanding of design yet it is appropriate to consider its relevance for it identifies that design is not the sole preserve of those with an appropriate level of skill and knowledge in design. This view of design and the connections made for it, especially with popular creativities, is in itself not a simple definable concept either and has many sub-divisions and sub-categories (new media; image; text; information) that may confuse the picture on an intellectual and creative level (Beverland, 2005). It can also be explained as the deliberate ordering of components where specific elements within a setting are presented with specific reasons behind them (www.worldtrans.org). As a cultural tool it can be used to design across cultures (Lipton, 2002) meaning it can be seen as a means for developing and planning for urban settings and environments where the design results in the geographic placement of and interaction between natural resources (e.g. topography, vegetation) and built elements (e.g. buildings, roads) in a specific area and where urban designers consider how people will perceive and interact with the human-made environments.

Ultimately the drawing together of popular views of design produces a list of explanations/definitions with a wide range of application. The following list shows some of the explanations that have been associated with design:

- the act of working out the form of something;
- plan: make or work out a plan for; devise;
- design something for a specific role or purpose or effect;
- an arrangement scheme;
- blueprint: something intended as a guide for making something else;
- create the design for; create or execute in an artistic or highly skilled manner;
- a decorative or artistic work;
- make a design of; plan out in systematic, often graphic form;
- purpose: an anticipated outcome that is intended or that guides your planned actions;
- answering immediate needs;
- create designs;
- conceive or fashion in the mind; invent;
- a preliminary sketch indicating the plan for something;

www.wordnet.princeton.com

What is apparent from the list is that design is embodied through a process of planned deliberation to produce a specific outcome or set of outcomes. It can also be seen that not all uses of design are associated with artistic creativity. A set of themes for discussing what is design is provided by Cooper (1996). Here design is discussed as art, as problem-solving, as a creative act, as a family of professions, as an industry and as a process. Some interesting observations emerge particularly the idea that design can be used to create values (in and for buyers) or that it is concerned to express lifestyle through products. By doing so differentiation is based more upon image and user requirements rather than function and enables us to begin to think about how an event image is projected to us so that we might make a choice on attending the event based around the value we place on it.

Activity 6.1

Do products and events hold values for us as consumers?

1 Randomly select a list of brand name products drawn from either memory or via research on the Internet or in magazines. Pick products across a wide spectrum so include TV, phone, cars, cycles, home-ware, pc, trainers and so on and select 2 or 3 brands from each category. Now assign your value of the image of the product so for example what would you say the image of Nike, Adidas and Puma was.

2 Choose 1 product from each category whose image you most associate with and so would buy that product. What do you think the product says about your lifestyle image?

3 Now do exactly the same thing for events rather than products, although the event could be a brand event. As before identify the events you would attend and those you would not. The added question here though is why would you not attend some events, can you pinpoint the image associations that different events project.

Case study 6.1

Event values

Focus of case study

Certain types of events carry more value than others

Interpretation of value is often a reflection of person's lifestyle or cultural interests

A seminar discussion with a group of students about the events they have attended or would like to attend produced some interesting responses. Attending the Ideal Home Exhibition gained a very low response and some very disparaging remarks for people who visit it, whilst the Vitality Show was regarded as a must do for three-quarters of the group. Attendance at the Cycle Show was moderately unpopular whilst the Daily Mail Ski & Snowboard Show (DMSSS) was a hit. The music festival Glastonbury was universally popular, whilst Tea in the Park only partially so. Attempting to explain this it was clear that the students made deterministic evaluations of the events, as they perceived them and the value they placed on them correlated with other lifestyle interests upon further discussion. When one student confessed he regularly attended business and technology events, most of the groups were aghast, placing no value on them at this point in their lives. The idea of attending the Crufts dog show was rejected by all of them.

Consumer culture

Featherstone (1990) in his critique of consumer culture would argue that such identification forms the very basis for modern culture where the associations and values we attribute to products and services is now a key determinant of identity. This is referred to as the aestheticisation of everyday life, and it operates on two levels. One is through a design as art perspective incorporated into images in everyday life where even surrealism is exposed via popular communication forms. The other is that visits to leisure sites, for example, are no longer attractive if they do not provide pleasure for the consumer, often in the form of something extraordinary to everyday life (Arnould & Price, 1993). Hence we have the emergence of ever larger, themed leisure complexes such as the Mall of America and Bluewater. Now there is relative affluence in society the choices we make no longer define our status simply because of their use-value or exchange value but instead through their symbolic value which we use to communicate our difference (Cooper, 1996). Communication tools are used to pepper us with images and lifestyle associations that it is hoped we will value sufficiently to embrace the product or service being promoted. In this way promotional events are used as communication tools but rather than appealing to us distantly they can appeal to us more directly, for example, to give a tangible quality, we can physically attend the event. The aim of these events is to promote a product, brand, organisation or idea and to communicate this to a specific target audience (Masterman & Wood, 2006). The event therefore has to be created specifically to meet this aim, and this requires carefully integrated design so that the setting produced works as a promotional tool. A key component of such an event is audience participation and inter-action (Cunningham & Taylor, 1995).

Interaction design

The extent to which this takes place can of course be a huge variable from high to low interaction, but events that have interaction rather than simply inviting an audience to absorb presentation information require detailed designing and scripting to ensure the interaction works. Without it, argue Masterman and Wood (2006) there is no point having an event since the advantage of a tangible encounter is wasted and such information can be sent via direct marketing or the mass media anyway. As has been demonstrated earlier in the book the quite rapid growth in brand event experiences that are promotional and interactive suggests that further opportunities arise for the study of these types of events where specific interactions are created and planned around the particular brand or brands being promoted. Such multi-promotional events then offer several layers of potential experience in relation to each brand and each interaction that is created. There are many ideas that event design can learn from both interaction and participatory design. Interaction design, for example, is based on ideas of user experience and aims to illuminate the relationship between people and the machines they might use. While interaction design has a firm foundation in the theory, practice, and methodology of traditional user interface design, its focus is on defining the complex dialogues that occur between people and interactive devices of many types – from computers to mobile communications devices to appliances (Bødker, 1991; Button, 1993). Designing interactions occurs from a research point of view and a delivery point of view. The former we might also refer to as participatory design (Kuhn & Muller, 1993) which looks at how humans interact with things like software interfaces and technology (Button, 1993) or how children interact with each other and with new toys and games as an aid to their (the games) development (Druin et al., 1998). Participatory design offers a more democratic model for design by attempting to actively involve end users, a collective resource, in the process so that the outcome meets their needs (Kuhn & Muller, 1993). Mostly used and applied in relation to software the concept has some applicability for public stakeholder involvement in voluntary organised events where the input of users influences the event design and may underpin its core philosophical values (Berridge, 2004).

Case study 6.2

Participatory event design: freedom quilt

Focus of case study

Participatory event design involves stakeholder groups

Participatory event design is most likely to take place where event stakeholders are involved in the process of planning and management and where the event has little or no commercial interests to consider. As a result there are less likely to be creative restrictions or conflicts in innovation that may arise out of tension between design ideas and commercial ideas (Beverland, 2005). In the Figure 6.1 we can see the result of participatory activity designing an event. A school project required each child within the school to create an image of pictures, words and symbols that the child felt epitomised their idea of 'freedom'. This had to be done on a 12 inch by 12 inch square piece of soft furnishing type material that is, cotton, hemp, wool, synthetic. The idea was that each child's contribution would then be displayed individually around the school hall, as was usually the case with such projects. However the school's pupil's committee wanted to do something different and the pupils put the idea forward that the display could be made into a special event and held somewhere else other than in the school. It was also felt that the pieces of work could be joined to together to create 'freedom quilts', thus displaying unity between all the pupils. The teacher leading the project accepted this as an excellent idea. With help from parents and teachers a shortlist of local venues was drawn up and members of the pupils' committee visited each one. They selected a venue that had strong historical associations with the area, but more importantly they felt that the architecture of the building would give their work a bit more prestige. The exhibition

Figure 6.1   Freedom Quilt Exhibition. Photograph courtesy of Lindsey Mellor.

space they chose within the venue had exposed brick walls (see Figure 6.1) and the pupils selected this because it was 'earthy and felt natural, and its nice and cosy'. They rejected a more formal and larger space available at the venue that had white smooth plastered walls and lighting. Three quilts were placed on one wall and three on the opposite with a table in the middle showing some of the pupil's early ideas and planning stages. The event ran for 3 days with a launch party on the first day between 4 and 7p.m. Over the 3 days 1231 people visited the exhibition.

Design can now be shown to be extensive in both theory and application and the extent to which design is linked in practice is demonstrated in Table 6.1 (Shebroff, 2004. http://www.nathan.com/ed/glossary/). Some inclusions of this list may not be completely relevant to all events but most are and they provide fuel for exploring more consistently the wider influence design has on events. Several stand out as being more immediately applicable to events such as interaction, service, information, communication, environmental, graphic, fashion, interior, theatrical, web and new product development. However if we look at the range and diversity of event types we can probably begin to make a case for including nearly all of them. Such design activity can be put into effect for any number of events.

Design can also be a set of fields for problem-solving that uses user-centric approaches to understand user needs (as well as business, economic, environmental, social and other requirements) to create successful solutions that solve real problems. The problem for any event is of course how to deliver the event experience and so here again a more visible link to design practices can be understood. The use to which design is put elsewhere in society has a far wider range of application than is often implied by event management. Design is often used as a process to create real change within a system or market. In other fields and contexts, design might only refer to Fashion design or Interior design. However, recognition of the similarities between all design disciplines shows that the more inclusive definition for design operates at many different levels.

Developing an understanding of design and its application is, as with most definitions, more complex than first seems. In order to truly understand more about the whole design of an event experience then

Table 6.1 Nathan Shebroff's design association list.

Architecture

Automotive design

Communication design

Computer-aided design covers drafting and other forms of modelling

Design research seeks to understand design in all its many fields

Environmental design and Green design

Error tolerant design

Fault tolerant design

Fashion design

Graphic design

Inclusive design

Industrial design

Information design

Intelligent design is a Creationism theory

Interaction design examines the role of embedded behaviour in human environments

Interior design

Landscape architecture

New product development

Packaging design

Participatory design actively involves the users in the design process

Service design

Software development

Theatrical design

Universal design

Web design

we need to be aware that design is not just a creative practice (of skill and technique) as that is too restrictive and it tends to associate the practice of design with 'drawing' and subsequently suggests a singular approach based around artistic skill alone. For design in art, this may be acceptable, but for design in events although it has value for some specific analysis for specific artefacts, in general, it is too limiting. This leads to the incontrovertible outcome that the most important part of any understanding of design is to recognise fact that it is a planned process, and one that leads onto a pre-conceived outcome from an original idea and one that can be estimated and produced and that this applies to any number of applications. In an event there is a clear intention to firstly identify a set of features and then to see them translated into a (temporary) reality (or fantasy) that others can then experience, and therefore the role of design should be regarded as of fundamental and central significance in this process.

Activity 6.2

1 Consider, for a moment, the number of events that now feature interactive elements in them, and then reflect upon how these are 'designed'.
2 How do you think you can analyse the purpose of the interaction?
3 How do you think you can analyse how it has been designed to achieve that purpose?

Design as experience

The result of the discussion up to now is that we are left with design having a broad and wide usage in society encompassing many different disciplines and forms. Certainly it can be regarded as a graphic activity, but it can also be seen as a process that influences and informs every action related to a particular project. In pursuing this latter line of thought we must also remember that design is not static as new ways and ideas on it emerge, especially in relation to technology (Druin et al., 1998; Shebroff, 2001). Design has a relationship, for example, with industry and society and any changes in those relationships can influence how design is applied. Mazda's design philosophy from the late 1990s asserted that it no longer wanted to be associated with industrial design but instead it wanted to make emotional cars (Cooper, 1996). As we shall see in a later case study this philosophy transferred to a car Trade Show can produce an event with emotional anchors that attempts to draw in buyers via a sensorial and experiential feeling rather than clinical and cold industrial design appeal. Locating events this way within a design and experiential framework allows for deeper appreciation of how individuals respond to stimuli they receive. In the later chapter predominantly devoted to Symbolic Interaction and Rossman's use of it in designing experiences, we look at several elements that have to be considered when envisaging the experiences people would receive from their attendance or involvement. This provides extremely useful tools for analysis and enables us to begin to grasp how individuals interact through designed settings. As a planning and perception tool it enables us to ascend into the middle where our prospective guests will move and envisage how they would travel through the event setting that has been provided. In order to fully visualise this process, Rossman suggests that the use of mental imagery in the design stage would enable a far greater realisation of this journey. Borrowing heavily from cinematic frameworks, where scenes are sketched out in some detail, Rossman indicates that it is possible to use imagery to reflect upon past occurrences and to predict how future ones can be designed.

Designing Events

The typical scenario for thinking about any event is to think of the space where the event will take place as four bare walls, or simply as empty space if outdoors. Now consider what has to take place in order to create an event within that empty space. Something has to fill that space, whether it is the production of in/tangible objects or settings, the environment has to be created. Whilst there unquestionably are management tasks that have to be followed in order to plan and organise the event, unless we know how we are going to fill this empty space all the planning and organising will not help us. We have to, at the very least, visualise how the space is going to be filled even if it just a case of laying out trestle tables for a School fete. We should be able to immediately see that this process is the beginning of a design one since we will be making decisions about how the empty space is filled and with what and we will be making those decisions for a reason. The decisions made will have a fundamental bearing on how the event experience unfolds. It is reasonable to say that the weighting of the importance of design and creativity may be more essential to some events than others and that subsequently the efforts made to create thematic elements can be a considerable part of the management and planning process. Even though some approaches to event management are uncertain where to locate design in this process, it is my contention that all aspects of the event have design decisions to be made. This encompasses relatively straightforward things like floor layout or entry system but extends to marketing and promotion as well as the physical décor.

It also includes, given the variety of event types, personal interactions and rituals since an event manager must address the manufacturing of the event situations for the range of people involved in the event. Whereas the application of management and business frameworks and concepts (e.g. project management) will show similarities with other subject areas, the very act of having to design an environment into which an event can occur creates a totally additional dimension to the practice of event management.

The decisions that are made about how a particular space will be used manifests directly into the kind of experience anyone attending the event will get. It indicates an emphasis upon event guests and suggests that any environment is for them and them alone. If you are not a guest at an event then what are you? (This is where the discussion on stakeholders and the multi-layered nature of the event experience begins and further studies of event management may begin to look into the different experiences of events from multiple stakeholders' perspectives.) At present we are in a situation where in our understanding of events there is the vague association of the 'shared experience' as a factor in social and cultural impact as suggested previously, but this is not consistently explored. What remains instead are a number of descriptions of events where both design and experience appear to be fundamental to the analysis but where, in fact, the analysis undertaken is limited in this respect. Full analysis of any event means considering the many features that are incorporated into the event to produce the environment and experiences associated with it. This means that there should be a way of reflecting how an event environment has performed. To do this means identifying the design components and analysing them as would guests. The question is how might we beging this process? later chapters.

Design and events revisited

Can design principles be established that will help any event manager or planner understand how settings and environments can be created? The answer is yes, and in undertaking this they will subsequently have a conceptual base from which to carry out detailed analysis about the nature of experiences at the event. The most prominent sources of material on events and design in practice are Malouf (1999), Silvers (2004a) and Monroe (2006), Gardner et al. (1989) all of whom, in general, contextualise underpinning design principles within an event management framework whilst Goldblatt's design blueprint also identifies key elements to be considered. As previously indicated, other studies of event management tend to give design an ambiguous role to play as part of the process of separating design out as a specialist activity concerned only with the creative process of artistic designing and decorating. Event design is often regarded as a different part of the event management process itself and it is not about what we might call the underlying problem-solving activity that will help generate an event. Design is not readily integrated with, for example, planning and organisational spaces of an event, exhibition or floor layout, queuing systems, payment isles, seminar structures, presentation platforms, seating, promotion and (sometimes) even food. This is not meant to provide a full list but to establish some principal areas of events that design appear to be excluded from. This is partly a result of such event activities being regarded as uncreative, and so not being a part of the duties associated with design. A key factor in many event successes is layout but creativity in terms of layout is usually given very little consideration (Van der Wagen, 2004).

Activity 6.3

Poor design nearly scuppers event

An auction gala was being held to raise money for a major international charity organisation and the guest of honour and 'auctioneer' was, at the time, a top UK comedian and television celebrity. The evening was a formal dress affair with silver service, and was high profile in terms of the guests. Like all such galas the object of the evening was to raise as much money as possible for charity. Adopting what is now common practice, tables for the evening were sold in advance to corporate companies as well as to individuals. In all just over 300 guests attended. The event was divided into three parts, a meet and greet opening with drinks then the formal sit down meal followed by the auction. During the welcoming session an auction list was made available for people to consider initial bids for a particular item. The role of the guest of honour was two fold.

Firstly to deliver a short 20-minute comedy routine, and, secondly, to conduct the auction. In addition to the listed items, several extra special items were to be introduced to spice up the bidding. The welcome and drinks took place just inside the entrance to the venue and the dining section was separated from view by thick black curtains. The dining lay-out was a series of circular tables seating 10 people, so 30 in all, headed by a stage that was slightly raised and flanked by two auction plinths, and two giant hammers. The décor was simple and functional to resemble a small cabaret function, with black and silver studded drapery hiding the actual venue interior, small chrome effect centrepieces, grey napkins and deep blue and white lighting, including stage spotlights. Guests were to arrive from 7.15 p.m. for an 8 p.m. sit down when there would be a formal announcement made before entry into the dining section. At 7.30 p.m. the guest of honour arrived and asked to do a simple stage check. Upon entering the dining section there was a look of horror followed by strong words to the organiser. The guest of honour refused to perform at the event unless changes were made to the dining section.

What do you think the problem was and how was it solved?

The case study used in Activity 6.3 illustrates how design considerations can be neglected and, as a result, have major consequences for the event. This is partly explained by the design function within this event being identified for certain features only and was ill considered in the context of the overall event setting and concept. It is a view of design that permeates many sources on event management. The concept of any event should lead automatically into design considerations, since once a concept has been established there has to be a series of design-based activities to provide the solution for delivering the event.

Events and Design practice

Study of design in events literature tends to be highly practice driven providing copious examples of how creativity can be used to design specific event settings (Malouf, 1999; Silvers, 2004a; Monroe, 2006). Each of them offers what might be considered sources of inspiration for design. There is more of an interest in accessing some of the tools and materials by which design can be developed and delivered rather than for any actual analysis of it. Malouf (1999) is by far and away the most illustrative publication and offers a whole host of practical examples of how to implement design ideas. In this sense it is very much a traditional graphic design view of how design creativity is used at events. To give some idea of the type of event design explained the main sections of the publication cover colour, design and décor, themes and their creations, special flowers and table settings. The principles and elements of art are also discussed and explained, giving again a clear sense that design is a singular creative component of an event to be carried out by, although not exclusively so, a designer. In an interesting pronouncement Malouf states 'these principles need to be considered for every event where décor and flowers are involved' (ibid., p. 99). Does this presumably mean they should not be considered when they aren't? Whilst this suggests a view of design as an art rather than as problem-solving it does align with Pine and Gilmore's ideas on the esthetic [sic] of experience. That is that there should be something fantastical (fantasy) about the event. In a similar approach to event design Monroe (2006) considers design principles, decoration and context. Design, although firmly rooted in creative skills as applied to decor, is also applied to layout of environments such as at conferences, conventions, exhibitions and tradeshows. Decoration here is mainly interested in backdrops, props, flowers, fabric décor, balloons, lighting and unique decorations. Context is understood to be the application of creative settings within the context of the events purpose and conceptual (thematic) premise. Basic event design then is said to involve a knowledge of how to use and apply focus, space and flow. These ideas on event design are beginning to show some connection with the overall experience of the event, and how a sense of experiential flow in an individual is a state of near perfect immersion and satisfaction with the event. Monroe uses flow more practically though, as opposed to a satisfaction construct, to consider how people move around any given space but in doing so begins to also suggest how design has a more involved application across the whole event. For example, planning interactions might not normally be within the remit of the designer, but here it is understood that it is both preferable and possible to plan the movement of guests in a highly structured way in order to achieve a specific goal and ultimately a specific experience. Monroe, significantly, also sets design within context stating that 'design does not exist in a vacuum, but first within, and is governed by, event management' (Monroe, 2006, p. xxv). This is an important point because it begins to establish the role and importance of design as an integral component of the event. In fact I would argue that neither event management nor design exist in a vacuum and that both are interrelated to such an extent that, if anything, design should govern the event. However I think Monroe's meaning is that event management is the starting point, we first of all think of holding an event then begin the process of from which our design ideas will begin to develop.

Event design blueprint

Both Malouf and Monroe's principles of design indicate the need to develop a design blueprint along some basic elements of design. They concur that:

- design must have a focus;
- design must consider the use of space;
- design must consider and reflect the flow of movement.

From these basic principles then the aesthetics of design can then be developed and this should take into consideration more technical awareness of the line of composition, form, colour, texture, pattern, dominance, scale, rhythm, harmony.

Using these ideas as a blueprint enables any event manager to consider how to start creating an event environment. In both texts there is a wealth of ideas and examples of how to create event settings and the uses to which the above design principles can be put. They tell us how event design can be carried out and place design in a central position for event management, as an essential and integral tool. Monroe, in fact states that event design is the 'conception of a structure for an event, the expression of that concept verbally and visually, and, finally, the execution of the concept (ibid., p. 4). In essence Monroe provides direction on how to manage the design process for a given event whereas Malouf provides more detail on the elements of design that can be employed. The final approach to consider is that of Silvers (2004a) who not only incorporates design as an integral component but also situates design as a provider of experiences. On design and creativity there are pretty clear similarities with Malouf and Monroe over how design should be understood and managed through reference to ideas on space, form, flow, etc. However the key points to emerge is that design is a creator of experiences and that such experiences can be envisioned from start to finish. To be successful in events it is most essential to be able to picture how a guests' experience will unfold. Design, as a result, has a pivotal role to play in shaping experiences, for the experience itself has to be designed (Silvers, 2004a).

We now have a picture of design's role in events, and whether this ranges from the barely acknowledged to the integral element, it suggests that events have to be designed. We have, in the shape of Malouf, Monroe and Silvers, an introduction to the skills of creativity needed to develop design ideas for events. We can begin to see that aligning these ideas of design with earlier concepts of experience and particularly experience design we will begin to get a much more profound understanding of how design needs to influence event settings and environments. What we now need is a mechanism for examining and analysing those ideas, to make sense of their application in events and to be able to understand the experiences event attendees subsequently get. This though appears to be the missing piece. There is very little in the way of insight, understanding and analysis of the three-way relationship between event, design and experience As a result each source stops some way short of analysing the event experiences created. This is not a criticism but an observation that extends to most of the textbooks on event management discussed as each one has its remit and focus that does not automatically include an analysis of the settings created. So what we miss, mostly, is why these suggested design settings work. There is a design framework for developing the creativity to produce settings, but there is no framework for conceptually analysing the settings.

Designing messages

Events provide opportunities to present messages, for example through brand events (Masterman & Wood, 2006) that give rise to creative flair in an attempt to articulate the experience of the product to the would-be consumer. In the case of say mega – events such as the Olympics the opportunities to design something that has personal, national, cultural and historical significance are considerable (Roche, 2000). One of the most understood and recognised elements of design at the Olympics, Football World Cup, Commonwealth Games, Rugby World Cup and events of similar stature is the opening and closing ceremonies. The design elements that are incorporated into the opening ceremony enable the occasion to be signified at the different levels suggested by Roche and therefore the careful selection of features (through symbols, artefacts and components) within such a ceremony require considerable thought. The interpretation placed on the images is never in itself uniform since we all view such occasions from a different context as individuals. Although there will be shared ideals and shared interpretations as a result, some features may be open to numerous varied and alternative constructions. The aim of the opening ceremony to the Sydney 2000 games was to present the world with a reflection and interpretation of contemporary Australia as expressed through cultural, social and political values. The range and depth of material presented in the Sydney opening ceremony for the 2000 Olympic Games provided an array of cultural and historical references that combined both global (western) images and sounds with colloquial Australian ones (White, 2006). Whilst there may have been a clear theme to the presentation the perceptual experiences of people receiving the images was varied and, it seemed, as credible as those delivering it. When the key features of the ceremony were presented to a multi-national forum there was a wide range of views expressed over what was presented in relation to the what the audience was told was the intended version. The point here is that in putting together creative events, we have to consider not only the conceptual underpinning we have used but also how any designs emanating from that are contextually interpreted.

Case study 6.3

A weekend at Dave's

Focus of case study

Design must consider the use of space

Design must consider and reflect the flow of movement

This particular case study is included because we have an example the pre and actual experience observations of the event. Therefore we can see how the event was envisaged, how it was delivered and the response from guests.

Communication

The event text ran as follows:

Weekend at Dave's, with title sponsor Foster's and media partner Nuts will bring together over 30,000 hard to reach, high spending,

18–30 year old men who will be attracted to our event in droves by 'shedloads' of entertainment and adventure. By creating the ultimate weekend destination for groups of lads from all over the UK, we will offer brands and businesses a truly innovative environment to reach this notoriously hard to reach audience. Bringing a broad range of male interests to life for the very first time, Weekend at Dave's will appeal to guys who are passionate about sport, games, cars, music, comedy, fashion, technology, adventure and of course girls.

The weekend at Dave's concept was simply to create a themed event destination based around several cultural indicators. With the brewers Foster's as the main sponsors, the event had an obvious outdoors/outback connection. However this was an indoor event attempting to recreate authentic outdoor environments. It is possible to see the rationale for this indoor–outdoor juxtaposition since over the last few years several traditionally outdoor sports have developed an indoor version. Snowboarding, Motorbike trials, Motocross racing, Surfing, Monster Truck Racing as well as several extreme sports have all bore witness to indoor versions, many with huge attendances that dwarf their outdoor counterparts. Thus for the event we had imitations of what some of the best cities in the world (Los Angeles, Dublin, Paris, Sydney, Las Vegas, Monaco, Tokyo) had to offer. Walkabout Sydney played host to a 'party down under' whilst Las Vegas consisted of a casino, fake Elvis and dancers, Monaco had cars, Dublin Guinness in a Jongleurs bar whilst LA offered a Playboy pool party.

The communication for the event was a projection based around a central hub, a central core of activity from which the various zones were linked. Like many events of this kind there was both an implicit and explicit indication of what the event would be like, in this case one big interlinked party albeit with different themed zones. It is suggested there is every possibility that multi-phasic experiences will be available, simply because there are different thematic zones, but that this will be part of one single continuous experience of immersion within the city zones. The choice of themes, cities and celebrations (all hedonistic) conjure up an image of intensity, of closeness between guests, of constant interactions and of mutual and complimentary enjoyment/entertainment. In other words the characteristics of urban environments. A way of thinking about how this might work is to consider Las Vegas's famous strip. The walk down the strip is an almost endlessly intense encounter with the possibility of pleasure and entertainment that succeeds because one hotel leads into another and so there is a linear procession available that all Las Vegas visitors wish to travel along. The flow of people between and within each hotel via the strip provides a series of experiences to sample. Thus we have crowds of people ripe for celebration coupled with a cluster of opportunity. The cluster of hotels is reflective of any similar urban environment where space is, technically, at a minimum (notwithstanding hotel grounds) and so the crush of people is complimented by the crush of buildings. To coin a phrase this is no walk in the park, with grassy vistas, ponds and gardens or animal sanctuaries.

The actual experience of Dave's was however different to this. Although the zones in their own right were credible and enjoyable the impact of the event was lost in the large hall of the venue, London's Excel. Rather than appealing as a series of interlinked city zones, each zone appeared to stand alone, in isolation from each other. The two key components of the urban settings the event looked to portray, the compactness of space and the pressurised flow of guests were lost due to the distance and/or space between each zoned area. So the guest, rather than be lost in this artificial world and carried along by the wave of revellers, was always struggling to maintain momentum. Exiting from one zone to another was not a seamless transition, rather it was a profound jolt to the senses as the guest was reminded they were actually in an event venue and not in an urban paradise. Thus space and flow interrupted rather than intensifying the immersion of the guests.

Activity 6.4

1 Reflect on how you use and interpret design in an event.
2 When planning an event how do you integrate design?
3 What do you consider to be the design elements within an event?

Factors affecting Design in Events

Design's inclusion as both an integral and discrete activity, within the event framework, is dependent upon many factors. Whilst there is an advocacy here that it should influence all and every stage of event planning and management, it is true to say that this is not nor will be always the case. From a practical perspective there are numerous reasons that might explain this variation such as budget, size, location, event type, aesthetic requirements, organisational skill level, and creativity. We might also consider who the event is for, is it a private company, individual, public company, charity, public body, educational establishment or trade association. There are no set rules that influence the extent to which design features will be present since there are so many variables to take into account. What we do find however is that there are certain actions or settings that are regarded as being design or designed and are recognised as such, and there are other actions that although clearly designed are not considered that way. This largely seems to be a result of history and tradition and probably occupies the same debate agenda as the question of 'what is art'. One way to think about this is to note that whilst many events do employ design consultants for specific creative effects, many others do not and the use of design and creativity is in fact sometimes seen as little more than an added extra. In the former the design features may be fundamental to whole event and they may even be the reason that the event is taking place. In the latter it is not unreasonable to say that design is not such a central feature, and indeed the idea of incorporating design into the event may be seen as irrelevant or unrecognised. These uses and interpretation of design are problematic though because they can still present design as a specialist minimalist activity in comparison to the overall event. What is it then that dictates the role of design for events? This question is not so easy to answer although we might feel that there are some prevalent circumstances as suggested earlier.

Activity 6.5

1 Take each point in turn and discuss how they might influence the role of design.

Example:
Budget – does a larger or smaller budget suggest design will be integral rather than peripheral? Viewing design as a tangible output, more money allows for more potential but does it allow for more creativity? It enables more creativity to be realised but it doesn't stifle it nor does it automatically assume design is a central element of the process simply because more creativity can be bought in. Less money may mean that design has to integral because we cannot adorn the event with 'extras' or creative professionals. Design may be reflected more subtlety and hence is less obvious to see:

- Venue
- Client
- Guest
- Event type
- Organiser skill
- Scale

Design and Pitching for the event

From the discussion of Activity 6.5 we should begin to understand the variables that influence a design agenda. Thinking about all the possible client sources, for example, indicates how wide a range there is and why the role of design is open to interpretation. In some cases it will be the solution to putting on the event, in others it will be a micro-event element where creativity takes place. There is much discussion in industry circles about procurement, pitching or bidding for an event. Whilst there are some minor definitional distinctions between the three, in principle they all allude to the same thing that is winning the contract to plan and run an event. In such cases selected companies will be invited to bid for a particular event and their job will be to put forward a proposal that persuades the client that their ideas for the event will be a success. The pitch for the event both in terms of the actual cost of bidding but also in terms of the creative input required can be considerable, equal in fact to producing an entire event proposal. Bidding for events is now a highly competitive area requiring considerable resources simply to be in the frame to bid for the event. As a result there is more demand for dynamic and creative bids leading to a situation where the actual 'bid' to win the event may well have been conducted by a design team or company and if this is the case we can say at this stage that the design concept is leading the planning and organisation of the event from the moment the bid has been accepted. Design here is most likely to be integrated into the very core of the event planning. As such the conceptual framework upon which all other aspects of the event are linked is then rooted to an initial design agenda established during the procurement.

However where there is no visible design input at the procurement stage, can we really say that there is no design to the event. The answer is no, since as we have seen design affects so many other parts of the event. However in such circumstances design is usually concerned with those parts of the event where creativity is evident. This means, to most people the visible and physical components that have been 'designed' to create a specific effect. It includes, for example, the 'decoration' of the venue, the use of lighting to create a setting, the use of objects to develop a thematic link, the design and creation of food. Perhaps a better way of considering how design is most commonly seen in events is to think of an event as a theatrical stage production where the design element is visibly apparent only in the stage setting and costumes worn by the actors.

Here there is ample opportunity to witness this in practice both for the whole event and sections of it. Events with large budgets (which can be almost any type of event) such as awards ceremonies, promotional launches, national celebrations, celebrity balls or private parties are where design consultation is going to be at premium because the event theme requires specific settings to create the 'wow' factor. In such cases considerable resources are utilised to create such settings. To put this into some kind of context: where a bidding contest costs the participants in the region of £30,000 simply to bid for the event we can assume that the actual budget for the event itself is considerably larger. Companies whose job it is to create, realise and provide components for specific settings form such an integral part of the industry that they not only provide such creative input but they also win the initial contract to run the event in the first place. Of course this process of pitching for an event depends largely on what type of occasion a client wants and creative event management agencies have to give careful thought before becoming involved in a pitch.

Case study 6.4

Creative pitching and winning

Assembled by Arthur Somerset, MASK event design and production

Case study focus

How to pitch for a creative event

Like any event the key to creating a successful design pitch is to know some essential things about it, namely: Type of event, Number of guests, Type of audience, Where & when, Objectives, What do they want to do, Budget. The next thing to consider is why pitch and whether or not you have the creative resources to deliver. There is no point offering a trip to Mrs if you are incapable of creating it. It is also useful to find something out about the client if possible, especially if they have run previous events and who organised them and what they were like. This helps give an idea of the design features that have previously been used and indicates the likely level of creativity required now. Following on logically from this is try to find out who you are pitching against, basically for the same reasons as above. Another question to ask is why is the client talking to you, and what do they know about you.

A seven-point plan to think about:

1 Cost
2 Creative
3 Chemistry
4 Credibility
5 Decision Maker
6 Venue
7 Outsourcing

There may be a particular event that you designed that has attracted their attention. A crucial point is the level of creativity they are expecting and the importance of the creative idea to the event. At this point you might also think about the chemistry between the two, especially with a corporate client, and if you can develop a rapport with their culture. This is sometimes easier said than done. It also helps to understand how credible the brief is, for some companies can run invitations to pitch and then use the ideas through their own in-house team. Not ethical perhaps but part of business. For pitches looking for design ideas it is important to know what the criteria for the final decision is going to be. Venue is a vital factor and you need to know if the client has one in mind or if you are free to select one. This will have a fundamental impact on any creative ideas you might have. The last point is the extent to which they understand outsourcing, since you will certainly have to bring in other agencies to complete the task.

Going ahead with a pitch may require other factors to be taken into account but assuming the decision is made to pitch, the next step is to present your ideas. The proposal should then include the reason why guests will attend in the first place, the experience they will get when they arrive and what the message of the event is going to be, especially if particular content is required. From here you need to understand the guest criteria such as how many, who they are and why they are coming to spend time with you and the age/gender ratio. On top of that we need to think about the venue, if not already selected. One important consideration for corporate events is the distance the venue is from their Head Office. It is amazing how many times this issue crops up. Finally you need to know what venue type they want such as historical, modern, prestigious. Blending these points together should enable you to create an effective pitch and also design a successful event that lives up to its promise.

If the event is of much smaller scale and the budget is unlikely to be attractive to professional agencies or indeed is insufficient to warrant a biding process it more than likely means that such an event does not utilise design creativity for the event simply because they do not see design as a feature of their event even though they are employing someone to actually create an event from scratch for them. In this context design is regarded as minor theming or staging where limited skills are required to produce a decorative experience. In a similar way functional but large budget events may also have a client who perceives there is no requirement for a designed environment as such, ergo they do not feel it appropriate to use design based companies. In this respect the traditional event management company or consultant is the one most likely to be contacted to bid for an event since the event type is categorised as being functional rather than creative. Events such as trade exhibitions, conferences, conventions, meetings, forums, some sales shows, sales briefings, training seminars or political rallies might be seen as (though not exclusively) design or thematically deficient under this interpretation. Very often such events do though have thematic micro-areas or zones within the overall event programme and this is the place where design and creativity are most likely to reside. A typical example is to have a 'themed' evening dinner or ball, possibly at a historic or landmark venue (museum, gallery, theatre, stadium, etc.) where the 'guest space' is decorated to fit the theme. This approach re-iterates the traditional role of design within events where it is seen as entertainment, an added extra set aside from the main, and presumably serious, function of the main elements of the event.

Creativity

By contrast there are those events that are the opposite to the functional event such as parties, festivals, weddings, milestone celebrations, parades, product launches, balls, awards, stage shows, fetes and galas. Here creativity is most likely to be seen as a major feature of the event. The components that contribute to such events are often drawn from what we might call creative resources and they consist of features such as food, drink, lighting, décor, furniture, flowers, dress, centrepieces, objects, sound and smell. Creativity at such events is almost limitless as concepts and ideas are developed to produce truly fantastic visual settings based on themes that use global culture as a reference point. The creative process of event design is, a bit like Hollywood blockbusters, a seemingly endless quest to do it bigger, better and brighter than the last time. Approaches to creativity have been briefly noted and there have been several indications of what factors, both experiential and design, should be touched upon. Most creativity requires some kind of framework to work from and several authors have outlined how to conduct the creative process (Malouf, 1999; Monroe, 2006; Silvers, 2004b). Creative development needs to be the result of a comprehensive overview of the whole event so that it is applied within context. How do we need to consider creativity? Malouf suggests the following process:

> We need to 'offset' our thoughts and eliminate negative thinking and remove perceived restrictions. This should lead us to 'reflect' and look back on what materials and methods

were previously utilized. Then we should 'isolate' our time, make free space so that we can go over all the details of the whole event. Find sources of inspiration and 'grasp' ideas and influences to help you. 'Navigate' possible and impossible ideas and write them down for reference. Size up the venue and 'appraise' its potential. Know the size of the room and its 'level's for creating a setting. 'Impress' to make things important and use 'tone' when considering colour. Finally use a 'yardstick' to measure the event for reference next time.

Edited version of Malouf's 10 point Creative Process Plan (1999, p. 66)

Activity 6.6

Themed Colour

Using colour as a theme has become one of the more challenging and illuminating ways of designing an event experience. One of the chief exponents is Matt James of DNA Productions who has produced a number of events based around a single colour concept. These events take the idea of colour to extremes so this is not simply a case of brightening up a venue or particular setting. The study of colour itself is a complex one originating from the theory of colours (Itten, 1975). Colour should not be seen as purely cosmetic and we should understand it for what it can represent. It is often seen, for example, as a source of life for it exists everywhere and the way we respond to it affects our mood. Understanding what colour can do to an event is sometimes critical to understanding the type of experience produced. Colour can be seen from a psychological perspective (Sharpe, 1982) and the use of colour can play a key role in communicating messages so its symbolism to any audience needs appreciation as well (Morton, 1998). Colour is ubiquitous and we cannot escape it so we might consider how we respond to different colour schemes. Are there particular associations that we make with certain colours? There are, for instance, seven different contrast effects in the world of colour and these can be used to create certain kinds of emotions such as neutrality, warmth, cold or subdued (Itten, 1975). Colour though is not uniform in its meaning and different cultures use colours for different things.

What do you think the following colours mean and how are they are used in popular culture to symbolise certain emotions, feelings or ideas.

Now take each colour and consider what type of events you would associate with certain colours and what type of experience you would envisage creating by using them:

- Black
- White
- Red
- Blue
- Green
- Yellow
- Purple
- Brown

Case study 6.5

Discovery Channel launch

Details supplied by Alexandra Munroe, Theme Traders, London

Case study focus

Use of colour to design a brand event

The original brief for this event was provided by Discovery Channel who approached Theme Traders to help launch 3 new channels. The brief required a re-branding with an event. Discovery channel had the idea they would do this via an exhibition based on PR photos. The budget was £3K minimum. The channels to be launched were Travel and Living; Home and Health; Real Time. In total ten meetings took place to finalise the event, and where the idea of a pure exhibition was discarded . The venue selected was Il'bottaccio, Grosvenor Place, London. Having decided on a V shaped room, with each corner of the V representing a different channel there were some main elements to include to represent them. At all time full branding was essential. One of the key ways this was achieved was through colour. Each channel was characterised by Discovery with a colour reference and it was important that this distinction was made at the event, especially for the press. Outside the venue flags in the colour of the relevant channels drew attention to the event and inside each V zone had a colour wash again to represent the colour associated with the channel. Another emphasis required by Discovery was one of quality that is they required the channels to be viewed as more than just schedule fillers amongst the rest of cable and satellite TV. For example, the channel Home and Heath was aimed at girls (Discovery's word) age between 20 and 35 years who were youthful in outlook, fun, lively, into trendy living and looking for something fresh. To epitomise this Discovery had used yellow for the channel and so the zone at the event had a vivid yellow look to it. The setting was a girls night in, and not forgetting this is a TV channel, this was augmented by plants, cream sofas and an ambience, provided by lighting, sound, colour and an image of relaxation. This was achieved and sustained by providing an interactive feature in the zone. In this case it was a bangle maker. The most important point of the launch was to connect the channel to the respective zone, hence the colour swatches used had to perfectly match those of the channel. Setting the event in the context of Discovery and each channels branding was the main aim of the launch and this was taken to exceptional lengths. Remember this was a triple launch and at no point was any colour theme allowed to dominate over another. To do so would have over emphasised one channel in relation to the others. So colour favouritism had to be avoided at all cost. This resulted in the toilets at the venue getting a temporary refurbishment in a plain neutral colour. The impact of the event was to create an informed experience for those attending, especially the press, and one that was subtle to avoid 'slamming' them with information about each one.

Case study 6.6

James Bond Celebration

Case study focus

Thematic experience

Reason for event: To celebrate the release of the complete James Bond Soundtrack for the first time, using all the original scores for the films. A party was held at Kensington Palace Gardens, London. The venue has an element of secrecy to it as it is located on top of a four storey building and so is not directly visible from the streets below. It also requires access via elevator (or stairs) not directly visible from the street. For those with memories of older cloak and dagger espionage adventures, the idea of locating a secret entrance via a discrete doorway is appealing as often the secret HQ of friend or foe would be behind such a hidden doorway. The lift operator was a large steadfast character that performed his duty perfunctorily, but totally silently as well. His dress was that of a service operative, a bodyguard, assassin or peace keeper who gave the impression that the guest should have a feeling of mild trepidation for the world they were about to enter, where mystery and secrecy were paramount. On exiting the lift, guests were met by another operative who guided them towards closed double doors.

A rap on the doors and they were opened to the music of Diamonds Are Forever. The entrance was set on a slight mezzanine section and the first point of contact were two women in cocktail dresses, naturally, who handed males guests a white silk scarf and toy pop gun, female guests a fake diamante power bag and both were given the soundtrack. One particular striking feature of the event was at one of the food areas. Adorning the walls was a high-resolution photograph of the ultra-baddie Largo's boat from the film Dr.No. Laid out on the table below were several huge salmons, slices of which were served by two men with eye patches wearing black round neck tops, a homage to Bond's opponent in the film. As we can see with the James Bond party the event appeared to have an integrated design approach but also used specific creative elements for the event setting. What is interesting is that even though this was a launch event, the actual purpose of it, the issue of the music soundtrack, took a secondary role behind the character of Bond and the films other characters. In fact, oddly enough, the soundtrack itself was barely featured during the evening.

At its most basic level creativity is often the only visual impact element of an event. There are clients who will be acutely aware of the ideas being propagated for any particular setting and will, in turn, have particular views on how they wish to see the event transmit these views or vision. Equally there will be clients who are open to creative interpretation and are interested in looking to see what an events team can create. Either way the concept of the event must be transmitted to produce a set of scenarios from which the event can then be further developed. Whilst this seems a perfectly sensible and rational and almost common sense type approach to take, it is a view that creates some limitations for event analysis since this design aspect of events is compartmentalised as being one solely for creative people and creative type activities. In adopting this approach it often treats events that do not have extravagant design as being of little importance (although I suspect this is not really the intended case) and, as has been previously discussed, consequently undervalues the range of design indicators that influence many more parts of an event.

Further it does not appear to leave any scope for an experiential analysis of events especially where such design is not so creatively or elaborately employed such as in what might be called lower status or lower complexity events or those with lesser funding, that is not hallmark, mega. Yet, it is the case, that even in these events the environment is still a designed and created one since there was nothing there before the event itself was created. Where events do not use professional creativity it does not mean they are not designed but it means that the design features emanate from a different source, namely the client, event manager or management team. What then becomes a useful analytical point is the way in which the experience of differently organised events differs, in terms of the features used to create the settings. On a basic level this might be the difference between a local community gala or festival and a sponsored or branded one. Is the gala any less of a designed event than the product launch? Probably, because the product launch has a single vested interest (the company) and specific purpose (the product) and just as likely a definite target (invited audience). It is more likely to have a conceptualised approach to the event setting, where the design is integral to any information and products that the event is looking to transmit to its audience. The gala has multiple interests (just within the local community alone) and tends to have general purpose (fun, but possibly fund raising as well) and has a general target (anyone who wants to turn up). It should also be remembered that the professional designed event must live up to expectations or at least exhibit the features of being well designed since it has been paid for by a client who is going to want to see some return on their investment in the event. In contrast the gala is the result of a group of volunteers with less need to justify their actions to a specific client but whose design is the result of a participative process that is as likely to include many of those attending the event. Anyone who has sat through the serious debate over the composition of a cake stall, its location point, it's layout and the type of cakes being sold will be all too aware of this. In a few instances there have even been verbal and written instructions on how to specifically present the cake stand with suggestions on the design of table, round or square, the covering and its colour (natural, white) and the precise layout of different cake types (colourful at the front, large chocolate at the back). With all these ideas at work within an event it raises a very fundamental question of how we can provide further analysis of these types of elements that make up event environments so that we can extrapolate meaning from them that can be expressed in more vivid and detailed terms than 'wow'.

Summary

With events design, we are talking about (a) the effect a whole environment, made up of many different elements, can have on a person or group of people and (b) the effect a single element of design within the event can have on experience at that particular point. The interactive and multi dimensional nature of many events means that designing for events is more than a single effect process, it is, in fact just the opposite since so many elements are required to create the event environment there is the potential for many different experiences. In the main most event environments are produced on the basis that the majority of attendees will experience as much of the event as possible although we can suggest that for example, mega events may not entirely be experienced that way and that they will have portions of them that not all event attendees will experience. When attending something like the Ideal Home Exhibition there is an assumption that you will spend a full day 'experiencing' all the features that are on offer in the different sections. The design of that particular environment (based around 'zones') has an overall approach in terms of layout and movement as well as an individual approach that is taken by exhibitors.

Chapter 7
The experience industry and the experience economy

Learning outcomes/objectives

Reflect on how marketing has been traditionally used for events
Identify the emergence of experiential marketing ideas
Reflect on how experience marketing is practised
Understand the concept of experiences through:
– experience parameters
– infusers
– enhancers
– makers
Establish a conceptual link between experiential marketing ideas and events
Be able to relate the six 'D's of experience to different types of events
Understand how use of experiential concepts can be adapted to analyse event experiences

Introduction

Whereas previously we looked at understanding experiences from a leisure and tourism perspective and drew attention to how this was studied via a number of participant responses to experience amongst others (Mannell, 1999) the purpose of this chapter is to draw attention to developments in our understanding of experiences via marketing, or communication, and in particular how a newer perspective on event marketing based around experiences and psychographics is relevant.

Event marketing

Approaches to event marketing has, by and large, been based upon traditional concepts of marketing that many people will be familiar with, and this has been the case whether it is a leisure, tourism or business event. Principles of marketing have been well established, whether in a service or product context, by amongst others Cannon (1996); Adcock et al. (2001); Kotler (1999) and Wilmshurst (1995). Applications of these to leisure and tourism (Middleton, 1996) have further embedded the principles and these have then been applied directly to events (Hall, 1997). Event marketing is often based around the eternal four Ps or slight variants and extensions of those ideas (Watt, 1992; Horner & Swarbrooke, 1996; Watt & Stayte, 1999; Bowdin et al., 2001; Masterman, 2004; Shone & Parry, 2004). These were first put forward by McCarthy in 1960 and called the marketing mix, a concept that consists of product, price, place and promotion (better known as the four Ps). The four Ps traditionally refers to:

1 *Product* that can be either a good or service and is sold to a customer or end consumer; it is designed to meet their needs. Customers buy products, and use it.
2 *Price* needs to be right. It is not just about cheaper but is about a pricing strategy and working out the difference between the cost of producing it and selling it on.
3 *Promotion* is about communicating with customers, giving them information so they can decide whether or not to buy the product or service.
4 *Place* is about location and where a service is delivered.

Kotler embedded them as principles of marketing through a now seminal text, Marketing Management, currently in its 12th edition (2006). There are though different views on what form of the marketing mix should be applied to events with Getz (1997) and Cowell (1984) proposing extensions to the 4 Ps, offering 7 and 8 P versions, respectively. As a further illustration of this point Bowdin et al. (2001) in a chapter on marketing considers the following areas to be now applicable to events:

- Marketing mix
- Event environment
- Event consumer
- Market segmentation
- Product planning
- Product development
- Pricing
- Promotion
- Place
- Market research

A number of sources now exclude promotion adding public relations and positioning to create the 5 Ps (Hoyle, 2002), whilst a 6 P version adds press releases to the mix (Shukla et al., 2005). Consequently it is suggested that the 4 Ps no longer address the needs of events or services and so we now need to add people, process, physical evidence, performance and profit (Tum et al., 2006). Whilst these aspects of marketing retain some relevance they are mainly rooted in the traditional view of the marketing mix and, as such, provide a limited conceptual depth and subsequently limited material for the study of events and experiences. Latterly the idea of the marketing mix is almost completely ignored as a concept and instead is replaced by an integrated approach to marketing communications that is specific to events and where events are themselves used as a marketing communication tool. This is based around events being transient in nature and where attendance also forms part of the event that is simultaneously consumed and experienced (Masterman & Wood, 2006).

This idea that events require specific consideration and involve experiences is beginning to develop and Shukla suggests that marketing for them now needs to address entertainment, excitement and enterprise, the 3 Es (2005). Where such factors are taken into consideration then we begin to see events as experiences where we need to tap into 'emotional hot buttons' that subsequently provide experiences of pleasure through events in relation to people, business, culture, fun, entertainments, desire and nostalgia (Allen, 2004). Now that we have acknowledged the growing importance of events in society so we now need to consider events in more detail, and one of the main ways of doing this is by understanding them as a designed experience and 'in relation to the 4th or 5th economy – the Experience or Dream Society' (Jackson, 2005, p. 1). To be able to do this, Jackson suggests we need to understand more about the characteristics of experience through not just experiential marketing, but also using the existing body of literature in consumer experience, service quality and relationship marketing.

Experience industry or economy?

Just as Toffler (1971) originally suggested, there is now a strand of thought arguing that management focus shifts beyond its perennial service remit and towards one that embraces experience (Jensen, 1999; O'Sullivan & Spangler, 1999; Pine & Gilmore, 1999; Petkus, 2004). The emergence of this 'experience industry' (O'Sullivan & Spangler, 1999), 'experience economy' (Pine & Gilmore, 1999) or 'dream society' (Jensen, 1999) argues that this shift in focus will see events having a significant part to play in appealing to and satisfying emotional as well as rational persona (Jackson, 2005).

Utilisation of the concept of experience has been expressed, in the main, through consumer and marketing contexts contained in the work of Pine and Gilmore (1999); Jensen (1999); Nijs and Peters (2002); Nijs (2003); O'Sullivan and Spangler (1999). Its specific usage in event-based publications remains limited, although that is not say that the notion of experience itself has been entirely neglected as we have discussed. Rather it is more accurate to say that it has been under-developed. Where there is acknowledgement (Getz, 1997; Bowdin et al., 2001; Shone & Parry, 2004; Allen et al., 2005) of experience as a component within events, the tendency is to see it as a feature that can be inserted (via theming and staging) rather than as the underpinning platform upon which the whole event is delivered. In order to consider models that would be useful for studying events it is necessary to look at the main

Table 7.1 Jacksons experiential characteristics.

Developing a cohesive theme

Consumption as interaction/engagement through full use of the senses (immersion, absorption, engagement)

Development of relationships

Emotions

Creativity/collaboration

Transformation

Theatrical analogy including scripting and story-telling

Visual imagery

Authenticity

sources that have identified the experience as a central element in the purchase and exchange of goods and services. Principally this has been done within a marketing and business framework where an emphasis is placed on how goods and services are produced and delivered. This inevitably leads into discussions around aspects of commodities and co-modification, the role and activities of the provider and purchaser and, as a consequence, the consumer experience. To fully utilize ideas on experience to study events requires that several key characteristics be understood and incorporated and these are set out in Table 7.1. It also requires a development, or subversion if you like, of some existing ones. The two seminal texts used to explore this are by Pine and Gilmore, and O'Sullivan and Spangler.

Experience marketing

O'Sullivan and Spangler (1999) use an approach to experiential marketing that is born out of ideas similar and contained within traditional marketing concepts, namely the marketing mix and the 4 Ps. Applying these principles to experiences they subvert and extend them to take into account a more involved notion of marketing whereby a product or service is equated to an experience that extends beyond simply that of function. O'Sullivan and Spangler provide an exploration of an experiential environment, the experience industry, that has very clear implications for the study and analysis of events.

In explaining the experience industry, they write:

> *Wherever you look, whatever you buy, the experience industry is present. The shift to experiences is more than on. It may have taken us decades to notice its gradual, but persistent growth but the experience industries are indeed here. Experiences have been introduced, integrated, and infused into all aspects of consumption and existence.*
>
> O'Sullivan and Spangler (1999, p. 1)

Experiences are viewed as a central part of everyday consumption of goods and services in areas of health, events, entertainment and travel (amongst others). Whilst it is possible to say experiences are everything, they suggest that there are 'some factors that make an experience or the experience component of a product or service uniquely distinct'.

For O'Sullivan and Spangler some of the key factors of an experience are:

- The participation and involvement of the individual in the consumption.
- The state of being physically, mentally or emotionally derived through such participation.
- A change in knowledge, skill, memory or emotion derived through such experience.
- The conscious perception of having intentionally encountered, gone to or lived through an activity or event.
- An effort directed at addressing a psychological or internal need of the participant.

An experience is not the same as simply buying something, it requires more involvement and they address the 'psychic needs of a society' (O'Sullivan & Spangler, p. 4). Using Toffler's idea that we will move out of meeting basic needs to meeting psychological ones, they argue that the experience industry is now divided into three different segments 'infusers, enhancers or makers' (ibid, p. 5). Each of these segments reflects the type of experience provided and later in this chapter we will look in more detail at what they actually mean.

4 Es

Using a similar platform but adopting a different set of headings, Pine and Gilmore (1999) outline their 4 Es of the 'experience economy'. Reflecting upon whether or not the economy exists or not they write:

> 'Of, course not everyone will agree that we are shifting to an Experience Economy or that such a development is a good thing. Consider Las Vegas, the experience capital of America ... Virtually everything about Vegas is a designed experience, from the slot machines at the airport to the gambling casinos that line the strip; from the themed hotels and restaurants to the singing, circus and magic shows; and from the Forum Shops mall that recreates ancient Rome to the amusement parks, thrill rides, video arcades, and carnival-style games that attract the twenty somethings and give older parents a reason to bring their kids in tow'.
>
> Pine and Gilmore (1999, p. xi)

Possibly the most significant point to make of this observation is their recognition that Vegas is a designed environment (virtually) and that the process of creating experiences within society is already happening. It is, I would contend, but one-step away from drawing a direct parallel with events, where the whole environment really is designed from a blank canvas. The point to be made here though is that in looking at events we need to be able to not only analyse the different component parts of an event but also the way each of them integrate to create the total, or holistic, event experience. Using this as a basis to move forward we can look at the ideas of Pine and Gilmore and begin to see how they can help us understand more about event environments and experiences. Jackson (2005) suggests that these 'seminal experiential marketing concepts' are able to provide the 'holistic view required to encapsulate the customer experience'.

The experience economy is the 4th economic offering that should be seen as different from services:

> When a person buys a service, he (sic) purchases a set of intangible activities carried out on his behalf. But when he buys an experience, he pays to spend time enjoying a series of memorable events that a company stages – as in a theatrical play – to engage him in a personal way. Experiences have always been at the heart of entertainment, from plays and concerts to movies and TV shows. Over the past decades, however, the number of entertainment options has exploded to encompass many, many new experiences.
>
> Pine and Gilmore (1999, p. 2)

Staging experiences

The key distinction they make, that marks out experiences from goods, services and commodities is that experiences are meant to be memorable, and that they are occasions that engage us in a personal way. Therefore in order to achieve this memorable occasion it requires someone (individual or company) to actively create it for us. This is achieved through the actions of the 'experience stager' who no longer 'offers goods or services alone but the resulting experience, rich with sensations, created within the customer' (ibid, p. 12). In characterising such experiences they draw attention to the 'inherently personal' nature of them, and the way they engage with individuals on an 'emotional, physical, intellectual, or event spiritual level' (ibid, p. 12). As a consequence of this approach no single experience is the same for different individuals, we each get our own unique set of sensations. At this point we can begin to see the parallels that exist between the idea of experiences and the definitions of events that were drawn out earlier. There is a crossover of terminology beginning to emerge here and whilst not an exact match it is certainly being applied within a similar frame of reference. Recurring themes are apparent such as feelings of sensation, creation of unique occasions and multiple levels of engagement that suggest a clear link between the two. To further cement this link they also draw out that these experiences are the result of interactions 'between the staged event and the individual's prior state of mind and being'. Here we can see a recognition of the essential element that marks out an event, that is the creation of a specific environment, or as is the case here the staging of one. Either way the message is the same that experiences have to be produced, they simply do not exist on their own and as such they require input into them in order to activate the required experiences. The experience then unfolds as a result of our own interactions within this staged or created environment. This last point now offers direct reference back to the earlier discussion of experiential studies in leisure and tourism that noted that the beginning of an experience starts from the moment information is acquired about it and a decision is made whether or not to engage with the experience in the future (Mannell, 1999). From the moment the decision to go ahead is made, then the initial pre-experience phase begins and anticipation develops. The basis for our decisions are made more on personal fulfilment related to the types of experiences we believe we will get rather than on any other factor.

Experiential theory

What then are the key components of an experience that enable us firstly to choose the specific experience and secondly engage with the setting itself. O'Sullivan and Spangler (1999) presents the experience as part of a marketing continuum that starts out with the first point of contact for the experience and continues through to its delivery and reflection. They also develop a 'customer continuum' model where a product and service moves into an experience. At the same time the customer involvement also begins to move from one receiving service into one of care that leads into one of connection and results finally in collaboration. Experience and collaboration occupy the same sphere at the end of the continuum. As the role of the customer is changed from one of service recipient to experience collaborator they seek to understand this change through their updated version of the 4 Ps. Their four Ps of experience marketing then are: Parameters, People, Peripherals and PerInfoCom.

Pine and Gilmore (1999) suggests a slightly different approach and is more interested in the nature of the actual experience and how it is created. In their view experiences engage guests in a number of different dimensions, which they refer to as the Experience Realm. Figure 7.1 sets out the components of the realm. The realm itself is not too dissimilar, at least in content, from earlier typologies of leisure expressed in Haywood et al. (1995) and should not necessarily be viewed as applying concrete categories for understanding experiences. As events are multi-layered and multi-dimensional in the range of experiences they offer, and it is accurate to state that events can overlap each of the characteristics at the end of the axis. Guest participation in the experience is viewed on the horizontal axis; where active participation is one in which participants personally affect the event and the experience it yields (network meeting), whereas passive participation is not a result of such direct interaction (art exhibition). The vertical axis describes the connection or environmental relationship that unites customers with the event. Absorption is more of a mind experience (music festival) whilst immersion is a more physical experience (sports competition). The four realms contained within the shaded circle are the 4 Es of experience namely – entertainment, educational, esthetic (sic), escapist – and they are described as 'mutually compatible domains that often commingle to form uniquely personal encounters' (Pine & Gilmore, 1999, p. 31).

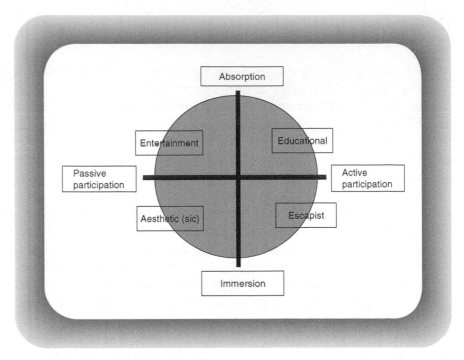

Figure 7.1   Pine and Gilmore's Experience Realm (reproduced from Pine and Gilmore, 1999, p. 30).

Having briefly identified the key points in the two approaches to experiences the task now is to apply these to specific events and present clear examples of their application.

4 Ps of experience: Parameters

O'Sullivan and Spangler's 4 Ps of experience marketing is made up of five segments and addresses what are seen as the essential components of an experience.

Five segments of experience according to O'Sullivan and Spangler (1999, p. 23):

The stages of the experience – events or feelings that occur prior, during, and after the experience
The actual experience – factors or variables within the experience that influence participation and shape outcomes

*The needs being addressed through the experience – the inner or psychic needs that give rise
to the need or desire to participate in an experience*

*The role of the participant and other people involved in the experience – the impact that the
personal qualities, behavior, and expectations of both the participant and other people
involved within the experience play in the overall outcome*

*The role and relationship with the provider of the experience – the ability and willingness
of the provider to customize, control and coordinate aspects of the experience*

For events management these five segments should be seen as a re-iteration of how much the role a constructed environment has to play in producing (event) experiences and so aid for a better understanding of the components and processes that are inherent in various experience types. Parameters of experience also helps us to be more aware of how events unfold during the course of an occasion and that, like most things we do, there is period of anticipation beforehand, the period of attending and the period after when we reflect. Each experience has a 'dimension' to it; the nature of this is a variable depending upon how and with what the experience is created. These experience variations relate to the elements within the experience, the interaction between participants and the type of outcome derived. O'Sullivan and Spangler offer some thoughts that might help in our creation of such experiences (1999, p. 29):

- Elements within the experience itself
  - Is it natural or artificial
  - Is it real or virtual
  - Is it commonplace or unique
  - Is it customized or mass-produced
  - What is the level of authenticity
- Interaction between participants and experience
  - Does it consist of concrete or disconnected episodes
  - Is it self facilitate or facilitated
  - Is the visitor role as a spectator or participant
- Range of outcome due to participation
  - Does it create a change in people that is temporary or transforming
  - Does it result in pleasure versus preservation

People

As we have suggested the role of people within an event is essential and the nature of their interaction an important element to consider. At the centre of the experience we have people, for it us they who are recipients of whatever it is we have created for them. Addressing people's needs is a key factor in understanding what types of experiences we wish to create. In fact event experience design in the modern idiom should be about the type of experience a client wants for their audience rather than simply creating a thematic image that looks visually impressive but fails to deliver the required experiential environment. O'Sullivan and Spangler suggest we concentrate on the people aspect of the experience by looking at it through the terms of core, culture, choice and change:

> *The core co-ordinate refers to central and unchangeable elements of individuals and includes age and stages of development, gender, race and ethnicity. The culture co-ordinate includes cohort grouping, household status, religion, EIO (education, income and occupation) and geographic location. Elements within the choice co-ordinate include values and attitudes, preferences, behaviours, and lifestyles, and the change co-ordinate contains factors related to health, life stages, life events, and seasonal and cyclical influences.*
>
> O'Sullivan and Spangler (1999, pp. 47–48)

It is not necessary to go into too much detail for each of these for our purposes here but we should be aware how people guide the very nature of experience and the variable co-ordinates outlined above. We can often see it practiced in simple examples such as sports events where we have age-related categories that create quite different event and competitive experiences, and are designed along lines that identify particle markets, that is the very different type of people who are available to who we can create event experiences for. Particle markets exist within previously defined categories. For example if we put on a youth event, what actually are we going to do given the very different types of people and experiences that would need to be catered for. We can have a number of possible experiences based on our interpretation or target group. Just consider, for a moment, the number of well-known particle markets that have been developed and to whom appropriate experiences can be targeted. The study of youth and sub-culture tells us there are endless variables to consider just based around the following nomenclatures of sub-cultural style and music such as punk, rockers, Rasta, old school, gangsta, b-Boy, metal head, gothic, garage and ska. Such a list tells us that there are wide and diverse interests to which we can direct our attention towards and create events for.

Case study 7.1

FHM Arms created by Brand Events

Event: Mobile Life

Chris Hughes MD of Brand Events, presented some of the following information at the ISES European Conference 2005.

Focus of case study

People interacting

Using people triggers to develop interaction

The FHM Arms was created as part of a multi-pronged promotional event aimed at the readership of the magazine FHM and was one of the exhibiting attractions that made up Mobile Life, 'the ultimate mobile lifestyle event' that took place over 3 days at Earl's Court, London and was presented by Carphone Warehouse together with a host of communication companies and associated sponsors such as Orange, Nokia, Metro, Honda, Kodak, KISS, Vodafone and FHM. Mobile Life itself offered event visitors the 'chance to experience how mobile communications can help you get more from your life, whilst on the move'. The experience promoted by the event was very much in-tune with the idea of fast, active lifestyles as the following introduction to the event suggests:

> *What do you fit into your fun-packed, rocket-paced, caffeine-fuelled 25-hour day? At Mobile Life you will have the chance to experience how mobile communications can help you get more from your life, whilst on the move. Held in Earls Court 2, on 13–15 June 2003 (10.00 a.m.–6.00 p.m.) you can spend all day visiting our Mobile Life Time Zones; Breakfast, Morning, Lunchtime and Afternoon. Drive-time, Evening, Late Night, Through-the-Night and The Carphone Warehouse will be at the centre of Mobile Life showing you how to find that extra 25th hour in your day.*

The idea of a '25th hour' offers a tantalizing glimpse of something unreachable, suggesting a very special component within the event itself. It was, of course, the core component for the main sponsors' (Carphone Warehouse) own activities within the event. Other event attractions were linked to current popular culture interests through the presence of professional footballers, celebrities and a radio station.

The FHM Arms was an attempt by the magazine to form a stronger bond with its own readership and also with any potential new audience generated through Mobile Life. Its core design concept revolved around a staple of British culture, the pub. This was one strand of the 'people' element of the FHM Arms, the target audience. The characteristics of the actual experience were dictated by ideas of what a typical 'British pub' was, as opposed to say the designer bar or pub/restaurant. Many aspects of British life are linked to the pub, but none more so than working class life where it serves as a focal point for local social and cultural activity. The characteristics of such a pub may be idealized to some extent but there are also very potent symbols that represent what such an environment may look like as is depicted in the television soap East Enders and it's central focal point, The Queen Vic (Victoria), named after a past British Monarch. Another obvious comparison would be between the TV series' 'Cheers' and 'Early Doors' both which depict, respectively, a US bar and a British pub. Although each have there own cast of regulars, the activities, habits and relationships are framed in totally different ways. More distinctly is the décor and ambience created by the two different environments. Therefore to create an authentic pub-type feel such as the FHM Arms it required not only the appropriate setting, but also the conspicuous symbols and artefacts of pub life. Importantly was the need to design in a people element that would help crate the atmosphere and that would generate visitors' interest and give the Arms an interactive element that would appeal to everyone, and in the process make it everyone's local. This was matched up with promotional literature that emphasized the type of people who might find the Arms an attraction:

> Visitors can meet up with their mates and have a swift half at the FHM Arms. A buzzy environment where you can sit and take in the entertainment, comedy and a selection of the FHM top 100 girls!
>
> In the Evening Zone you can call in at your favourite local, the FHM Arms and be served a pint by a glamorous babe, play pool with a snooker legend and step up to the oche with a five-times World Darts champion.

The latter of the two examples gives us our 'people' element for this event. Using recognisable and well-known faces from British sporting life and recreating staple pub sports games namely pool and darts, the FHM Arms offered visitors the chance to play sporting legends, something that is not an everyday occurrence. The people, Eric

Bristow former World Darts Champion and Dennis Taylor, former World Snooker Champion, thus provided a magnet for visitors looking for something 'special'. This people element for the event was then rounded off by the use of a former England cricketer, Phil Tufnell, to be the 'local' in the pub who was reportedly paid several thousands pounds to sit and the bar, chat to visitors and simply get drunk with them.

Case Study Activity: Research events past, present and future and describe how 'people' are used to create an interactive experience at the event or within the event. Is the model of the FHM Arms as an experiential promotional strategy replicated elsewhere?

Peripherals

This refers to 'multiple factors and variables related to and involved in the entire (experience) process. Peripherals add to the substance of the experience. They provide meaning for the participant and can be used to differentiate experiences from one another' (O'Sullivan & Spangler, p. 107). In some respects the peripherals relate directly to Rossman's (2004) artefacts and Barthes (1977) signs and symbols in that they provide the physical and textual evidence that helps us make meaning out of the event experience. Our response to these then controls how we view that experience. Peripherals incorporates a whole host of things related to the chosen place of something and also the price for involvement, but also brings attention to some of the multiple little elements that make up an experience and so includes:

Place (time and location)
Price
Packaging (physical evidence, personalisation, perks)
Participants
Policies and procedures
Public image
Patterns of demand
Popularity cycle

O'Sullivan and Spangler (1999, p. 112)

The combination of these elements ultimately begins to shape our experience of an event and the way it impacts upon us as participants.

We can consider each one of these individually and show how an experience is framed by how the peripherals mentioned here have been applied.

Activity 7.1

Using the list above select either one event or several different events that you are familiar with because you have worked on them, have knowledge of them or have visited them. Alternatively you can target a specific event and study it from promotion through to delivery and gather material on it before you make a visit.

For each of the eight elements then describe each one as they have been designed for the specific event(s) and analyse how each one shaped and impacted upon the experience that you had.

PerInfoCom

The last P to consider deals with the materials we use to make decisions about the type of experience we want created. This includes developing the idea of say the promotional process by which an experience provider makes contact with potential stakeholders. Commenting that traditional promotional material is not able to exploit any experience potential, a 'hybrid' term, PerInfoCom has been used to explore how the specific needs identified in experiences are met/matched/reached. It is a relatively simple term that incorporates' the need to 'communicate with people and to inform them about their needs as it relates to a particular experience while simultaneously doing so in such a personalized manner that will encourage them to take action' (O'Sullivan & Spangler, 1999, p. 133). In this we can begin to start an interpretation or deconstruction of the information provided and assess whether or not it will brings us the experience we want. A key approach in PerInfoCom is positioning (Ries & Trout, 1982). Positioning incorporates 'the actual design of the experience specifically to meet the needs of a particular group of people' (ibid, p. 138). Marketing an experience in this way is ensuring the message of an experience is directed at the targeted group, conjuring up a sense of need identification with the recipient. Positioning is the way in which an experience is framed in our mind with a particular distinctive feel or flavour. The creation and projection of the experience presents people with an image of what they think it will be like, this image can then be further enhanced by additional benefits linked to the image. We can see this in the communications used, for instance, in holiday and property exhibitions or destinations that use events and festivals to promote themselves or use events as to celebrate a particular country or culture. Ischgl, Austria, was one of the first ski resorts to promote itself through a free rock concert. In 1995 Elton John played a free concert at the resort and has since been followed by other rock superstars such as Sting and Bon Jovi. In 2006 Lionel Ritchie, Status Quo and Pink played to the largest ever crowds and Ischgl is now positioned as the party town for skiers coming from Munich and Stuttgart. Many resorts have since followed this approach of mixing a music festival and winter sports. The Telus World Ski and Snowboard Festival, Whistler, mixes freestyle events with live music, the Canyons area of Park City, Utah hoists a series of winter music events and Snowbombing, Mayrhofen is a blend of club cultures evidenced by its slogan 'piste by day, beats by night'. The aim of this is to connect people with an idea of a place, and using image associations such as music helps this. The suggested framework for putting this into practice is dubbed the 6 Ds.

6 Ds of experience

Using the six Ds of experience positioning will allow us to fully connect the experience with potential participants (O'Sullivan & Spangler, 1999). It is argued that consideration of these points will enable us understand how to frame an experience in people's minds, and importantly, enable us to carefully deliver the right kind of experience in reality. This understanding of event experience forms the pre-experience phase of our experience and, other than assumed knowledge or preferential tastes, is the initial point at which we consider what type of event experience we are likely to get. When we attend the actual event we inevitably begin to measure if the actual experience is what we anticipated.

The 6 Ds are outlined below with accompanying examples from events. They include how events have developed their experiential aspects in reality as well as promotional material.

Detail the specific needs or range of needs that can be accommodated within the type of experience. For an event this means being fully aware of the limitations to what can be done within a particular space and to understand what type of physical evidence needs to be present to fulfil the experience, for example fantasy events around an Xmas theme often require certain symbolic artefacts and symbols and these form part of a recurring set of images used in promotional material around that particular time of the year. Yet the ability to recreate, for example, a pure white fantasy scene is not easy and is not cheap so event managers have to be careful in what type of experience is promised (promoted) set against what they can actually deliver.

Depict the specific groups of people who may well be seeking to fulfil the needs that are provided by your experience.

Special events generated for and by specific groups often require needs fulfilling. A clear example is a one of the myriad of partner finding events or dating events aimed at single adults. As one female researcher put it 'I went along looking for a male partner, out of 120 people there were six men, and it was not a lesbian convention'. This is straightforward observation on the part of the particular participant and is a fairly obvious failure of promise on the part of the event organiser. Events offering 'interactive' elements also need to be carefully assessed as the reality of the interaction is often designed via specific control or booking mechanisms that inhibit many people's take up of them.

Delineate the exact benefits target market groups seek to take away from the experience. As stated above, going to a dating event and coming away without the slightest hint of either date or contacts is clearly not providing the right experience. Experiential tension, as we might call, is at its highest when an event offers something at odds with what we expected such as product events having both trade and public access on the same day. Delineating the target market that makes up a trade visitor and a public visitor is relatively easy to do, and from an event operational viewpoint this can be achieved by having limited access days. So for example an event that runs Thursday–Sunday, may have trade only access on the first 2 days, followed by public access at the weekends. This solves the operational issues of mixing the two markets up, but it doesn't solve the experiential differences. Public visitors often require a fundamentally different experience to the trade visitor, primarily because they are not there to buy in bulk or negotiate trade deals. Their 'viewing' of product is consumerist and is, by and large, emotional (notwithstanding the chance to buy the odd single item bargain). The trade visitor is more practical, concerned about things such as the profit margin they can get when selling the product on at retail value, whether the product fits their own target retail market or sits comfortably within their own retail range as well as making an assessment of whether or not the product is going to be a popular item per se. Although this requires obvious access to the product and information, the trade buyer doesn't need to get any other real experiential outcomes. For the public though this is not the case. One of the inherent weaknesses of some trade/public events is the simple inability to actually try out what is on offer, especially so if you are there as a member of the public who is there for precisely that purpose. We can all stare at the object and we can absorb information but often we cannot try it there and then or see it working. Of course in many cases there are perfectly sensible reasons for this, and it is up to us participants to perhaps follow up the event by finding access to the product. This, after all, is the purpose of most promotional specific events that are looking for subsequent return on investment through follow-up contacts. The benefit of such events to participants is that an array of products and services is on display under one roof, often from a particular industry (i.e. cars, furniture, PC technology), and so we can gather information on a range of them with little difficulty. But the fundamental exhibiting approaches for trade and public are not the same. As public we are in a live event experience, and surely we want something more than a glorified shop window. Many events have been stultifying, to say the least, in their desire to keep us away from display objects whether it is by glass partition, barrier or exclusive access. This is mostly where a trade show has a public day(s) and in terms of exhibiting style, nothing changes between the two. In this respect the events are little more than (poor) versions of retail outlets which display, like the shop window, the product for viewing only but actually offer little else that we cannot get from a visit to a shop, where often we can either use or see in use the actual product. Of course this view is industry, or product and service specific. Nevertheless the limitations of such event experiences has been recognised as events like this have started to become more interactive and more hands-on than in the past.

Until recently mainstream bicycle shows were like this, lots of displays and technology but nowhere to actually ride a bike or see the equipment in operation. Some even mixed trade and public access days, leaving an unsatisfying experience for all concerned (product manufacturers do not want the public to know the trade price of any item and a degree of tension builds up around a simple question such as: how much is this product). This has now begun to change partly for several reasons. The Las Vegas and Milan Bike shows, probably the major annual cycle shows in the world, have not only wonderful displays of machines and equipment, but are now a far more interactive experience that a decade or so ago. Manufacturers are more open to allowing their product to be seen 'in use', whether through a display of working arts on a stand or through the simple process of allowing a person to ride and test the equipment. They have also introduced visitor appeal activities such as trials circuits, BMX displays and jump arenas thus giving the events a far less static feel to them. This has influenced newer events, with the UK Bicycle Show 2002 winning the Best New Exhibition award at the annual UK Events Awards, as a result of its attempts to create a more special event experience as opposed to a functional trade display. In 2005, moving to London's Excel centre from the Business Design centre the event expanded its experiential qualities making a truly trade (1 day) and public (3 days) event that was full of interactive displays, activities and within-event shows. In addition to stand displays there was a catwalk show (for bikes!), an excess post oxygen exercise consumption test machine, a Tacx time-trial computer course, an Endless Pool where bicycles could be test ridden, a cycle circuit race and a safe cycle challenge.

Decide on the image or position you want to create in the participants' mind as it relates to your experience. Imaging experiences requires us to be able to project into the participants' mind an environment in which they will feel excited by, motivated and comfortable being in. Events promoting such experiences attempt to do this by depicting a 'flavour' of, say a geographic region, or even a brand. They also do it by directing lifestyle connections and connotations towards people that they can relate to. This is an important feature of all events but especially new ones that need to capture our attention for the first time. Whilst by no means all music events are subject to this cultural entrapment many are as it gives a distinct identity to both music and the subculture that surrounds it.

Design the experience as well as the communication message accordingly. The very essence of this book, how exactly is the experience delivered. This point will be examined elsewhere as well but it implies that there is more to event design that simply the idea of theming or staging. Much of what occurs within an event is about getting people to interact in the way in which the event client and/or manager wanted them to from the very beginning. The challenge is not to throw in a few flashes of colour, drapes, flowers and comfy chairs that a light system is then projected on to create an impact. This is simply ornamental dressing and although it is quite essential it is only one part of the whole design process (as is argued elsewhere in this book). The challenge for designing experiences is to make decisions with a conscious knowledge of how they will impact on guests and how the experience will then be created as a result, leading to the planned interactions that the event set out to achieve. Too often the promise is far greater than the reality. Design embraces all facets of experience but, it is true to say, that we can also take a more one-dimensional view of design and treat is as that part of the event that deals with creative artistry (often dealing with graphic elements) as witnessed through colour schemes, table dressings, ornamentation, displays, etc. and it is a very important feature of many events. Harnessing the technical skills available to them, the event manager has to be able to put into practice the image created and provide the right setting for it. We can see an example of this in the film the Fast and Furious, when towards the end of the film the main characters of street racers descend on an underground race meet. The means of getting there is surreptitious, secret, and well protected yet the event exhibits all the important features required for an off-street racing event. Rather than describe it to you in detail, I suggest you watch the film.

The finale: *Demonstrate, deliver and delight* by providing people with what you promised.

This is the outcome, the experience that was promised. Or better still more than was promised. It's a bit like going on a ghost train ride and wondering if you will be scared. The answer is usually no, since there are very few genuinely scary ghost trains, in fact there are very few scary events per se, yet we promise some of the spectacle of scariness through the events imagery. Halloween, for example, is a celebration associated with scariness yet events hardly ever achieve the experience of being scared. This is now being addressed and the UK theme park, Thorpe Park, utilised the skills of an event company Weird and Wonderful to help create 'Fright Night' and its main scare attraction 'SE7EN' which was promoted with the following slogan 'Repent for your sins with the arrival of a new and bloodcurdling horror maze, SE7EN'. So how do we deliver this? Delighting audiences, participants and guests, all at the same time can be a huge challenge to say the least but at this point the reputation of the organiser is at stake. The imagery of the earlier promotion or the promise of an organisational outcome (e.g. technical, skills based or learning events) is now going to be tested by its delivery and the actual experience that results. Sports clubs and franchises often run touring events (or road shows) during their out of season and the promise of many is direct access to the star players. The experience is sometimes a poor one because the promise of meeting the stars never materialises and instead second-string players fill in, disappointing many who had attended to see the main ones:

Experience Realm

• Pine and Gilmore's 4 Es of the Experience Realm
• Entertainment

In most cases we attribute entertainment experiences to passive consumption where we view, for example, someone performing for us, and people absorb 'the experiences through their senses' (Pine & Gilmore, 1999, p. 31). Watching and listening (television) provide the basis for passive absorption but it is pointed out that 'while many experiences entertain, they are not all, strictly speaking, entertainment' (ibid, p. 31). Entertainment today is highly developed and is almost routinely familiar to most of us. From this premise it is argued that as the experience economy develops, then 'people will look in new and different directions for more unusual experiences' (ibid, p. 31). As a consequence of this such experiences are likely to develop elements from other realms (educational, escapist and esthetic (sic)). Such events now exist in abundance as they have sought to meet the new expectancies of customers and guests and, of course, add a new dimension to events that otherwise may retain similar experiences year after year.

Activity 7.2

Choose an event that has developed the experience by adding an entertainment element to the event package. Analyse the entertainment element and explain how it contributed to the overall experience.

The educational

There is a degree of absorption within educational events, but there is also individual participation and interaction. Two foci are suggested for this to be truly achieved, one the engagement of the mind, the other the engagement of the body. The mechanism for doing, we could suggest, only limited by the creative imagination of those planning the event. In truth limitations of budget and technology will play a part but if we consider special events and exhibitions in, say museums, then the nature of interaction is being increased all the time. The result is the emergence of edutainment, where educational information is presented in an entertaining way (Addis, 2005). Education though may be viewed with limitations, especially if taken to mean the formal process of (teaching and) learning. But if we take education to mean the mental absorption of information that we otherwise were not aware of, then we can see it in a different light. Take, for instance, the role of trade shows and exhibitions, events where the purpose of the experience is to introduce either new ideas, new technologies, new product models and so on to either trade guest or public guests then we can consider some of the mechanisms used to create experiences linked to new product information.

Activity 7.3

Before reading the following Study case (7.2) complete the activity below:

Think creatively! Consider the archetypal trade show for car manufacturers, which take place in just about every country in the world. The experience of such events has historically followed a typical pattern and that is one of show and display where cars are put on display to show to the public. Sometimes you can sit in them, sometimes the hood may be opened and sometimes you can simply stare at them. More often than not, there are glamorously made up women on display to allure the male guest. Is it unfair to say this is a fairly dated form of presentation, set squarely within a gendered interpretation of male and female roles in terms car interest and buying. It also has an air of preciousness to it, with the untouchable car placed on a pedestal to attract the 'oohhs' and 'aahhs' of the passing guests. Occasionally there might be a 'seminar' on the car and company with drinks and canapés for guests and there will be the usual array of leaflets and glossy brochures.

Consider this scenario: The challenge now is to come up with an entertaining way of getting your message across at such an event. How would you provide an experience for guests to a car show? Try to think of one or two unique experiential components that you could put in to make a guest visit more than simply one of passively absorbing information.

When you have given your answer(s) and committed them to paper, only then should you read the following case study.

Case study 7.2

VW Cars, Geneva Motor Show

The following material was presented as part of a seminar session on creativity held at the International Special Events Society (ISES) 2006 European Education Conference, Novotel, London. Colia Vok Dams Group, MD of Vok Dams Kommunikation Direct, an event, live-marketing and communications company gave the presentation. The slides from the conference were made available on the ISES website:

Case study focus

Creative engagement of public with product

Developing mediated experience

The challenge facing the group was how to present cars in a new way to the public at the Geneva Car show. Their clients, VW, wanted something more than a display and show trade stand, and the brief required that guests and visitors to the VW stand left with an experience that they could remember and also left with knowledge about the particular model they were interested in. The standard approach to car sales is mostly show, display, talk and brochure where a combination of all of these is employed to pass on technical information to the potential buyer, or as is often stated, to help the guest identify their needs within our range of products. It was regarded as a viable goal to attempt to create an emotional link between guest and car, in other words try to engage with the public in a way that would make their visit to the VW stand memorable and, lest we forget, consider purchasing the car either now or in the future. Vok Dams solution to the problem was both innovative and daring, and required a high degree of technological input in order to produce the experience. A key aim was to engage the guests in an emotional exchange and information and knowledge transfer. One of the key ingredients for any motor show event is access to the product and although this can be fairly static in terms of display creativity, it usually involves touching it, sitting in it, inspecting it or even (but rarely) using it.

In order to do something different Vok Dams decided to make the VW stand and cars an 'once-in-a-lifetime' experience by providing a mediated individual product experience. This was achieved with 'speaking cars' via an interactive dialogue between the product (the car) and visitors. The dialogue was delivered via 16 international speakers who were assembled out of site in a back stage technical area. When visitors sat in the car, the car talked to them via the link. But this was no pre-recorded set of responses that played the same thing on a loop to each person. Instead, with a two-way audio pick-up in the car, the link voice was not only able to both direct the conversation towards the personality of the visitor but also attempt to match that personality with the personality of the car that the voice demonstrators had been given. In effect this live interaction was emotionalizing the guest/car relationship by giving the car a real, live soul and creating a sense of individuality for the guest, thereby moving them from a primarily mass event into one that was far more personal. The process is an attempt to produce a 'creative positive' within an event of this type which more often than not is a 'creative killer'. The crucial element here is the exchange of information about the product and that is achieved through the highly personalized interaction with the visitor allowing the technical features of each car to be integrated into a casual exchange. As a result of this creative approach to product information and education Vok Dams won the Gala Award for the most outstanding spectacle at the show.

The escapist

Their level of immersion characterizes escapist experiences. Whereas entertainment experiences are regarded as passive, escapist ones rely on the total active involvement of the guest or participant, in other words they are immersed in it.

Such immersion begins to draw us into ideas of experiential flow that Csikszentmihalyi (1991) amongst others has suggested is an essential part of experience and with it the optimal satisfaction gained from active involvement in an event or occasion. They become a factor in affecting the outcome of the experience. This suggests an added dimension to the movement or action that takes place. Pine and Gilmore point to the use of simulator rides as an example of this immersion experience whereby the act of consuming, say a movie, is augmented by the thrill of movement that enables customers to participate in the experience. As a result of such 'motion-based attractions' we can become immersed in a different perspective to the one we normally get:

> 'One such attraction is part of the American Wilderness Experience in California, where a film that presents the world from animal's point of view is supplemented by the sensation of the flowing forward and backward, pitching and yawing, shuddering, lurching and sometimes even rotating 360 degrees'.
>
> Csikszentmihalyi (1991, p. 33)

Such attempts to immerse us in these escapist realms is no longer the sole preserve of attraction-based experiences, it has also evolved into event based ones as well. When the UK company Virgin owned by entrepreneur Richard Branson branched out into operating a rail network they opted to promote the experience of travelling Virgin by creating an immersive experience on their stand at business and travel shows. Visitors to the Virgin stand at Business Travel held at London's Business Design Centre were invited to sit in a high-backed leather bound chair and stare at a TV screen. After a few moments a short journey of the train began with a screen showing a view as if the guest in the chair was strapped to the front of the engine. The chair itself was set on a small plinth and responded to the movement of the train and as it raced along the track. The point being made was that Virgin trains and newly laid lines accompanied by comfortable seating proving a traveling experience unmatched by other train operators. With the guest immersed in the simulation they could experience some sense of what this would be like and how superior, in terms of comfort stakes, the journey on a Virgin train would be.

We can take this idea of immersion one stage further by drawing some parallels with how video game technology has developed this feature of immersion through first player roles, interactive AI figures and environments. Ultimately it has created immersive 'worlds' through online interactive gaming such as World of Warcraft. Now consider how many events have attempted to incorporate this element of immersion in them. Event companies promoting particular brands, for example, attempt to create an immersive brand environment, as we saw earlier in the example of the FHM Pub. Immersion can result when people are not content with the immediate purpose of their experience and subsequently want something more out of it. Pine and Gilmore suggest that such escapist experiences 'do not just embark from but also voyage to some specific place and activity worthy of their time'. Therefore we can begin to understand how events and their interactive features have begun to evolve, since we as guest want something more than just the straightforward experience. So networking events, parties, celebrations, exhibitions and conferences amongst many others incorporate some element for an escapist feature that enables the guest to immerse themselves in another frame or place within the moment of the main event they are attending. This doesn't though have to be a simulation as it can be any kind of physical and mental immersion that allows guests to gain an experience. We might add that for events whilst this immersion may be the very event itself it can also be some part of the wider event concept, a single or series of elements and components that make up the total experience.

The ISES UK 2005 Xmas Ball was based around a TV programme 'Stars in their Eyes' and as a first phase of immersion this allowed ISES members who would have normally attended the event as a regular guest to play a participant role in the experience of their fellow members. The Stars in their Eyes show itself is an opportunity for members of the public to mimic a performance of their favourite musician or singer. The person is given full technical back up, make up, costume, music and support dancers if required and they then deliver the song of their choosing. Linking the main feature of the 2005 ball to this event afforded members a great opportunity to themselves be in an immersive situation and participate and shape not only their own experience but also those of their peers. Escaping into the world of a music performer allowed a person to experience a moment of being a star. For the record the performances delivered were Elvis, Britney Spears, Peggy Lee and Mariah Carey. Phase two of the immersion occurred afterwards when the ball continued with drinks, food and music. Set off to one side of the main event space was the chance for guests to experience an element of 'play'. A small arena had been set up and radio-controlled cars could be raced or crashed around a mini-race track. This small escapist component enabled a diversionary aspect of immersion to be integrated into the event and took people away from the fairly routinised feature of food, drink and disco. It offered another place or zone that, because of the nature of the activity, was worth escaping to, and could be seen as a place for mingling, hanging out, drinking, watching and participating. A further aspect of the experience could also be developed as small groups of people linked by their working relationship 'challenged, each other to a race and crash duel, especially once they had some food and drink inside them'.

The esthetic (sic) (sic)

This fourth realm is seen as an escapist world, but one where 'individuals immerse themselves in an event or environment but they have little or no effect on it, leaving the environment (but not themselves) essentially untouched' (Pine & Gilmore, 1990, p. 35). There is an element of 'gazing' about the esthetic (sic) realm (and the nature of the gaze has been a subject of tourism experiences through the work of Urry (1990)):

> *'While guests partaking of an educational experience may want to learn, of an escapist experience to do, of an entertainment experience want to – well, sense might be the best term – those partaking of an esthetic (sic) experience just want to be there'.*
>
> Pine and Gilmore (1990, p. 35)

Such experiences can be gained through gazing at authentic natural wonders such as the Grand Canyon, Mont Blanc, Old Faithful, Ayers Rock and so on. These are the esthetic (sic) of natural experience and so are not, in there natural standing, a part of events. However, they become a part of an event experience when they are used to provide a setting for an event that then combines the aesthetic (sic) with some other realm. Using natural backdrops begins to provide us with a two-dimensional aspect of experience where the setting provides the 'being there' element, whilst the event itself offers something else that is a more staged event experience. Whilst examples of this kind are not in abundance simply because the very best gazing experiences are not available for events there are some that can be used. Sporting events that use natural terrain can provide this backdrop and here we might think about ski events that take place in truly spectacular scenery and, on a similar note but in a different season, we might also look at road cycle racing such as the Tour De France with certain stages taking the riders through major alpine passes. We might also suggest that surfing events in Hawaii may have a similar quality attached to them and that celebratory events such as those around New Year that take place around Singapore beaches and the islands of Thailand offer a very spectacular location and esthetic (sic). Whilst the physical occasion of the actual event has to be created for us, the esthetic (sic) of the location provides a natural, authentic situation/location in which to achieve this.

An alternative way of developing an esthetic (sic) experience is to use the built environment to provide the gaze like quality (Robinson, 1990). This esthetic (sic) uses visual, cultural and architectural environments to accentuate the event experience. We have seen it in virtually every Olympics ever held as the host city uses its dominant landmarks to provide settings that are memorable. Some of these already existed, others were newly built for the event. This allows guests to just be there, to relish the experience of the setting itself and then the event that unfolds around it. For the 2004 World Cup held in Japan and Korea there were a number of highly sophisticated attempts to create stadia experiences like nothing previously offered. Perhaps the Sapporo Dome was the pinnacle of this, an indoor multi use arena that had a 'floating' pitch. Although not actually floating whilst in use, the grass pitch was grown outside of the main stadium, adjacent to it like a car park. On the day of the game, the pitch was floated on a hydraulic frame into the stadium, rotated 180 degrees then lowered into place and locked. Once the game was finished it was taken back outside again. Such design settings created within venues for specific parts of the major games, such as say the opening and closing ceremonies, although not offering any participatory component to guest and spectators, provide opportunities for engagement with that specific situation. Here interaction occurs in a social situation where we are immersed in an experience that is not purely about participation but is a result of a 'personally interpreted perception of a specific situation that is construed through interaction in a social occasion' (Csikszentmihalyi, 1991;

Rossman, 2003). We are now moving into the esthetic (sic) realm of, in the first instance, venue selection, and, in the second instance, environment or setting creativity. In the first case the focus is to regard the built environment as a special feature in it's own right and that provides an additional moment.

Activity 7.4

Using the typical profile of event types, research within each one a venue or location that provides an esthetic experience that augments the actual event itself. What particular innovative or inspiring locations can you discover?

Authenticity

Instead of a natural setting here we are considering venues that have been built. These obviously exist in their own right to provide a range of facilities to enable the event to take place. Within this existing environment we can then begin to create the experiential setting for the specific event. In creating such environments and settings, the issue of authenticity is raised. This suggests there is a problematic encounter with regard to authenticity that all events must face since by their very nature they are created rather than natural. Leisure and tourism natural experiences may be the target of experiential inauthenticity where there is an attempt to create a faux natural setting but we cannot say that the experience itself as it is felt emotionally, physically and psychologically for individuals is lacking authenticity. Pine and Gilmore suggest that there is no such thing as an artificial experience, even if the setting itself is. Every experience created within the individual is real, whether the stimuli are natural or simulated (p. 36). We might suggest here that if this is the case it alludes to the intrinsic satisfaction that we might get from an experience forwarded by Csikszentmihalyi (1991). So therefore successfully creating, for example, immersive event experiences, artificial or not, should provide intrinsically satisfying engagements that result in an optimal experience. Csikszentmihalyi wrote that 'the key element of an optimal experience is that it is an end in itself (1991, p. 67), it satisfies us as individuals. This approach points to the variable nature of individual responses to experiences and although we might be able to offer some conceptual analysis of the event, we must also reflect on the range of these variable responses in our analysis. Simply put an event that appeals to a 6-year-old child may be viewed by an adult differently. As in the case study on Xmas experiences whilst it is possible to offer an analysis of the experience from an adult perspective we must also consider doing the same from a child's perspective and attempt to interpret the event as they experience it. Neither analysis is devalued because of this, since as we have seen events operate on a multi-dimensional and multi-faceted level so they are open to multiple experiences. This range of potential experiential outcomes provides a formidable challenge to the event manager who has to consider which ones to create within the event. Inevitably this leads event managers into selections about target groups, target markets, particle markets, psychographic markets, lifestyle segments and so on. So we have some events that adopt a more holistic approach attempting to attract as wider audience as possible and provide experiences that can touch all of them at some point during the event or we see events broken down perhaps via branding or theming in order to appeal to particular groups of individuals.

Pine and Gilmore argue that in order to successfully produce the experience such groupings require they are more likely to be achieved when all four realms of experience are present, what they call 'the sweet-spot' (p. 38) of the Experience Realm:

> 'To design a rich, compelling, and engaging experience, you don't want to select and then stay in just one realm. Instead you want to use the experiential framework as a set of prompts that help you to creatively explore the aspects of each realm that might enhance the particular experience you wish to stage'.
>
> Pine and Gilmore (1999, p. 39)

They ask pre-experience and reflective questions that should address each realm and how it can be improved:

> What can be done to improve the esthetics for the experience? The esthetic (sic)s is what make your guests want to come in, sit down, and hang out. Think about what you can do to make the environment more inviting, interesting or comfortable. You want to create an atmosphere in which your guests feel free 'to be'.

Once there, what should your guests do? The escapist aspect of an experience draws your guests further, immersing them in activities. Focus on what you should encourage guests 'to do' if they are to become active participants in the experience.

The educational aspect of an experience, like the escapist, is essentially active. Learning, as it is now largely understood, requires the full participation of the learner. What do you want your guests 'to learn' from the experience? What information or activities will help to engage them in the exploration of knowledge and skills?

Entertainment, like esthetics (sic) is a passive aspect of an experience. When your guests are entertained, they're not really doing anything but responding to (enjoying, laughing at, etc.) the experience. Professional speakers get them to listen to ideas. What can you do by the way of entertainment to get your guests 'to stay'? How can you make the experience more fun and more enjoyable?

Pine and Gilmore (p. 40)

In addressing this idea of the Experience Realm we can begin to see how a sense of 'design' in the wider context than simply that of graphic interpretation, as suggested earlier in the work of Shebroff, Brown, etc. becomes an essential part of the landscape of the event. Creating settings and environments that help the event develop into a combination of experiential realms provides opportunities for creativity and experiential outcomes. It suggests an all-embracing approach to event planning, management and organisation; design a delivery in order to produce an extensive and enriching experience. This requires event planners and managers to think instructively about the use of, for example, space and the means to which it can be put in order to deliver a certain experience. It suggests a constructed and insightful approach to how environments can be used to enhance event experiences so that the sections and the totality of the event offers the potential to produce, in a guest, a state of optimal experience.

The examples we have looked at here merely touch the surface of possibility for understanding more of what events are about but the general premise that events can deliver certain experiences is clearly prevalent. The possibility of using events to market to key audiences is becoming more widespread as key operators in the advertising field, for example, shift some of their budget away from a more traditional approach towards a live one. Events can be used to attract direct sponsorship and companies can link themselves with markets that otherwise would be difficult to access. On a global scale probably the most successful example of this in recent years has been first of all the emergence of the extreme sports events and secondly the development of the X-Games phenomena. In this way events are used to target very specific groups of people in a way that TV advertising, for example, cannot. Innovative road shows such as Nokia messaging Frog Road-show (which in 2004 won an Industry award) work in this way, promising exposure to new technology and a chance to use it before purchase. Events such as these created for specific companies, products and services are often tagged lifestyle events having clear audience connections in mind.

Venue experience

In a similar away corporate sponsorship of event venues is a development that is attached to the idea of experience, linking a business name to a venue that is already rich in iconic imagery. Naming rights for event venues has become a popular way of associating business with specific audiences and this corporate naming infusion has reduced the number of independent and culturally associated venue names considerably. And, some sports fans might add, totally destroying that imagery in the process. It is odd that in an attempt to link a brand with an experience, the brand owners in effect undermine the strong cultural experience associated with a venue. Consider how many 'sponsored' stadiums have a connotation that goes beyond the name, whereas stadiums named after a place or person carry greater cultural impact and reverence. In some cases though this is not significant, in others it is. The brewers Carling have a nationwide list of prominent music/ theatre venues branded with their logo and named Carling Apollo. Most were built in the last century but frankly it doesn't really seem to make much impact emotionally as such venues have often had name and/or ownership changes and play host to numerous performers. One of the most prominent name changes has been in sports venues that have seen traditional names being replaced by those of commercial organisations. Whilst this is often a result of refurbishment or new development it is not exclusively so. Either way the names now being given to large stadiums is devoid of the soul and, some might say, culture, which the original venues had in abundance because they were seen as representative of the fans and spectators who follow their team. There is argument that such branding activities attempt to create a 'brand bubble' (Brown, 2001) around spectators so that there is no dilution of message between or clutter.

Activity 7.5

Think for a moment what the name Madison Square Garden conjures up. What does it represent in terms of a sporting venue and legacy and what connotations do we see in the name.

Now do a comparison with the stadium 3 com. How do you analyse the difference?

Venues of this kind are often named after the area they were located (Wembley, London), after some individual who at least had some association with the game (Wrigley Field, Chicago) or as a reference to the immediate culture (Aztec, Mexico). Now it is simply whoever pays the most gets the rights to call the stadium what they want. It acts as a calculated promotional route as opposed to an emotional attachment to a locale or person. In the accompanying chart we can see some of the significant changes that have occurred in US sports, in baseball and American football.

Some of the main changes have occurred in the NFL (see Table 7.2). In the UK the trend is mainly for new stadiums to be named after sponsors rather than older ones to be changed so Arsenal FC's move from their original Art Deco structure at the Highbury Stadium led to the new modern high-tech one being called the Emirates Stadium after the airline of the same name. The conclusion to be drawn is that we can begin to think more articulately about how we market such experiences through, in the above case, positioning and that this offers us many different approaches for study. Where this leads us is towards a better understanding of how events are communicated. The range of techniques being adopted to attract audiences to events is now clearly recognized (Masterman & Wood, 2005) and that the nature of event types lends themselves very well to suggestive and interpretive communication activities. The promise of a live experience is the essential quality that all events have to offer but the decision to choose one event over another is a part of our complex rationalisation of choice. For subject matter we are familiar with then the choice is far easier and often based on ticket availability, peer group influence and our own motivation to attend (or repeat attend). For something we know very little about the choice to be made is influenced initially by the type of information we receive through promotional activity and the extent to which that stimulates our interest (Masterman & Wood, 2005). According to Mannell (1999) the experiential values from which we

Table 7.2 Sports venues name change (USA).

Old Name	Team	New Name
Patriots Stadium	New England	Gillette Stadium
Mile High Stadium	Denver	Invesco Field
Oakland Coliseum	Oakland	McAfee Coliseum
Jack Murphy Stadium	San Diego	Qualcomm Stadium
Jack Kent Cook Stadium	Washington	FedEx Field
Silverdome	Detroit	Ford Field
The Ballpark in Arlington (1994–2003)	Texas	Ameriquest Field in Arlington
Chase Field	Arizona	Bank One Ballpark
Comiskey Park (New) (1990–2002)	Chicago	US Cellular Field

will gleam our satisfaction are constructed in our minds (at this initial point of contact) and then remain and form part of our ultimate evaluation of the actual experience we have. Therefore, the ability of marketing to instill a pre-experiential sense of anticipation is crucial in the initial choice we make, but it is not left behind and forgotten. Our pre-experience phase is awaiting a cognitive response from us from the moment we arrive at the event and where the extent to which it is satiated is then dependent upon the relationship between promise and reality. At this point the event has to deliver the type of experience anticipated, or delivers one beyond those expectations, otherwise the experience will fall flat often in direct relation to the marketing pre-experience we had been exposed to.

The question this raises is how we make sense of these marketing experiences that are created for us and how they can be studied. What we can see is that they create an image that we either respond to or ignore. Notwithstanding other social, economic and cultural influences we base our response on the type of experience we believe will be offered, in other words we instantly begin to interpret the promotional material and deconstruct the messages we are presented with. If we refer this process to experience marketing of a product it suggests that it is intended to give it a presence that is more than just the physics and quality of using it but to give it life and experience beyond that. So, for example, buying a pair of Nike Air Jordan is more than just a functional sports shoe, it is imbued with other qualities, other connotations that give it desirability and status beyond its functionality. This is how an experience of a product is formed and we can see this everyday in advertisements on television where the product is targeted at a lifestyle and an image associated with it (O'Sullivan & Spangler, 1999). Honda's Lexus ad transmitted throughout 2005 exudes corporate smugness, in the way it identifies with the business person who needs to look the part, to be smug and self-satisfied about their job and role and to locate themselves on the hierarchical ladder through the car they drive. This homage to the business executive exemplifies the way the experience and message of the car takes over from the physical aspects of it, hardly any of which are featured in the ad other than the car's appearance. It is this approach to advertising that is now being mirrored in event marketing where we have, say, experiences of event participation being imbued with images, qualities and features that go beyond just physically being there. Let's consider how this takes place.

Experience infusers

As I mentioned earlier, O'Sullivan and Spangler describes this process as one where by products and services are subject to activity by infusers, enhancers and makers of the experiences. Infusers help mark out an experience as distinct, these are the things that enables us to be different in our choice of engagement. Infusers are there to facilitate the experience we seek. It is easy to get drawn into believing that such elements of an experience only apply to large-scale hallmark or mega-events, but this is not the case. Whilst these may be the ones with the most noticeable and high-profile examples, more locally based events carry infusions but on a smaller and more discreet basis. Infusing an experience does not have to be a spectacular element, but quite clearly it can be. Events such as La Dolce Vita sponsored by Alfa Romeo cars, with its slogan 'calling all lovers of Italy' carries such strong infusers in their attempt to create a realistic experience of Italy for the event attendee. The extract from the website winedine.co.uk used below was the result of press releases by the event organizers and the information included here was pretty much mirrored elsewhere word for word by other online and hard print publications and they give a strong indication of how such an event is experientially promoted. Such obvious location and geographic attachments allow an event to be created in a particular way, in this case, an entire country. The promise of an escape to a false Italy can only be achieved through marketing of a live experience that connects with our understanding of what Italy represents. Of course this itself is a problematic area, for there is no-single true Italy, and so the event organizers have to project an image of how the event will be infused with indicators of a symbolic Italian experience.

Delectable delights at La Dolce Vita

With its wealth of stunning landscapes, passionate hospitality and diverse regions, Italy has long offered food lovers an array of gastronomic pleasures. There is no need to go all the way to Italy, as hundreds of mouth-watering specialties and traditional flavours will be available closer to home this spring, when Italy comes to London, with La Dolce Vita. La Dolce Vita, sponsored by Alfa Romeo, will take place at Earls Court 2 from the 8th–10th April and will showcase Italian lifestyle at its best. This three-day event will encourage visitors to taste the best that Italy has to offer and really embrace the Italian way of life. A traditional cobbled piazza will be recreated at the centre of the show to reflect the true heart of every Italian city. Surrounding this piazza will be a selection of restaurants, including Locanda Locatelli, Zilli Fish, Etruscas Zuccato City and Zuccato, Sardo, Little Italy. Visitors can purchase tickets to exchange for starter portions of dishes from each restaurant, thus giving them the opportunity to taste their way around the best that London offers in Italian food. For the ultimate authentic Italian beverage, visitors can choose from the selection of cafes that will also surround the piazza. These will include Fratelli Deli and Bar Italia relocating from the hub of Soho to the heart of mini Italy at La Dolce Vita.

Budding gastronomes can benefit from demonstrations given by well renowned chefs in the Buongustaio theatre and can learn skills from Giorgio Locatelli, Aldo Zilli, the head chef at Rick Steins Seafood Restaurant Padstow, Jose Graziosi, Valentino Bosch from Percento and Steffano Stecca from the Brunello who will all be showing off their culinary skills using Alessis special range of La Cintura di Orione and Mami pans. Food lovers can chat to the team at Caffe Caldesi to discover a truly authentic Italian experience at their excellent cooking schools in both Marylebone and Tuscany. Italian Secrets will also be revealed by Anna Venturi who will be talking about her gastronomic cookery week that she runs from her own stunning Tuscan villa.

The Food & Wine area will offer an array of specialties from Italy. Brands include: Savoria, the home of Iveri sapori dItalia (the true tastes of Italy), providing a spectacular selection of the finest Italian food from each region, Dress Italians delicious home, made pasta sauces, Extrav Cozzicioti Salvotores extra Virgin olive oil from Puglia one of the exciting up and coming areas in Italy and Morellis creamy Italian gelati served extravagantly in designer Italian glass wear, with an abundance of glorious toppings and adornments! Winecellars of London will offer an iconic selection of wines including Planeta, Fontanafredda and Castello di Brolio. Divinus will also be present with stunning wines and olive oils from Puglia. Beer and grappa fans can tickle their taste buds with Peronis Nastro Azzuro and Nardini Grappa. They can learn more about this classic Italian spirit that is a perfect complement to bitter chocolate and espresso coffee, from the expert Nardini family skilled in making grappa since 1779.

Extract from FoodWine& Dine: retrieved 10/12/05 from winedine.co.uk/home/ lifestyle.htm

Socially, the idea of transition tracking has taken us from purpose to pleasure and though we have functional business and organisational events, even with them there is a need for it to be mixed within an element of a pleasurable remit. One example of this is the global competition for business exhibitions and conferences where a supply of services (venue, hotels, leisure facilities, etc.) is an attractive part of an equation in which several cities are chasing the dream of 10,000 dentists descending on them for an annual gathering. This in turn extends to event exhibitors who can find many different ways to display either services or goods in way that is pleasurable as well as purposeful as we have seen earlier through the FHM Arms. In a similar way the ice-cream manufacturer Walls once had a stand at Ideal Home that consisted of a walk-through adventure for making an ice cream. Visitors entered a huge stand that looked like an industrial ice-cream maker set on two levels. Once inside guests were taken on a walk-through of research, design and production of a typical ice cream, in this case, a Solero ice lollipop. There was no hard sales pitch or sell by any of the staff, and at the exit door there was free ice cream.

Experience enhancers

Experience enhancers are used to develop the services at an event. We might see this as a shift into more personalized experiences for people, where they can experience a service as it should be; perhaps as they wished it would be as well. In this way we can begin to identify what feelings a person may get from coming to a certain event. Emotive appeals to ours senses can reflect this approach through marketing slogans linked with the event. One way of explaining this is to consider it from a transition tracking point of view that shows how experiences have changed. Instead of just choosing something for its tangible qualities, we do so on the basis of inner values, where choices are made as a reflection of what we might be dreaming, thinking or feeling. For example attending music events, which have a great capacity for anecdotal recollection, becomes more about identifying with the self-expressive uses we can put it to than simply being there for the music. To attend Glastonbury is a fundamentally different experience as a feeling and a reality compared with T in the park, V Festival or, in the past, Reading Festival. European festivals such as Roskilde carry similar attachments that are recognized by the audience. Of course this is not always a static entity, and the transformation of Glastonbury from free, alternative music festival to one that is expensive, security patrolled and more populist in its musical programme shows how this evolution occurs. It is both a reflection of the changing nature of outdoor events, of the ambitions of the organizers and, significantly, of the changing demands and needs of the audience. Choosing so-called credible (or fashionable) events over less credible ones is based on a perception of their cultural value as much as there practical value.

Activity 7.6

Are some events more credible (fashionable) than others? Try to draw up a list of event types for either and then identify the factors you feel makes one event more credible than another.

As with infusers so too enhancers have seen changes in the way we experience them. Provision of service is no longer expert to novice, but is about partnerships, where we share knowledge and desire. Academic conferences have, in some but not all cases, changed in this way from being Plenary directed with select academics being put on a pedestal, to being more integrated with workshops, seminars, debate councils, forums, panel discussions to involve everyone in the debate rather than simply to be addressed by the singular expert.

A quite fundamental shift may be emerging as we move from introvert to extrovert people. Rather than simply acquiescing to the protocol of recipients, more people want to be heard, want to have a voice. This is most notable in areas like cinemas and theatres but is apparent at exhibitions also where the serene and silent reflection of art is being challenged, not only by visitors but also by the nature of exhibitions that are, by design, dynamically active rather than passive. In 2003 the Tate Modern in London. Exhibited Olafur Eliasson's installation the Weather

Figure 7.2   Visitor interacts and creates a silhouette at the Tate Modern.

Project in the vast expanse of its Turbine Hall. The project itself is a part-illusion for the image (photo 7.2) above shows a full sun spreading light in its darkened hall. In actual fact the installation of the sun was only a semi-circle, the other half of it was a bank of mirrors reflecting back.

Here is an extract from the Tate's own website about the installation:

> *In this installation, the Weather Project, representations of the sun and sky dominate the expanse of the Turbine Hall. A fine mist permeates the space, as if creeping in from the environment outside. Throughout the day, the mist accumulates into faint, cloud-like formations, before dissipating across the space. A glance overhead, to see where the mist might escape, reveals that the ceiling of the Turbine Hall has disappeared, replaced by a reflection of the space below. At the far end of the hall is a giant semi-circular form made up of hundreds of mono-frequency lamps. The arc repeated in the mirror overhead produces a sphere of dazzling radiance linking the real space with the reflection. Generally used in street lighting, mono-frequency lamps emit light at such a narrow frequency that colours other than yellow and black are invisible, thus transforming the visual field around the sun into a vast duotone landscape (www.tate.or.uk).*

What was the experience of visitors to this installation and how did they interact with it? Rather than be inconspicuous or introverted exhibition visitors the vast majority made the space their own and developed a more extrovert approach that resulted in an experience of the installation slightly removed from that intended. Many people lay down on the floor of the hall, formed into ad hoc groups and saw reflections of themselves off of the ceiling in any number of bizarre ways – stars, circles or just sitting – so that the focal point of their experience became less the sun but more their own, their friends and their physical neighbours interaction with the physical environment. Far more photos appeared to have been taken of people's reflections and in relation to the sun rather than simply of it. This interaction between the visitors and the exhibition appeared to be spontaneous and not the result of any designed process. Although the mirrors formed part of the installation it's purpose was to communicate ideas about the weather and landscape but visitors used them to develop their own additional experience.

Experience makers

As a historical point we can see this as the main domain of the event manager. The craft of making events happen is not a new phenomenon but its significance in both business and entertainment is growing as events are used as tools for all manner of activities. Tracing events back in time to the ancient Greeks and the Romans, to the pagan and religious festivals people have had a desire to be entertained. This historical starting point for event management is based on celebrations for religious dates, marriage ceremonies, victory in battle and similar occasions. Events with a relative long history can be viewed over time to identify changes in the way the experience has been made, but this is not so easy since we don't have a lot of data on events or a lot of studies for comparable information. Certainly analytical descriptions of events are not in abundance and so we can often only rely on descriptive anecdotal accounts if we want to show how the important elements of an event may have changed. The Olympics offer some opportunities, but it is really only at the level of spectacular openings, of which all Olympics have them. Nevertheless making an opening statement is now a feature of many modern sports events, especially so for global ones and the impact of such events is highly significant for galvanising interest in event management. This globalisation of events raises awareness of the practice of event management at all levels. As I have mentioned earlier, the celebrations of the millennium were a great catalyst for interest and activity in the process of making events happen and how different parts of society interpreted the millennium showed off the wide range of creative ideas employed in these events from choice of location to range of actual occurrences both leading up to and at the point of midnight.

O'Sullivan and Spangler (1999) argue that such experience makers in society are less concerned with making a social contribution than for making an entertaining one. This point though indicates that we should therefore look with more insight at exactly the mechanisms used for the entertainment, and begin to dissect the elements used in the experience creation. In events where there are several overriding aims, we can use tools to explore them, and explain some of the 'average' elements we encounter. For instance in village fetes or galas, situated as many are in the public or voluntary context, where communal aims or messages are the essential experience we do not necessarily expect truly spectacular wow type encounters, for these types of events are run with a different purpose in mind. However, where an event is situated within a public/private and profit-based context, and where the primary aim is entertainment, then we have to be able to look at them differently. This does not main though that these events are devoid of any other kind of analytical component, but more that we should consider how the experience has been made within some kind of relevant context.

For instance in looking at experiences made for entertainment, the following short list could be used in identifying what the main purpose and intention is and against which we can begin to measure the events success (as an experience):

- escaping from reality;
- interacting with others;
- facilitating a sense of belonging to a larger group;
- meeting inner or psychic needs in a safe and socially acceptable manner.

So we might now begin to look at some of the experiences made for us in this light and ask to what extent these factors are achieved. As with enhancers and infusers so there have been changes in the way experiences are made for us. Mass participation and technology has brought most things within the grasp of the majority of people so we have experiences for all. One of the biggest single changes in experiences has been the rise of extreme activities coupled with a reduction of the risks associated with the activity. Within the event framework this is, actually, less of a concern than it is for packaged type activities which if only for insurance purposes have to be integrally safe. But there is a crossover particularly to event expeditions, which offer extremeness, but within well-established safety parameters. For example, signing-up for an expedition event to Mount Everest is seen as both attainable and safe for people who have enough money spare, and the expectancy is that nothing untoward will happened. This despite the fact that scaling Everest is one of the most challenging physical activities anyone can do, set in the most hostile of environments where weather and climate can change abruptly and there are very serious health risks. People, in ever greater numbers, undertake expedition events across the Sahara desert, along the Inca trail in Peru, across back country ski areas and along mountain bike routes with very little concern for safety issues because the 'extreme' experience of danger is all but removed by the provider of the excursion. Experiences are both coming together and separating as we want newer individual ones for ourselves but also want shared ones with others, ones that are memorable because they are a celebration of togetherness and communal.

These ideas on the creation and formation of experiences have been drawn from within a marketing framework, establishing a number of central themes that help us understand a little bit more about the factors that go into making them. We can use these ideas to offer further insight into event marketing experiences to demonstrate how the experience has been presented to us and the likely experience we will get as a result. The purpose of an event management analysis is to then interpret both the promise and how the experience unfolds in reality. In this way we can begin to identify the features of the experience that will have formed the pre-experience and think about how those relate to the actual and post experience.

The questions we might ask are quite simple. With repeated implementation we can begin to understand more about the evolution of specific types of events and also about significant differences between events based on their design and the experience they produce. Infusing and enhancing events can be charted and these moments of change explored, event experiences should then be seen as part of the wider change in experiences sought by people and we can already identify some of these. The clearest approach is with the term special event, which conjures up ideas of uniqueness, and how an event with repeated calendar date, develops and changes as an experience. This does not automatically suggest that these changes will be better, but our conundrum, at present, is to be able to make a meaningful analysis of such changes and offer some kind of assessment of their worth, both in relation to the events history and also in comparison to other events. For example, no-one doubts the spectacular nature of the opening ceremonies of the World Cup and Olympic Games but the never-ending search for a uniquely designed ceremony results in an elongation of the event running time which is often uncomfortable to sit through or watch on TV.

At this point we might now begin to draw out some points to reflect upon such as:

- What type of people do certain events attract and do these change for each version of the event?
- How are themed events used to create experiences?
- What aspect of an event experience makes it unique?
- How do event experiences change over time, either for specific events or events generally?
- What types of experiences make for the best exhibitions, sports events, wedding ceremonies?
- How can experience be developed from the existing interactions of people to embrace newer ones?

Summary

By utilising the idea of experiences as they have been understood in the context of leisure, tourism and business and by employing some of those ideas on the marketing and developing of experiences there are a number of ways that we can now think more coherently about events. With the examples used in this section we can recognise the importance of the experience as a fundamental component in creating events, and that there are a number of pointers we can look to in order to further our knowledge about how experiences are projected towards their likely audience. The next stage is to provide further ideas on some of the specifics of an experience and how we might attempt to explore them within the occasion itself. In this respect there are perhaps two questions: (1) how are experiences created and (2) what tools can we use to help understand these designed experiences.

Chapter 8
Experience design

Learning outcomes/objectives

Understand what is meant by the term 'experience design'

List the different elements of experience design

Describe its different applications in practice

Appreciate how experience can be forecast

Understand how design strategy produces experiences

Reflect on the role of design within events

Introduction

In previous chapters we have looked at what is meant by events, design and experience and sought to draw correlations between the three so that designed event experiences can be more meaningfully analysed. In order to advance this discussion further it is necessary to explore the relationship between experience and design. In this chapter we will identify what is meant by the term 'experience design' and consider its applicability for events. So far we have explored the concept of experience and the concept of design but how do we connect the two together. What we need to know is how does design relate to experience, and how are environments invested with this experience. Understanding the link between the two offers some indicators for how events can be further understood for part of this process incorporates and can be applied to business and management as well as creativity.

What is experience design?

'Experience design is a new emerging paradigm, a call for inclusion: it calls for an integrative practice of design'.

Jackson (2000)

As a new and developing term it draws upon historical ideas of various disciplines to help give a greater understanding of how design and experience are interrelated to help explain the processes involved in designing for experiences.

'The design of experiences isn't any newer than the recognition of experiences. As a discipline, though, Experience Design is still somewhat in its infancy. Simultaneously, by having no history (since it is a discipline so newly defined), and the longest history (since it is the culmination of many, ancient disciplines), experience design has become newly recognized and named. However, it is really the combination of many previous disciplines; but never before have these disciplines been so interrelated, nor have the possibilities for integrating them into whole solutions been so great. Experience Design as a discipline is also so new that its very definition is in flux. Many see it only as a field for digital media, while others view it in broad-brush terms that encompass traditional, established, and other such diverse disciplines as theatre, graphic design, storytelling, exhibit design, theme-park design, online design, game design, interior design, architecture, and so forth. The list is long enough that the space it describes has not been formally defined'.

Shebroff (2001)

Whilst there has been a general adoption of experience design as a tool for developing and understanding web-based technology experiences

(Krug & Black, 2000; Nielson, 2000; Sterne, 1999), it's use and application is not restricted to these areas and it can be applied to many forms of design-based activity. As a new paradigm it is becoming more popular, precisely because it does offer some models for analysing and interpreting web-based experiences as well as analysis of more physical environment-based experiences. For events this has potential application in general but also because we have seen the rise of web-casts for music, sport and other events in recent years. The activity that is associated with it is spelt out below in a glossary of terms, but we first need to see how many of the general principles that experience designers operate around have direct parallels with event management and the creation of event experiences. The main focus for experience designing is to create desired perceptions, cognition and behaviour among users, customers, visitors, or the audience (Jackson, 2000). Expertise and skill is drawn from many specialisations and their sub-fields and the key to success is the ability to work together and, importantly, to also work with non-design professional. As a result there are clear synergies in cross-disciplinary associations. All of these are features that could be applied to event management.

According to AIGA (American Institute of Graphic Arts) experience design is characterised as follows:

Experience design is:

A different approach to design that has wider boundaries than traditional design and that strives for creating experiences beyond just products or services

The view of a product or service from the entire lifecycle with a customer, from before they perceive the need to when they discard it

Creating a relationship with individuals, not targeting a mass market

Concerned with invoking and creating an environment that connects on an emotional or value level to the customer

Built upon both traditional design disciplines in the creation of products, services, as well as environments in a variety of disciplines.

(http://www.aiga.org)

Unsurprisingly there is synergy here with the characteristics of experience expounded by Pine and Gilmore (1999) and O'Sullivan and Spangler (1999). We can see from the Table 8.1, how these statements have overlaps for event management.

This similarity of purpose is based on both approaches' need for some semblance of creativity, since each has to develop something that otherwise does not exist. In this respect both are attempting to provide solutions to a perceived problem where the challenge of the solution is to create an experience that connects with people. Key points to emerge

Table 8.1 Experience design and event management.

Experience design	Applicability to event management
A different approach to design that has wider boundaries than traditional design and that strives for creating experiences beyond just products or services.	YES. Different to other routine activities that strives to create unique event environments.
The view of a product or service from the entire lifecycle with a customer, from before they perceive the need to when they discard it.	YES. Overview of event from start to finish with client, but does not occur prior to client, although does occur prior to guest/consumer.
Creating a relationship with individuals, not targeting a mass market.	YES and NO. Depends on event size and type but brand events, private arties, charity balls have target not mass market appeal.
Concerned with invoking and creating an environment that connects on an emotional or value level to the customer.	YES. Central to event management, creating an environment from nothing to connect with guests/customers.
Built upon both traditional design disciplines in the creation of products, services, as well as environments in a variety of disciplines.	YES and NO. Event environment requires multi-disciplined approach, creates service and multi-experience environment for example taste, smell, sound.

are: (1) Both can quite rightly claim to be solving problems of organisational connection and communication. A case in point is the notion of event stakeholders providing a multi-layered array of potential connection and communication challenges that an event has to overcome. Stakeholders are in effect any relationships that form between an organisation and its external/internal constituents, solving problems between these groups can require complex multi-dimensional solutions due to the variety of constituents – employees, investors, volunteers, suppliers, partners even competitors. (2) What is the purpose of attempting to solve such problems? One of the main purposes of any event is its' ability to understand people, since they are the vital ingredient that creates uniqueness. If we know something about lifestyle, for example, we can design events to fit with such preferences, for example X Games. In a similar way experience design, by understanding people – character, behaviour, context – can apply ideas and concepts that help business match up. (3) Event managers decide what they want to create, within the context of the first two points; they solve the problem of how to celebrate a birthday party, product launch, homecoming. As we have seen in earlier chapters events are about a concept, an idea of the type of event experience we want to take place. In order to achieve this we have to at least envisage how that might occur and then we have to decide how to communicate that to people. This can be a mixture of many components entirely dependent upon the event type. By the same token experience design helps make decisions about what products might be made, the types of service offered and the communication mechanism. The goal is of course to make them at least useful to people, and on top of that they should be usable. If they can be made desirable as well then the problem of communicating is solved.

Experience foresight

Event management is a predicative skill, one of attempting to predict what people will want from an event and how then to design that event. It is very much about future reading, putting a scenario together that will produce a successful event setting. In the case of the Olympics this future reading has a 7-year lead in time, almost 10 if you include the period leading up to any actual decision to bid and the bid competition itself. Each of the final list of five cities bidding for the 2012 Games attempted to project an experience of what the Olympics would be like in their city. This involved using images of venues, historic sites, landscapes and visions of what any visitor would experience. Morello writes that design predicts the future when it anticipates experience (2000). How though do we predict event experience? One way would be to develop a tool that would serve as reference point in understanding what features people might want out of an experience, a way of forecasting experience needs. A possible way of achieving this might be to develop an ontology, a knowledge domain, of experience or event experience that we could draw on. In the meantime, until such an ontology exists, what else might we use? Any tool, to be successfully applied to events, would have to have some central core that included people as a pivotal strategy in any decision-making process. The following matrix, produced by Zoels and Gabrielli (2003) provides such a human centred platform so that foresight of experience can, in theory, be planned (Table 8.2).

Table 8.2 Experience matrix.

Sensory
Tactile responsive, flowing
Visual pleasing, current colours, lush
Photographs
Auditory mystical, enticing, hip
Intellectual
Emotional adventurous, intimate, authentic
Functional resources, geographic
Information, product information
(Cultural) self-actualizing
'Core', non-pretentious, aspirational, personal image

Source: Zoels and Gabrielli (2003).

This particular model is classed as a human-based strategy fundamentally concerned with the experience derived from products. Is it applicable to event management? The answer is yes, because although product originated, events are used to project the experience of the products via launches, promotions, road shows and so on. Earlier we discussed how Jackson (2005) identified the experiential characteristics that could be applied to events and we can see that there are several clear correlations between the two. However in our understanding of these experiences there was a greater range of categories suggested. This is to be expected given that events , by and large, are a more complex equation to solve than the development of a single product notwithstanding technical issues of product development. Zoels and Gabrielli's matrix suggests the central concerns that should be addressed in designing experiences, with an appeal to sensory and intellectual stimulation a driving force. Events, that have both a perishability and intangibility to them, are also concerned with appealing to people in this way since for certain event types the mental and sensory experience is all that remains once the event is finished. This lives on in memory as we very rarely have a specific product to take away with us, although there are exceptions to this with brand events and populist exhibitions that have a retail component.

In adopting a strategic design approach we can initiate foresight and innovation processes that can enhance 'scenarios of the future with the visual, the spatial, and the experiential (Zoels & Gabrielli, 2003)'. Such processes cover a wide range for, as with events, they have complex subjects to deal with. Ultimately design as a practice can offer numerous techniques for depicting and predicting future scenarios and allows for a deeper level of understanding from and of stakeholders. Conducting research amongst designers Zoels and Gabielli found that by mapping findings visually they could establish relationships between different concepts. From this they identified five themes around which they could develop the concept products:

1 An awareness of the senses
2 Space and how to address the choice of location of an appliance
3 Ritual, social interaction
4 Fabrics of the future
5 Environmental concerns.

If we refer back to the earlier discussions on experience and events that established the link with design we can see that these themes here have some compatibility. We can now establish solid connections in terms of process and purpose that link the ideas of event, design and experience. One way of understanding this is to see them as three interrelated circles. Event is the main dominant circle with the two interlinked circles of design and experience located inside it. The truly integrated event will be a perfect balance of all three where event concept, design creativity and experience setting blend equally, that is at the point where design and experience overlap. Linking experience and design enables us firstly to begin thinking about a framework for developing event experiences and secondly, a way of analysing and interpreting them.

Therefore having looked at some of the ideas that influence experience design, we will now look at some of the means for putting it into practice. Shebroff (2004) is one of the strongest advocates for seeing design as more than a visual graphic solution to problems and suggests a range of practices that can and should include design. The following glossary of terms and definitions on experience design (in bold) offers an account of numerous definitions to help explain their purpose in the context of designing to create experiences (Shebroff, N at www.nathan.com). The glossary is not reproduced verbatim but the definitions and explanations have been para-phrased. For each one I have added an additional observation offering a way of linking them to event settings. To begin with **Design** is regarded as set of fields that solve problems. It uses a user-centric approach to predicting, perceiving or understanding the likely needs of users in a particular setting. User needs can be more than just personal/individual they can relate to business, economic, environmental, social and other need requirements. The idea behind employing design tools is to offer a solution, hopefully successful, to solve whatever problems are presented. If we limit ourselves to a view of design as simply a visual medium for these solutions, then we limit its potential to create and to make a change.

A starting point might be to have a Design Strategy that is concerned with the ability of a company or organisation to respond and perform well in the long term, rather than for a particular design project or goal. Think about how reasonable it is to suggest that nations considering bidding for any Olympics adopt this approach, since the lead in time after a successful bid spans 7 years allowing a whole strategy for the experience of the Olympics to unfold over time. The design strategy is not just about how the Olympic Stadium will look, it is about the multi-dimensional significance of the whole event as a cultural phenomenon. **Design Strategy** develops strategic policies, usually at a high level within a company or organisation in order to better realise the ongoing creation of successful Design created for users, audiences, participants or customers. Design Strategy is more concerned with outward market forces and how these impact an organisation's ability to perform and serve its customers successfully, than with the creation of individual experiences. Is there such a thing as design strategy for events? The answer is yes, but not for every event. Where might we see a design strategy in place – in road shows, touring exhibitions, music tours and even exhibition stands where the design strategy is the start of the process, followed by the selection of the medium into which the experience will occur. Design Strategy is most often performed only in visual fields and the wider aspects of experiences are rarely addressed. This is where the interface of design with events can be at its most critical for we see design being deployed as a dressing rather than as a strategic tool. So within the realm of experiences, where designed environments attempt to project a specifically planned encounter, what are the areas that can be further investigated? Shebroff provides an expanded taxonomy of experience that he describes as 'infinite' in terms of the different types (ibid., 2001). However in order to make some sense of an infinite number of possibilities there needs to be some measure of containment that will enable us get to grips with experience and design as follows:

Emotions are the feelings we experience and attach to events, people, products and services. Emotional attachment to people, things and events help form the platform form which we often develop our 'lifestyles'. Many of our lifestyle timelines are frames by specific events that leave an emotional impression upon us. They help us identify periods of our past and are used to give meaning to periods, people, places occasions, etc. (Roche, 2000). Meaning, when deconstructed via shared understanding based on social or cultural indicators can engender powerful emotions. Personal specific events such as weddings, coming of age celebrations, graduations, anniversaries and the numerous cultural events that individuals celebrate provide a source for these emotions. The basis for emotion is though built upon features within such occasions that are designed either from tradition that is passed down through generations or newly designed to provide an abstracted version of it.

Environmental Design consists of physical and spatial solutions and whilst most widely associated with architecture, landscapes and interiors it applies to event design. Consider the environment of expos and how they resemble and are resembled by theme parks. One is permanent, the other temporary but the connection between them is based on environment or landscape that offers similarities in experience. Disney's theme parks were based on the old nineteenth century expos and have since been imitated the world over. They offer very similar types of experience excitement and sensory stimulation borrowed directly from expos (Davis, 1996; Roche, 2000). **Information Design** is a field and approach to designing clear, understandable communications by giving care to structure, context and presentation of data and information. In practice this relates to all experiences, regardless of medium. The purpose should be clarity and we can see it being applied to events in two ways. It might take the form of internal event signage including floor layout for exhibitions and conferences and external communications via pre-event promotion and publicity. **Interaction** is a response experience in which both actor and reactor are engaged in a mutually affecting experience. The cornerstone of interaction is that there is a dual relationship that creates the interaction. At its most simplistic such an interactive experience can be produced simply through conversation.

Interaction Design is concerned with interactive experiences that occur in several mediums, one of which is events. They require time as an organising principle and relate to user, customer, audience or participant's experience flow through time (Sukaviriya, 2004). Shebroff says interactivity should not be confused with animation as the latter is concerned with the way objects move. Interaction is the opposite of passivity and we can see how many events now have an aspect that is interactive such as trying out products, sampling service, etc. **Interactor** is a term for an interactive participant in an interactive experience. Other terms could include: user, participant, actor and audience. **Meaning** operates at the cognitive level; it gives significance to an occasion that represents how people understand what is happening. Meaning is a distinct level of cognitive significance that represents how people understand the world around them – literally, the reality they construct in their minds that explains the world they experience. Meaning and significance, whilst individual can be shared via common understandings inherent in cultural values. But they can, as semiotics suggests, be open to interpretation. This makes meaning a precarious element within an event experience for its interpretation is not set in stone and depends very much on how we make sense of our own reality. For instance the British Labour Party held a pre-general election rally in 1994 that was supposed to represent the party's emergence from over a decade of Conservative government. The idea was to make the party leader, Neil Kinnock, seen as the avenging leader who had brought the party back to power and the event was based on the idea of the personality of Kinnock as the driving force for change. At the time of the rally, Labour held a lead in all opinion polls and it was widely expected that they would win the election. However the rally was interpreted in a different way to that imagined by the party, receiving severe criticism for its heralding in of new 'demigod' style leader and some commentators suggested parallels in presentation with past unpopular dictators. As a result, votes haemorrhaged away during the last few days of the election and the Conservatives won the election. Meaning is the deepest level of this understanding and is distinct from Values, Emotions and functional or financial benefits:

- *Meaning* (our sense of reality)
- *Values* (our sense of identity)
- *Emotions* (our sense of feeling)
- *Value* (our sense of what something is 'worth')
- *Features* (functional benefits)

Sensorial Design is a term used to include the presentation of an experience in all senses. For events we should consider how our senses are appealed to across the whole spectrum of possibilities. Researchers attending the Ideal Home exhibition have noticed that attendance at the afternoon mezzanine section can be challenging because there are eyes and nose are assaulted by a clashing array of scents and smells, a result of numerous cooking displays designed to show off new cookware and other kitchen equipment. To one person the effect resembled a cattle sale or fairground for in addition to smell the sense of sound was invaded by simultaneous multiple announcers and demonstrators. So audio design, whilst traditionally focussed upon the creation of music, sound effects and vocals to communicate and entertain in the aural sense (hearing) needs to be designed so that it is not a cacophonic display of noise rather than information. Likewise, all of the other human senses (touch, smell, taste, etc.) are elements of an experience that can be designed. **Service Ecology and Design** is a system of interactions and actors that, together, create a sustainable and successful service. Service Ecologies often include several companies or organisations that specialise in delivering one part of the total service. This is clearly the case for events – think of a relatively low complex event such as a local fete and consider the number of people and organisations taking acre of different sections of the event – the easiest is to think of those providing the 'cake stall' or similar which is coordinated and supervised by either a specific person or committee whose remit is to procure, deliver and display the food product on the day. As a fund-raiser their role at this level is probably crucial. As a food outlet, the types of food on display will have a direct bearing on the former. Sometimes events may need a pre-emptive display of this kind. For example student groups have been known to raise in excess of £200 to help fund an event simply by running a cake stall. Whilst this may fit outside of the actual event, it forms a part of the overall process that enables it to actually happen. Distinct service providers within an event play a part in helping the overall event experience and can help sustain the service ecology, fracture it or embellish it.

User Experience is very much the total immersive outcome that combines all the various elements that are experienced, as individuals and as a collective. It amounts to the holistic event experience, but for large-scale events where we cannot reasonably expect to visit every possible zone or stand or encounter or attraction it can be the result of a percentage of exposure. This re-affirms the point that event design must be treat as a total package, for if we neglect some element of it, that could be one that many people will view as a poor experience and the event will reflect this, most probably negative way. So the overall experience, in general or specifics, a user, customer or audience member has with a product, service, or event, the experience encompasses more than merely function and flow, but the understanding compiled through all of the senses. **Values** are the significant beliefs we hold about how ourself and how we should behave in the world. They govern our judgements and understandings about our own and others' identities. **Visual Design** is the field of developing visual materials to create an experience. It spans several fields such as typography, layout, colour theory, iconography, signage, photography, etc. and any medium, including online, broadcast, print, outdoor, etc. Visual Design is concerned with the elements of visual expression and style.

Event design decisions

In order to understand more about the role of design in event management there requires an appreciation of how many of the decisions about an event affect the design of an event environment. As has been outlined earlier, the approach of event management publications is often focussed on guides of how to do it rather than analysing the impact of the way it is done and the experience that results from any particular event design. The argument being put forward here is that event design should be viewed and understood as a much wider more embracing concept than one that is limited to the very specific creative parts of the event. This view is based on the premise that an event is a totally planned and conceived entity that has to be singularly created as an idea or concept before being transformed into reality. So in this case design will not be seen as the sole preserve of the creative artist, such as a person who operates within the confines of a design studio, or who is a trained professional exhibiting the skills of technical design. This type of person, inevitably, forms a part of the use of the term here, but is also applicable to the event management process itself where there exists a responsibility for ensuring that the event itself is created as it was meant to be (or better). The relationship between an event manager and design or production team can be both close and distant or indeed non-existent depending upon the circumstances of the event.

Experience strategy

A starting point for utilising this approach is to begin to develop an experience strategy which is the field and approach of developing strategic policies, usually at a high level within a company or organisation, in order to better realise the ongoing creation of successful experiences created for users, audiences, participants or customers. Experience Strategy is more concerned with outward market forces and how these impact an organisation's ability to perform and serve its customers successfully' (Shebroff, 2004). The more carefully developed use of events as a strategic tool for promotion shows evidence of this approach and it, in turn, provides a relationship to the creation of the individual event environment and the experiences that consequently accrue. This, suggests Shebroff, results in the idea of experience and design being employed at several levels whereby it is also concerned with the internal organisation, structure, culture, processes and values within an organisation that allow it to successfully create experiences and respond to both market and customer needs. This is in itself not a single medium tool, but one that transcends several in order to create successful experiences. Any strategy should be understood through a reflection of how to utilise all three spatial dimensions, all five common senses and 'interactivity, as well as customer value, personal meaning and emotional context'. All of these do not need to occur all at the same time, especially within events, since there may be particular focal points for one event compared to another. By having knowledge of their existence and relevance though we can begin to make strategic judgements about how to feature them in events. This would indicate that adopting a strategic experience design philosophy would allow for some key indicators to be developed that could analyse the success of the strategy. However such an experience design strategy is not so straightforward for events as it is for the design of web pages or other interactive media or on-screen digital content where there is a much clearer and tangible element to analyse.

Identifying superior experiences

So where does this put the discussion. At this point it would not be unreasonable to restate that everything, technically, is an experience of some sort, but it has been established that there is something important and special to many event experiences that make them worth discussing. We might ask what they are? Having attributed some aspects of the definition of events to importance and special (but not necessarily always unique) it is therefore pertinent to consider what the elements are that contribute to superior experiences. And this is the central and fundamental question that any event management individual or team has to be able to solve for the answer(s) lie at the very core of an event. Event management requires an understanding of experience and its replication, so that questions can be asked about what elements are needed, what is it that is knowable and reproducible, for the event to be replicated with similar experiences for a new, different audience. If such elements can be identified then that makes them designable. The question now, of course, is how are they identified and that is not such a clear or obvious task because of the multi-layered nature of the mass of events that are put on. And whilst it has been stated that events are, in their own right, one-offs, this does not mean to say that the elements in them are not to be reproduced to attempt to re-create a similar experience. The extent to which that happens though is a variable and a direct result of the nature of the interactions that occur within that replication. That does not mean however that an event manager cannot attempt as far as is possible to seek some replication, especially where the event is believed to have recognisable characteristics that whilst not physically identical may be symbolically so.

Meaningful experience

So if the design and experience elements aren't always obvious how do we discover them? How we know what particular types of experience people value? If we can begin to provide an answer to these questions we can begin to incorporate them into a design and experience strategy. The Experience Matrix offers some points of what we should be looking for and we can certainly start to use this as one method of providing more insight into what takes place at an event. It is though something of a conundrum since even though they may be identified the resulting solution is not going to be foolproof for every variant of its application. That is the very essence and nature of events and experiences, they are contextualised by groups and individuals and so every version of the experience is different as a result. Designing for experiences presents interpretation challenges for the creator, especially when the event runs across several days and there are repeat versions of it, simply because each version will have different people. Still we must realise that great experiences can be deliberate and can be based upon principles that have been previously successful. According to Diller et al.

(2005) there are meaningful experiences that people value from any kind of engagement. Based on research with over 100,000 people they produced a list of the 15 most recurring types of meaningful experiences:

Accomplishment
Achieving goals and making something of oneself; a sense of satisfaction.

Beauty
The appreciation of qualities that give pleasure to the senses or spirit.

Community
A sense of unity with others around us and a general connection with other human beings.

Creation
The sense of having produced something new and original, and in so doing, to have made a lasting contribution.

Duty
The willing application of oneself to a responsibility.

Enlightenment
Clear understanding through logic or inspiration.

Freedom
The sense of living without unwanted constraints.

Harmony
The balanced and pleasing relationship of parts to a whole, whether in nature, society, or an individual.

Justice
The assurance of equitable and unbiased treatment.

Oneness
A sense of unity with everything around us.

Redemption
Atonement or deliverance from past failure or decline.

Security
The freedom from worry about loss.

Truth
A commitment to honesty and integrity.

Validation
The recognition of oneself as a valued individual worthy of respect.

Wonder
Awe in the presence of a creation beyond one's understanding.

Diller et al. (2005)

The extent to which this list is useful and applicable to event management is open to debate since some of these experience meanings may not be so easily transferable. However if we think about them not as specific meanings but ones that can have some adaptability we might begin to see their relevance for events.

Activity 8.1

Take the list of meaningful experiences people value and try to apply them to events. Use specific event examples to show how they can be applied.

- Accomplishment
- Beauty
- Community
- Creation
- Duty
- Enlightenment
- Freedom
- Harmony
- Justice
- Oneness
- Redemption
- Security
- Truth
- Validation
- Wonder

Summary

The most important concept to grasp is that all experiences are important and that we can learn from them whether they are traditional, physical, offline or whether they are digital, online or via other technological features. What any solution to experience design requires is that those creating the experience need to understand the elements that make a good experience in the first place. This is a fundamental part of the qualification for ceremony and ritual, it worked previously and so has been replicated several times over with a similar level of success. In looking at a management – design relationship for events, there should, of course, be no tension or difficulty between the two. Invariably we are looking at a close relationship between event manager and event designer to work on their clients' behalf, and so the creation of the event environment is a mutually beneficial one, where the vision of the designer can enhance the initial idea. But there are other relationships with the event organisation that can influence the design of an environment. There is also the fact that a good many events have no specific designer input but are the product of either committee decisions or the event managers' own perceptions of the environment. In adopting a narrow view of design does it suggest that if no 'design team' is employed at the event then no design has taken place? This would seem to be an erroneous viewpoint from which to understand events as it would, in effect, indicate that such events have neither the capital nor intellectual capability to use design teams are redundant of design concepts. If design were to be taken so literally, it would leave us with very little to explore as some events may only have a small portion of this kind of design. Thus we may end up studying relatively minor elements of the event such as invites alone or party napkins or food or the colour of the walls but not other aspects of the event that have helped create the experience but are not classed as design.

Instead of studying events this way, we need to re-align our understanding of the event experience to reflect the experience design relationship as a principle tool for both foresight of event experiences and analysis of those experiences. All events requires foresight and a subsequent ability to reflect on the decisions made in creating the environment, taking into account the totality of the event and, where relevant, specific parts of the event. It is appropriate to identify the key aspects of event design that require consideration. The next step having worked from a model forecasting experiences is to develop the model to analyse it. Despite my assertion that event design has a more central role to play, we can still consider the design (or maybe themed is a better word) segments of any event individually for they will also tell us much about how we experience events.

Part Three

Analysis of Events

Chapter 9
Analysing event interaction and experience

Learning Objectives

- To understand and explain the concept of symbolic interaction
- To explain the different elements within it
- To describe its application in designing leisure experiences
- To apply the model to event experiences
- To reflect upon how event experiences are analysed
- To reflect and analyse how experiences are affected by variation in interactions

Introduction

Having so far discussed the principles and relationships between experiences and design, and how event experiences are formed as a result of multiple rather than a singular design process, this section seeks to explore and understand more about the way such environments can be analysed. There are several stages that need to be considered here that would help our understanding. One way is to see the design as the delivery experience, an approach that suggests a method for visualising the experience as a staged or thematic concept where design is focussed on decoration and aesthetic (Monroe, 2006). This approach is more grounded in design as a decorative activity – embellishments of the environment that are delivered through food, lighting, sound, materials, backdrops and so on. Another way is to see the application of design in a wider sense, where the concept is not simply an embellishment of an interior but is in fact a principle underpinning concept that influences the whole event (Brown & James, 2004). This understanding of the role of design is one where it occupies a central role in the planning stages, the delivery stages and the evaluation and analytical stages of the event. The general context then of this chapter is to emphasise design as an overall factor in the production of event experiences rather than a singular component, and to develop awareness that it can influence the nature of experience in a multiplicity of ways.

More than a wow factor

One of the difficulties we have in event management is a meaningful way of deconstructing the event experience itself so that we can see how anyone attending or involved with the event interact with the environment and each other. The only real way of doing this is to develop a more theoretical method of analysis. What is needed is a way of conceptualising the design of the experience so that the concept itself can be used to also make an analysis. By adopting a more conceptual approach we will give some continuity in terms of the values for analysis that can be applied to different events and the experiences they provide, thereby giving a more structured understanding that goes beyond simply saying an event has a 'wow' factor, which as, I have argued, seems a fairly limited view of the role design has to play in event experiences.

Experience analysis

Analysis of experiences per se has been primarily undertaken via experience and satisfaction constructs as previously noted (Mannell, 1999), often within a leisure framework. As we have seen this analysis can be done in several ways such as via participant feedback in situ and retrospectively, and it can also be conducted ethnographically in a similar way to the study of popular culture. The value of the tools used are that they can involve participants or not, they can view experience from a subjective and objective perspective, they can be studied in isolation through post-event indicators and they can be studied as active observation, either as participant or not. There are some considerations that need to be taken into account.

The crucial factor to be aware of is that any kind of experience is not a simple occasion or simple activity it is a complex series of relational components, neither is it uniform for the length of time that it occurs (Ryan, 2002) and it is not the same for all those involved due to the circumstances under which people have chosen to attend. An experience is in fact a combination of a multitude of components and occurrences that have, or should have been, consciously designed to create the event and its environment. According to Rossman (2003), who looked at the design of experiences from a leisure perspective (that included events) the act of participating and experiencing (in leisure) is itself a complex interaction form that is the result of numerous processes simultaneously occurring. It follows then that any attempt to facilitate such experiences through the provision of designed environments requires equal complexity in the planning and construction. The importance of understanding this experience is central to Rossman's approach to designing experiences and he draws heavily on social science to aid him in understanding more deeply what people get from participating in leisure activities and events. The relevance of the approach for event management is that, in the first instance, the expectation attributes that define leisure can apply equally to a great many events as the leisure dimension is one of the four main event types used to categorise special events with the others being personal, cultural and organisational (Bowdin et al., 2001; Shone and Parry, 2004; Goldblatt, 2005). This suggests that Rossman's approach to designing leisure experiences can be utilised and applied directly for the design of leisure event experiences and that the model can be used both as a tool for not only planning but also for evaluation and analysis. The relevance of the approach in the second instance is that as it is derived from social science, it can also be applied to the three main other categories of event types for not only do they often share some of the features that might be described as 'leisure' anyway, but also because the very nature of the interactions proposed by Rossman form essential characteristics of other events as well. The important point to remember is that in studying events we are dealing with planned occurrences, interactions and experiences where the environment itself is the result of creation and manipulation of this physical and human space (Murphy et al., 1973).

Symbolic interaction

In drawing out the knowledge and skills needed to construct experiences in the first instance Rossman advocates that those engaged in producing experiences need to understand the phenomena they are dealing with, hence his focus on a leisure context which allows him to draw upon his own personal knowledge, skills and experience in that area. In understanding this point we can then begin to understand more about how humans engage in and experience the particular encounter or engagement. Developing the idea on from here means we can start to anticipate (or predict) the results of this engagement, and consequently begin to analyse how that can be facilitated. The final phase is to then investigate how we might facilitate an individual's experience within the particular engagement. Rossman posits the question of 'how individuals experience leisure' as the key to better provision and applies the symbolic interaction (SI) model developed by Goffman (cited by Denzin) to aid in the understanding of this experience. Whilst Rossman's interest is confined to leisure there is nothing in the above description of engagement and interaction that suggests it should be limited to this area and as we have seen in previous chapters, one of the essential qualities of any events is the engagement and interaction that occurs. The theory that Rossman uses identifies six key elements that make up any planned occurrence that are named as follows: interacting people; physical setting, objects, rules, relationships and animation. During the course of this planned occurrence each element may constantly change as participants interact and interpret for themselves the meaning of the elements they encounter and so the nature of the experience itself may constantly change.

The sources for using this approach lies in theories previously developed on SI namely the perspectives of H Blumer and NK Denzin. SI, as one of the three major approaches in sociology, examines the different dimensions of the construction of social reality through the seemingly autonomous activities of individuals (Rossman, 2003). The value of using SI theory is the recognition that any reality is constructed – ergo as are events – and that it enables us to explore the different levels of and types of interactions that take place in any given environment. As a tool it seeks to examine human behaviour in face-to-face interactions, and it is these interactions that form the mass of leisure. They are also the essential ingredients of any event. The key to understanding more about any participative activity is to be able to understand more about how the individuals experience the occasions they participate in Iso-Ahola (1980) and Samdahl (1988). Any occurrences that are experienced through specific facilities tend to have a more static experiential offering whereas events, given the variation in location, types, space, size, aims and so on are much more dynamic and problematic to study especially for comparative purposes. This is in itself a significant challenge but it does not mean that we cannot apply some ideas to the study of event experiences.

To give clearer outline of how this approach is used for leisure, Rossman refers to the work of Blumer (1969) and Denzin (1978), respectively:

> *'SI rests on the three basic assumptions. First, social reality as it is sensed, known and understood is a social production. Interacting individuals produce and define their own definitions of situations. Second, humans are assumed to be capable of engaging in 'minded', self-reflexive behaviour. They are capable of shaping and guiding their own behaviour and that of others. Third, in the course of taking their own standpoint and fitting that standpoint to the behaviours of others humans interact with one another. Interaction is seen as an emergent, negotiated, often unpredictable concern. Interaction is symbolic because it involves the manipulation of symbols, words, meanings and languages'.*

Integral to this perspective is the view that the social world of human beings is not made up of objects that have intrinsic meaning. The meaning of objects lies in the actions that human beings take toward them. Human experience is such that the process of defining objects is ever-changing, subject to redefinitions, relocations and realignments. The interactionist assumes that humans learn their basic symbols, their conceptions of self and the definitions they attach to social objects through interactions with others (ibid, 2003, p. 18).

Nature of interaction

One of the key aspects of SI is the nature of interaction and the way that all humans act toward and in relation to things. The responses that result are a consequence of meaning, that is the meaning anything has for them. Such things include everything that the human being may note in the world – physical objects, such as tress or chairs; other human beings, such as friends or enemies; institutions, such as school or a government; guiding ideals, such as individual independence or honesty; activities of others, such as their commands or requests; and such situations as an individual encounters in their daily life. The second premise is that the meaning of such things is derived from, or arises out of, the social interaction that one has with other humans. The premise is that these meanings are handled in, and modified through, an interpretive process used by the person dealing with the things they encounters (Blumer, 1969, p. 2 cited in Rossman, 2003, p. 19). So we become aware that human beings respond to meanings, either ones they have themselves or ones that are given to them and when an occurrence is constructed the meanings that are presented to them help shape the experience they have of that occurrence. So for example, we can identify a specific type of event, one that may be based around some central or inter-linked set of themes, and begin a process of interpretation of the meanings those themes have for people. There are numerous potential interpretation perspectives of course, as reflected by the range of people engaged with the experience, but this does not mean we should not attempt to unravel some of these, or analyse what appear to be the core meanings that emerge and that a majority of people may recognise.

As we have seen in the section on experiences the attempts to imbue a service or product with meaning beyond their functionality lies at the core of experience marketing. One way of considering therefore the type of interpretation and meaning the experience has to offer would be through the symbols expressed in the experiential marketing components. This could relate specifically to the event type, its' name and most obviously in the event sponsorship. Live brand experiences, for example, which more often than not consists of new events being created to promote a brand, require some connection with the potential audience and one of the ways we can understand how this works would be to deconstruct the message that the promotional activity projects (Masterman & Wood, 2006). Such expressions of meaning and our response to them are, for many people, the first point of contact and therefore potential interest in the event is aroused through this initial encounter. It is then through interaction with other event attendees we derive further meaning from the occurrence, reflected also in the physical environment we engage with. Using a model like this allows for the development of a distinctive theoretical perspective on events, where we can understand how experiences are promoted and delivered, and where there is the prospect of analysing how humans respond to symbols communicated to them. Symbols can be communicated in many different forms but they ultimately lead towards one point and that is that we choose to attend the event on the basis of what we think the symbols mean for us. We might of course see the symbols in a different light and choose not to attend, but in that case we are obviously not going to be part of any interaction or analysis, although we can, of course, analyse the failure of the communication to attract people to the event. However attending the event then places us in an interaction with people who have some semblance of a shared meaning, because they have also chosen to attend based on the symbols of communication. Adopting a theory to both predict and explain this should enable anyone involved in event management to channel attention towards the nature of this interaction and to concentrate on what they are doing to construct it and how it will occur. In relation to leisure, such interaction is seen as attributing a 'unique meaning to specific social occasions that are created by the individuals involved through interaction with objects in the occasions' (Rossman, 2003, p. 19). We have earlier established how unique meanings do form a core element of most, if not all, events and so we can begin to see how the model has some currency of studying interaction at events.

SI is not without it's critics or flaws and there is some adaptation of the theory (Kuhn, 1964; Hochshild, 1997; Collins, 2004). The main strengths of SI are its ability to provide a concept and method for study of the dynamics of interaction that can be undertaken at a micro level so we can focus very specifically on certain subject matter. It also enables the study of creativity or creativeness that is a unique feature of any human conduct and interaction. However it is because of this focussed study that one of the key criticisms of SI theory has emerged, the lack of any emotional element (Hochshild, 1997). The question of how emotions influence interactions is a debate between, on one hand, socio-psychology that says emotions are representative of the relationship between the environment and the self whilst, on the other hand, sociology argues that the emotions we feel are a result of social factors. This view explains that emotions exist that we can express because they are known, they are pre-conceived ideas of what emotions we need to express at certain times for example, how to grieve and show grief following the loss of dear one. They are appropriate for an occasion and we adopt them as a result of this and not because of any interaction. In the interactionist model, our emotions are an expression caused by interaction and so they can be highly personal as a result of the various influences we have from the interaction. The answer would seem to be that, for events, both approaches can be adopted for we can see that there are norms of emotion that people appear to express and there are also interpretations of that are influenced by environment and are not, as result, pre-conceived.

Applying the SI model to events

How might these ideas on the study of experiences be applied to events. I have suggested in the introduction that there are clear connections between leisure and leisure events, as events are included in Rossman's analysis. But there are also connections between the ideas he uses and other types of events, as all events exhibit some form of interaction and engagement. In Rossman's work these ideas are specifically applied to aid the study of leisure programming, so that it can be used to explain and predict the design, development and operation of any facilitated leisure programme and experiences. If we examine the main tenets of SI we can see significant parallels for events and begin to appreciate how the approach can be used as one strand of an analysis of event experiences. Table 9.1 shows the emergence of a progressive adaptation of SI, firstly to be applied to leisure, secondly to events.

The key to the applicability of SI is the notion put forward that experiences have to be designed, developed and delivered. Events, without these essential attributes, simply do not exist and so we can begin to frame a way of exploring how events are 'designed, developed and delivered' in the same way that Rossman does for all leisure activities. Taking this as our perspective we can see that the interactions that result from these events will ultimately greatly influence our experience of the event, allowing us to sometimes reinterpret it over and over in the passage of time. When we first set out to create the experience it is imbued with meaning, the meaning we have integrated into it from concept to delivery. However as a result of interaction that have occurred at various occasions of the event, the meaning of the event can change for example, Notting Hill Carnival has moved from being a local event to a race riot event to London pageant and, now, a hallmark event. If

Table 9.1 Symbolic interaction for leisure and events

SI attributes	For leisure	For events
Social reality is a social production	Leisure activity, in most cases, is produced for us	Social reality for events only exists when we produce the event
Interaction between individuals produces own definitions of situations	Leisure is intrinsically free and open to spontaneity and interpretation	Events can be construed by individuals for their own purpose
Humans interact	Ditto	Ditto
Interaction is symbolic through manipulation of things	Leisure activities carry symbolic meanings that we interpret in different ways	Events require symbolic characteristics to enable us to derive our meaning from them – these must be created though
Meanings are derived through interaction and can be reinterpreted	Leisure is interactive and the activities we undertake often develop via our interactions	Events can be redefined via interactions of people for example, Glastonbury from sub-cultural hippie to popular culture

we develop the idea further we begin to understand much more about how to create and construct experiences on the basis of what the event means to people. The important point here is to recognise how people will react to what we present them and they do so on the basis that the objects we use in designing the event hold some meaning for them (Blumer, 1969). Taking this position as a starting point we can begin to ask questions about events and the meanings they have. Our perspective on any event will then be established by the context from which we interpret and ascribe meaning. This is the point we will pick up later in the section on semiotics so for the moment here this is an initial part of the discussion.

The SI model is intended for two purposes, one to help those creating experiences to learn more about those they are creating for and, second, to provide an analytical and practical framework by which both providers and recipients can derive meaning from such occasions.

Paraphrasing Blumer (1969) Rossman asserts states that in order to fully understand and apply SI we must first recognise the three points that need to be developed. These are the nature of objects, how meaning is derived, and how interaction unfolds and permits the ongoing interpretation of meaning. The key to exploring meaning and experience is to understand that by the term objects we do not mean just physical entities. Objects can be a series of things (physical, emotional, sensorial, structural and organisational) that can be indicated to have meaning, although usually the implication is that they are physical and in which case we tend to be in their presence. We can say that the presentation ceremony for a trophy at the end of a sports event carries with it the physical presence of experience. This is exhibited through the podium itself, the person making the presentation, the crowd (if present) and the actual trophy itself. There are also obvious symbolic meanings to the presentation. It acts as an indication of achievement and success in the competition that is recognised by all competitors, officials and crowd. It also symbolises closure of that particular competition, and it serves to demonstrate that the organiser respects the efforts of the participants by formally acknowledging success. There are of course other types of presentations that have different meanings. Some also have developed their own particular attributes through the actions of the participants.

Case study 9.1

Formula 1

Case study focus

Emerging ritual/symbolic actions

Interpretation of celebration by participant(s)

Animation of celebration

Perhaps one the most notable podiums in sport is that at a Federation Internationale de Automobile (FIA) Formula 1 Grand Prix. All Formula 1 drivers who finish in the top three positions at a Grand Prix ascend to a podium to receive their trophies and then they indulge in the, now, ritualistic spraying of champagne over each other and the attendant crowd of press, fans and VIPs. This ritual and symbolic act, led by the winner of the race, is the defining post-race moment for a Grand Prix winner in the eyes of spectators, both for those live at the event and watching on television. As the case material below explains, this celebration is an occasion for both joy and elation, yet it also has several additional layers of meaning and representation as the physical elements of the ceremony are given away as symbols of prestige. The ceremony can also be manipulated by the drivers and used to convey a message of some kind to particular viewers. In the main, to have acted out this celebratory scene is also a sign of having experienced success with the fraternity. Imagine then the feeling of elation experienced by the Italian driver Giancarlo Fisichella in March 2005 when he won his second ever Grand Prix race and celebrated, in the time honoured fashion, albeit a bit more exuberantly than usual. Why, though, when this was his second win. The answer may partly lie in the idea he was acting out the preconceived norm of emotion for a winner but it can also be explained in the context of the interactions he had as a result of his first win and his responses to that. This had come earlier in the season but was the result of stewards investigating discrepancies after the race finished and altering the finishing positions. Thus he was awarded first place after the race had finished and, significantly, after the podium celebrations had taken place with someone else in the winner' spot. In other words he became a winner after the closure of that event. Why? This first win was awarded 2 weeks after the race had finished and so consequently he was not the one to receive all the laurels of the winner at the time he most likely got the news in a letter, telephone call or message via his management. In short not really the occasion or situation where you might leap up and down and pour champagne over people. Thus the defining moment of many sportsperson who wins, the ascent to the top of the podium, had been denied him. The importance and significance of the podium ceremony is explained below.

Writing for grandprix.com Joe Seward explained what happens at a Formula 1 podium ceremony extracted 12/12/05 from http://www.grandprix.com/ft/ft00274.html

'For many years the podium ceremonies in Formula 1 were organised by French aristocrat Baron Gerald de Bar de la Garde de la Michardiere, who was employed by Paddy McNally's All sport Management, which also looked after many of the promotional activities on the periphery of Grand Prix racing. De Bar's job is to make *sure that everything runs smoothly with the ceremony and that the right sponsors appear, the right music is played, the correct flags are flown and that everyone is where they should be. The flags and the music for the ceremony are transported from race to race. The flags are put behind the podium and normally those of the men most likely to win are set aside so that the flags can easily be found. Other flags are available if, for example, there is a surprise face on the podium. As soon as the results are known the flags are fitted to the ropes on each of the flagpoles. Three people are then designated to raise the flags at the right moment in the ceremony.*

The music is on either cassette tape or compact disc and is selected in the same way and played over the public address system. Usually the recordings are shortened versions of the national anthems so that the ceremony does not drag on because of a lengthy anthem. The podium ceremony is a triumph of organisation as not only are there three drivers needed but there must also be a representative of the winning team. In addition there are normally at least three VIPs who present the trophies and the Moet and Chandon silver trophy. The choice of VIPs is made by the FIA and Formula 1 Administration combined. This is not always easy because traditionally the FIA likes to have the important people from the local automobile clubs while Bernie Ecclestone *prefers to have visiting celebrities. These can range from politicians such as Malaysian Prime Minister Mahathir Mohamad to the state president of a German state. Sometimes visiting royalty will be asked: Prince Rainer of Monaco regularly presents the trophies at Monaco – despite the fact that he and his entire family were once sprayed with champagne by a very excited* Ayrton Senna. *There are also presenters such as the late Princess Diana, who presented* Damon Hill *with his trophy at Silverstone in 1994. In addition there are international stars such as Sylvester Stallone, chat show host David Letterman and Michael Douglas. There is actually an FIA regulation which states that drivers are not allowed to talk to any journalists until the podium has been completed'.*

There were other problems when *Eddie Irvine* was on the podium for the first time. Eddie comes from Ireland but as he is from the Northern part he is considered to be British and so a Union Jack was flown. This upset the Irish nationalists who demanded that an Irish flag be flown and threatened Eddie and his family with violence. When an Irish flag was flown there were threats from the Irish extremists who want Eddie to be British. Irvine asked the FIA to fly a neutral flag and play a neutral song! There have also been problems with the use of champagne – a Formula 1 tradition. Back in the 1980s *Alan Jones* used to spray orange juice – a rather sticky substitute to champagne – because the *Williams* team at the time was sponsored by Saudi Arabian companies and alcohol was forbidden by religion. In France there is currently a law forbidding all advertising of alcohol products. In theory, the use of champagne on the F1 podium is an infringement of that law and this year (1997) the French refused to supply champagne. Annoyed, *Bernie Ecclestone* sent one of his assistants to a local supermarket on the morning of the race with instructions to buy bottles for champagne for the ceremony. If there was any legal action, Bernie said, he would face it. The champagne was sprayed and nothing happened.

Normally there is not much champagne left in a bottle when an F1 driver has sprayed it over the others on the podium and even over himself. The bottles can be very valuable, however, and are sometimes kept and then signed by drivers for charity auctions. A signed bottle can raise a great deal of money. The rest are given to mechanics as gifts by which to remember special events. They are rarely, if ever, left lying around. The trophies are normally given by the drivers to the teams. Some teams even have it written into the contracts that the trophies won belong to the team and not to the driver. Most of the big teams have display rooms full of all the trophies they have won and, in the case of *McLaren* or Williams, these can take up an awful lot of space. *McLaren* has an enormous display room at its base in Working while *Williams* has an entire museum to display its cars and its trophies.

If drivers want the trophy the teams normally arrange for copies of the trophy to be made. These are expensive but it is only fair that the driver be allowed to keep his trophies as well. Some drivers do not care. *Niki Lauda* used to give all of his trophies to his local garage and they would be displayed there. Other drivers, such as *Nigel Mansell*, have their own trophy rooms in their houses to impress their guests. There are occasional hiccoughs in this system. At the end of 1989 when *Alain Prost* was leaving *McLaren* and was angry with the team management he deliberately gave away his trophy for winning the Italian Grand Prix to annoy team boss *Ron Dennis*. He simply dropped the trophy off the podium and into the crowd of tifosi. Not surprisingly, the trophy was never seen again.

We can see from this that the meanings derived from the podium presentation are multiple and are subject to interpretation directed (or animated) by those taking part. Overt and discreet actions, such as Prost's dumping of the trophy, give a new meaning to the situation from the perspective of the team's management. In the normal course of things the physical elements of the presentation are given meaning beyond their functionality as awards by the fact that they are passed on to the winning driver's team as tokens and emblems of mutual respect. The recognition of the value of these things is what, over time, helps generate a sense of occasion about podium awards and establishes, in turn, some of the protocols adopted such as sponsor's display, VIP guests and so forth. We can see some of these becoming established elements of the event environment when they are repeated over a period of time and they form part of a tradition that helps give meaning to the occasion. In a similar way the presentation and donning of the green blazer by the winner of the US Master's Golf gives meaning to audience and players as the mark of the champion, a more significant event perhaps than the awarding of the actual trophy itself.

There are potentially lots of other ideas at work in looking at the physical nature of events in this way. Objects, by their very real presence, can be things that can be pointed out, by observation or identification, and this suggests a more social aspect, and is often undertaken with other active participants within an occasion. These objects can influence the nature of the occasion, as we have seen above, such as in a conference or meeting where a dominant or influential figure is identified in status perhaps by their seating or placement within a programme of activities. These objects are seen as being prominent and having possibly leadership or authority to influence the occasion. Finally they can be referred to abstractly as (perhaps an idea under which we experience the occasion). Such events might be those that carry more philosophical tags such as Promise Keepers, a personal catalytic type of event, that seeks to identify groups and individuals looking to embrace, renew or develop faith and also to fund raise for the principles for the organisation promoting that faith. Events like this and similar types where the interaction between stakeholders is shared through an abstract object, the idea of the faith, tend to occur where there is unquestionable meaning and status to the objects used. Therefore we end up with objects being a means by which experiences can be unfolded. The objects are physical, social and symbolic and all interactions that take place are a direct result of the way people act towards them. Physical objects are those tangibles of an interaction whilst social objects are all other people in the interaction. Symbolic objects can be philosophies, ideas or doctrines (Rossman, 2003, p. 20).

Moving on from this relationship, we can appreciate that human beings act towards objects on the basis of the meanings that the objects have for them. The meaning is not necessarily locked but is gained through interaction or through the ideas conveyed by them. The different situations that we find ourselves in can influence the meaning derived from the occasions. This is certainly the case with leisure events, but is perhaps less convincing for other types of events. Rossman recognises that the notion of 'freedom' and 'satisfaction' are crucial in characterising the interaction for leisure, and we can certainly therefore apply it to leisure events. The element of context here is central and we might link this with thematic ideas for events where symbols and artefacts are borrowed from other aspects of life and re-interpreted for an event, resulting in a change of meaning. Similarity of symbols used in heterosexual and homosexual events for instance convey totally different meanings to the audience or participants.

Whilst event managers may plan for certain experiences, the way individuals then respond to them is not always certain. Meaning through interaction can be changed as a result, take the case of the 1968 Olympic 200m medal ceremony. To all intents and purposes it was like any other award ceremony, but the moment that Tommy Smith raised his right arm, wearing a black glove and clenching his fist the whole meaning of the ceremony took on a new dimension. Smith's celebration of Black Power was a comment on the current sate of civil rights in America in 1968 and he wanted to send a message to the world that, whilst he represented America, as a black American there were issues in society that were not being addressed. At this point our experience of this particular ceremony was transformed, not by the organisers but by a stakeholder who, in this case, interacted with the objects of the occasion, interpreted them in the way he felt was appropriate and provided his own object (the black glove) as a symbol for a new meaning and interpretation of the ceremony.

Meanings are therefore developed and modified through a process of interpretation during occasions of interaction. One of the differences for looking at events is the singular nature of them compared to other activities, where repeated interactions build up the meaning of things. For routine events these can be repeated daily, for events they take a much longer period of time. With events such interactions are more immediate and the cycle of repetition is not so spread out, but occurs in the immediate fluctuations of the course of the event. Planning for a business meeting is more than just setting out tables and laying out an agenda, the whole purpose of the meeting can be constructed in advance yet its nature can be transformed by the way those present interpret their interactions during it. Meeting Professionals International organises thousands of meetings each year and the guidelines/templates they provide for members to use suggest how we might construct a meeting to achieve desired goals. More than any other, given the very close physical interactions likely to occur, the briefing for such occasions contributes significantly to its outcome. Such meetings may operate at the lower end of the events organisational spectrum but they nevertheless incorporate many of the skills we associate with event management. The whole tone of such meetings is heavily influenced by environment, by the construction of the physical and social setting and by the actions and interactions of those present. Individuals play a part in shaping the course and direction of an interaction and they direct the episode and the meaning of interaction for them (Rossman, 2003).

Having established that event management is all about producing the environment for the event to function, we know that it is a fundamental part of this process that we seek to control to whatever desired effect we want, how this functions since we are designing and creating it for a purpose and for others to consume. Nevertheless no matter how well we plan such things, the ability of others to interpret what we have planed in a way different to that intended is always a presence. It is through such actions, for instance, that we get unruly behaviour or violence at some events and we know that these events have not been designed to generate violence. As different occasions unfold, interacting and self-reflexive individuals enter them. They subsequently become a highly significant part in the way they are shaped and, as a result, the outcomes that we predicted are shaped by them, sometimes with undesired results.

Just like leisure planners and programmers, event planners and managers have to consider how to facilitate a successful event. Within a leisure dimension this necessarily has to also reflect the perceptions of freedom associated with leisure experiences, with non-leisure events this is less of a concern but we also have events that are a combination of business and leisure and so the considerations required here can be complex. If as suggested, events are a manipulation of time and space to create a specific moment the extent to which we manipulate that is a major factor in the design of the event. The question of how to advance our understanding and analysis of events revolves around how we begin to develop a model for the more complex appreciation of the event experience. Drawing once on again on the work of Denzin and Goffman there are six key elements to producing effective experiences. These are explained and based on the argument that place is the point where co-orientation of the self occurs. This place is some kind of social occasion that has an identifiable structure to it and that we can extract meaning from. Once we begin to affect changes, so that the elements that make up the occasion change than the experience that was planned will also change as a result.

The cornerstone of this approach is the interaction of individuals and its applicability to events becomes highly resonant. The main factors to consider in this approach are:

> 'Experiences are developed by creating and/or manipulating the environment, both the physical and human aspects.
>
> Interactions occur, and these are linear in fashion 'with only one action being attended to at any given time' and that these interactions are made up of sequences of orderly processes.
>
> Planning interactions, from the design point of view, is done vicariously as the planner attempts to image how the experience will unfold before it takes place.
>
> These planned interactions are though ideals of what experience should unfold since individuals' interactions can impact on this'.
>
> Rossman (2003)

Summary

Using the above platform Rossman defines the six elements of SI as a model from which all planners can develop experiences. In considering this model the purpose here is to use the model to reflect on how experiences have been constructed. Rather than just employ it as a method for 'imaging' experiences, the purpose is to use it, with some adaptations and extensions, to identify the elements and then reflect on how they can be used to examine the experience that has been provided as the reality of an event unfolds. Whilst it is clear that planners will most likely not have used this model in their planning, by adapting the model for critical analysis we can begin to see what the result of their planned experience is from a conceptual viewpoint and understand more about un/successful experiences.

Chapter 10

Using symbolic interaction to analyse event experiences

Learning objectives

- Understand the meaning for each element
- Apply the elements of symbolic interaction to the analysis of event experiences

Introduction

The preceding chapter laid out the basis for using an interactionist model for creating and explaining how event experiences occur and sought to explain how interaction shapes the meaning and outcome of experiences. Here we will look specifically at Rossman's six elements of symbolic interaction and apply them to event settings and environments.

Symbolic interaction

The six elements identified by Rossman are:

1 interacting people,
2 relationships,
3 rules,
4 objects,
5 physical setting,
6 animation.

We will now look at each one of these elements, using case studies to illustrate how they can be applied to the study of event experiences.

Interacting people

An essential element of all events, the interaction of individuals covers all those likely to interact and so would extend to include Bowdin et al. (2001) list of stakeholders. For any experience to be effective, the planned programme of delivery needs to consider who will be involved and design the environment accordingly, for either a specific target group or in order to recruit a specific target group. This whole project management process must be dominated by the desire to market the event to all necessary parties, not just spectators and participants, but sponsors, media, VIPs, staff, advertisers and the public (Watt, 1998, p. 60). Interaction here does not have to be on a direct communicative level that is of conversation but is where those involved in the event are, simultaneously, sharing exchange of information.

This element is a central point in the study of events because it also enables us to understand how experiences can be investigated and researched with a range of targets in mind, and great care is taken by those providing for events to ensure they know who their audience is going to be. As we have seen in the section on marketing experiences there is a clear need for us to understand as much as we can about people and to understand what benefits they expect to get from the event experience. Supovitz (2005) writing about sports events states that modern event marketing is about 'recognising current market sensitivities and ensuring that your sports events are being managed and marketed with the application of sound and current business practices are essential to achieving the objectives of your programme' (p. 14). In brief there is a need to develop away from the classic SWOT/4 P's approach and into a more complex approach that can be best summed up as 'psychographics' and offers us some deeper insights into how experiences are created for consumers. This has been discussed in detail earlier and we can assert that individuals are a vital element within any event and thus the design of it needs to reflect this accordingly. Whilst the ideal is always to link the correct groups of individuals with an appropriate experience, sometimes it is not possible to do this perfectly.

Activity 10.1

1 In what ways are events targeted at specific individuals by anticipating who will come along and how they will behave.
2 What events are created around known target individuals and then promotional attempts are made to recruit them.
3 Can we tell the difference?

Case study 10.1

The Motion Picture Association of America Academy Awards – The Oscars

Focus of case study

Symbolic experience and interaction

The Academy Awards ceremony offers potential for study and analysis on many levels from tabloid celebrity social commentary through to more serious cultural, social and anthropological study. It is also an event experience that can contribute to many of the symbolic experiential categories we are looking at here. Whilst this example mainly looks at the nature of interactions, it will also include a note on the nature of objects within the awards as well. The experience of the Oscars is constructed on multiple levels of experience which results in a carefully designed programme of interactions that involves the media, fans, guests, television audience, costume designers and staff amongst many others who together with each of these groups' assorted sub-divisions provide a multi-layered, multi-level and time extended experience. We should never forget that despite all the elements we can consider that make the Oscars, by far and away the most important of all are the people themselves and the interactions that are created for them with each other, with the audience and with television. The Oscars ceremony experience itself is preceded by preview events, these then lead into the main ceremony but then the show is extended by post-Oscars events, that in themselves offer a new range of experiences. Whilst many of these events are not linked or co-ordinated as a total package, nor necessarily involve the same organising companies the end result is a series of Oscar-related events that result in an experience that is elongated across time and space and which starts and finishes long before and after the actual ceremony itself. Pre-events, often taking place the night before are casual, informal and remain largely unknown to the vast majority of the public. Mostly these are not showcase media events and the stars that do attend are interacting in a far more casual, intimate, environment than the publicly exposed Oscar ceremony itself. These pre-parties are designed to be relaxing enjoyable affairs, devoid of ceremonial protocols, despite the attendance of A-list celebrities. By contrast the main event is the very opposite.

The interactions of all of the aforementioned groups produces, at its basic level, the three G's of the Oscars namely Glamour, Glitz and Gossip. And it is these interactions that feed the frenzy surrounding the event. Anyone tuning to watch (on TV) is treated to well over 4 hours' worth of celeb entertainment from build-up to the stars' arrival as they make their way down the red carpet and into the auditorium itself. In the past thousands of fans would gather to share the red carpet moment, acting as gazers and gossipers at the same time, and interacting with each other and, superficially, with the glitz and glamour unfolding before them.

The history of the Oscars is well documented so the purpose here is to look at how some of these interactions take place within the event. A useful staring point is 2002 when a change of venue took place and the awards moved to the new purpose built Kodak Theatre having zigzagged for the past decade or so between the Shrine Theatre and the Music Centre. The Kodak itself is a landmark venue. It was billed, at the time, as the worlds only live broadcast theatre. In other words a venue designed to deliver a live televised event, and more importantly designed for the specific needs of the Oscars. Whereas at the previous venue physical changes had to be made to accommodate the awards night such as seating removal the new venue has a flexible seating arrangement.

Kodak Theatre basic facts:

- 136,000 sq ft space,
- flexible seating from 2000 to 3600,
- live broadcast media cockpit,
- large stage at 120 ft wide by 75 ft deep,
- press room for 1500 linked directly to the winners' podium,
- three balcony levels to keep audiences close to the stage,
- twenty opera boxes.

In order to keep the prospect of interaction within the theatre open, the boxes, for example, remain exposed, without glass or curtain partitions. However they provide the celebs with a passage away from public interaction via separate entrances to the theatre and a direct connection to the adjacent luxury hotel.

The actual interior design of the Kodak Theatre is not dissimilar to the some of the Old Opera houses of Europe. The difference is that this is a high-tec version.

> *The balconies are decorated with rich blue and wine fabric and a glass material on the front that will 'glow'. The giant silver leaves that make up a stylised crown near the theater's ceiling can be lowered to form columns. In an attempt to capture the light and transparency of projected movies, designer Rockwell's emphasis is on glass and sparkle: while entering, visiting celebrities will pass through glass curtains at the gate, past glass panels etched with the titles of Best Pictures, by wall-sized lobby windows offering a panoramic view of the Hollywood hills, down hallways studded with shimmering, star-filter beads … all to simulate a symbolic move past the screen and into the movies (OscarInfo.com).*

The new venue has also resulted in a new relationship emerging between fans and celebrities as the interaction between the two is played out via the now ubiquitous red carpet. The role of the red carpet is synonymous with high-profile VIP treatment, bestowing status, prestige, recognition and respect for those who are invited to walk across it. It is also a massive PR exercise for all concerned allowing the stars every opportunity to gain massive public exposure. The process of arrival by limousine followed by parade across the carpet in front of the world's media is carefully orchestrated. Here the interactions are based on several requirements that an event of this type needs to fulfil. Pre-eminent amongst these, and reinforced by the Kodak Theatre's technical facilities, is feeding the media's almost rapacious desire for images, both still and live, interviews and stories associated with stars (the 3 G's). Orchestrating this process requires detailed timing and segueing so that each arrival becomes, in turn, centre stage. Outside of being nominated, receiving an award and the occasional TV shot, this is the main chance for a celebrity to be in the limelight on their own as they move through each section of the red carpet. This is the point to acknowledge their fans, to adopt promotional dress (as many often do), in the style of their latest movie or, in the case of many women, to show some drop-dead gorgeous (or not) designer dress. Each celebrity performs as expected, waving to the crowd, sharing a joke with someone, stopping for photographs and briefly giving the odd quote to TV crews before entering the theatre. It is these recorded moments and images that will fill countless TV screens and magazine covers and articles over the next few days and weeks immediately after the event has long finished.

If we think about this situation with the Oscars (Case study 10.1), it almost seems as if this is in fact a different part of the event and in truth it probably is. Since only a small percentage of stars actually feature during the awards themselves, for the rest their moment of exposure on the red carpet becomes quite critical. It alone offers a chance for interaction, however brief and however stage managed, it nevertheless presents them in the flesh. For members of the public this is also their moment to be within the same space as the people they idolise and to, almost, be within touching distance. And there always remains the possibility that something will happen to make interaction more personal and real. At past Awards for example when held at the Shrine Theatre, large grandstands were built to accommodate spectators and allow them a view of the stars, as they exit their limousines curbside and walk to the auditorium. The stars make their way up the red carpet, running the gauntlet of photographers, and stopping to give interviews to the horde of TV news crews and entertainment reporters, before entering the Shrine. These Bleachers seating, as they are called, were free and indeed, just like the infamous queue to get into the All England Tennis Championships in Wimbledon, so scores would camp out on the streets for days in advance, in order to secure a spot in the bleachers – which were first come, first served. However two things have happened to change this relationship between stars and fans, one is the move to the new theatre and the other is a result of 9/11 and increased security.

Practically speaking it would now be a lot more difficult for fans to camp out at the new theatre, situated as it is on the busy streets near Hollywood and Highland, and with new security concerns now prevalent at all major events resulting in the need to pre-screen any fan likely to sit in the bleachers, then a new arrangement had to be made. As a result the spontaneous and personal pilgrimage for seats in the bleachers gave way to a far more controlled access system. In 2002, for the first time, reserved seat tickets were given away, guaranteeing a seat in the bleachers and no need to wait in line. Whilst organisationally a sound move, this particular act takes away from the public a quintessential experience of attending the event in the bleachers and one that is common to many open and free-to-the-public events (see Tour De France) and that is the dedication and commitment (some might say madness) to queue for several days. Such acts are, of course, a feature of many events for they signify the truly dedicated fan and they provide another layer of interaction that organised ticket allocations avoid. In this case the relationship between stars, event, place and the public is, to a certain extent, bonded by this experience for only those members of the public who really want to be at the event will queue in this manner.

The alternative is the modern trend for pre-booked, pre-arranged and pre-allocated tickets that are limited by number and are, often, controlled in their dispersal. In 2002, the Academy received about 5000 applications for the 400 seats that they made available to the public. The view of the Academy on those who do not get a ticket is simple, don't turn up, don't queue and watch the show on television (because they might add that's what $170 million theatre is built for). There is now no public area for fans to informally congregate except through the formalised arrangements for the bleachers. The plus side of the system is that anybody can apply and providing they get their application in on time there name will go into a draw for a seat, which means that everybody has an equal chance. But does this mean that an element of the experience of the Oscars, for fans anyway, is lost forever? We might also ask whether or not this development adds or takes away an experiential quality. There is an organisational logic to the system but it lacks spontaneity, it reduces the act of fandom to a simple process of mechanical ticket allocation and, in the process, reduces the number of fans who can have live interaction with the stars, in turn reducing expressions of fandom and the idiosyncrasies that come with that (such as camping out for a week to catch a glimpse of their favourite actors).

The presence of the stars is essential yet it is the extraordinary lengths that the Oscars go to ensure their presence that marks them out for attention. The truth of the Oscars is clear to everyone to see, without the stars in attendance there is no show and as I have indicated previously their arrival is a prime experiential component. The other key areas of presence are in the attendance in the auditorium itself, as guest announcers who hand out the actual statuettes and, of course, as award nominees and ultimate recipients of the Oscar should they win. Running at well over 3 hours the ceremony takes its toll on those in attendance and, quite naturally, many will want to leave their seats and, euphemistically speaking, stretch their legs. This creates a problem however since the auditorium has to remain full, to maintain the sense of occasion, because the last thing anyone wants to see is empty seats. On top of that is the need to maintain a presence of stars, some of whom may well be shuffled around in terms of seating throughout the evening to ensure that key 'actors' are always visible (especially to the TV audience). So the solution to this problem is body-doubles, a host of look-alikes waiting in the wings, prepared at any moment on the instructions of a co-ordinator, to quickly fill an empty seat. In doing so the illusion of a full and star-studded audience is maintained together with the experience of an attentive (and complete) set of peers. Anyone who has been to any ceremony where there are audience gaps and people leaving before the end should recognise the elaborateness of this solution to what might be called vacant space syndrome, an experience that can leave such events devoid of ambience and atmosphere.

What does this tell us about modern events? That the nature of interactions between those involved in an event has to be fist of all appreciated by event organisers and planners when there is relationship with the public involved. Interactions can be planned and orchestrated but it is essential we know what impact such plans have on any experience, otherwise we may end up with the ultimate sterile event, where no public are present. This should not be viewed as fake or masquerade no matter how stage-managed, it is simply showing an understanding of how an essential element within the event is structured to the satisfaction of everyone. The public feels involved, it gets its chance to be there and it gets its pound of flesh as the stars arrive and wave to them. Without this then the 'live' event would become little more than a television show, and if that is the case it doesn't have to take place on a single day it can be filmed, manipulated and edited over a period of time and delivered as yet another show on TV. So the need to retain and manage the public realm element of the event provides has to be seen as a vital component.

Physical setting

The very environment in which our event takes place and the components used to fill that space provides the physical setting. Earlier in the book we looked at some of those components, those were our objects and there is some overlap with physical setting. The decisions made for the setting and the objects therein, affect our sensual environment, affecting our taste, our smell, our vision, our hearing and our touch. Not all are necessarily active elements within the setting and often it is the case that taste and sight (e.g. food creativity) are given higher significance than say smell and touch. The conscious need though to design these aspects of an event is made more glaring because these are usually the main elements that will immediately impact upon people. And it is usually in this element that we get that moment of cerebral impact when an instant impression can be made. Physical setting as used here is mainly focussed on venue, its setting and location. Venue selection can often provide us with a unique quality that makes the event different.

Case study 10.2

ICE space

Case study focus

Physical setting and sensorial experience

In the summer of 2006 one of the most original event venues appeared in London. What made the venue unique was (a) the material it was made of – Ice and (b) it's limited existence as a venue during the summer months. Situated on the banks of the river Thames, London the structure was located between Tower Bridge and City hall and, appeared to some, to be like a Zeppelin. Apparently made from 200 tons of Canadian ice (?) the integrity of the structure had to be maintained by keeping the temperature at minus 0°C. Any temperatures at this point or lower, say minus 5 or 10, presents the possibility of frostbite or hypothermia and the ensuing problems that result and so both staff and guests had to be protected. This added to the physicality of the space, since not only was it cold but guests were given a thermal jacket and gloves to wear whilst inside. To alleviate the effects of cold hot chocolate was available from the ice bar. The Ice Space created perhaps the ultimate in physical setting experience for, unlike the famous Ice Hotel, it was artificially maintained and having left the space the guest returned to normal summer temperatures.

This relationship between event and location is often fundamental to the experience, and one useful categorisation is that given to 'hallmark' events where the event has become linked and identified with the spirit of a particular place (Allen et al., 2005). Such events are synonymous with the town, city, region or even country where it takes place. This is a geographic reference point but it can also extend to a specific venue reference point where a venue becomes synonymous with an event, a link that is normally a result of several years' versions of the event at the specific venue. More often than not however this is less of a feature than location due to the fluctuation in venue selection as we design events within venues, and often whilst an event title or type remains, the actual venue itself changes from 1 year to the next. The reasons for venue changes are varied based on what the clients and organisers want to achieve out of an event.

Typical reasons for venue changes:

- Strategic – to open up new markets or market to potential ones.
- Financial – prohibitive cost of venue or incentives to use alternative venue.
- Facilities – existing venue has limited capability, especially technology.
- Size – larger audience/attendance/exhibitor space required.
- Personal – change in event management company.

- Trend – a cyclical issue where some venues are seen as 'fashionable', others are not.
- Catchment – closeness to client HQ.
- Unavailability – venue already booked.
- Transport – inaccessibility of existing venue.

Despite these reasons, some venues and events attain hallmark linkage. This is most likely to occur in specialist venues that, if not purposely built for the event, are nevertheless ideal for its purposes and over a period of time the event is indelibly identified with the venue. The most obvious venue: event linkage occurs in sport simply because many sport venues do not have high flexibility, they are built for a purpose and whilst some may host non-sport events by far and away the vast majority do not.

Where venue and event are synonymous

Example: United States Masters Golf Championship at Augusta National Golf Club, Georgia, USA

It is inconceivable that the Masters would take place anywhere other than at Augusta National. There is a rich history and tradition associated with the venue that affords modern golfers a comparison with the past. As one of the four major golf championships in the world, the Masters is the only one to remain at the same venue. The other three – The USPGA Championships, the British and US Opens, all change venues each year.

Example: The Proms, The Royal Alberta Hall, London.

For prestige, uniqueness of design and tradition the Proms remain at the Albert Hall and despite the fact that demand for tickets far outstrips capacity the event is not likely to move to a multi-purpose venue such as Earl's Court where many more tickets could be sold. The circular structure of the hall is itself at odds with most modern, square or rectangle designs, and, in similar style to amphitheatres, there are several levels of seating, with colonnade supports separating different areas. It would be almost impossible to replicate such an environment in a multi-purpose venue and the cost to do so would be exorbitant. Apart from that aspect, which we might call the internal performance area, the outer zones of the hall, the separate bar areas and such, could not possibly be done on a temporary basis to provide even a close replication of the Albert Hall.

Activity 10.2

1 Identify events that are synonymous with their physical location and venue
2 Could any of these events be re-located to another place or venue?
3 What would be the impact on the experience if that happened?

The most common association though for hallmark events is to do with the geographic location rather than venue. Table 10.1 suggests a way of thinking about this relationship between event and location. Whilst lots of events exist that are infrequent in occurrence but similar because they are physically based at the same location there are also many events that are infrequent but occur in different locations.

If we look at the table above, which is not meant to be exhaustive but illustrative only, we can understand a little bit more how the physical setting might influence one element of the experience and also the significance in changes in experience that either event type or location might make. A similar location producing a similar physical event is Notting Hill Carnival and Glastonbury music festival. A different location producing a similar physical event is a World Cup Final or Super Bowl. A different location producing a different event is any event that is, literally a one off. Finally there is the same location producing a different event such as a multi-purpose venue like the Paris Bercy, Frankfurt Arena, King Dome or NEC.

Events that have very specific physical settings carry a degree of uniqueness about them in relation to other events, and this is often the basis for the events success. For example, there have been numerous discussions

Table 10.1 Event occurrence and setting relationship.

Occurrence	Event type	Physical setting
Event frequency	Similar	Same location
Event frequency	Similar	Different location
Event frequency	Different	Different location
Event frequency	Different	Same location

about re-locating the Notting Hill Carnival away from the tightly packed streets of Ladbroke Grove in West London and surrounding areas into the more open and expansive area of Hyde Park. There may well be good safety concerns for doing this but in one stroke, the essential element that the experience of Notting Hill is built upon, that of the rolling parades and sounds systems occupying the streets will be lost forever and it will never be the same Carnival. Creating, re-creating and duplicating physical settings is an essential part of event management and the success of many events rests on the ability to do this. Sometimes this involves accepting a locations limitations and not pushing too much to create an environment in an unsuitable location. However it also involves understanding how creativity can be used to transform an environment into something else. Sensitivity to people's attitudes and views can play a part here, although this is often a highly subjective viewpoint. Nevertheless we sometimes have to think about the use a venue can be put to as opposed to what we want to do with it and respond accordingly. I have attended many rock concerts held in wholly unsuitable venues, and despite the best efforts of engineers, the sound emanating from a stage becomes a melee of clashing overlapping and rebounding unintentional noise because the venue's acoustics are not equipped to deal with the music. At other times however we have to be daring and innovative enough to challenge these limitations as happened during the Paris Fashion Show in the early 1990s when one catwalk show was re-located to an abattoir. Finally, of course the physical setting itself is open to manipulation and distortion as we alter its shape to suit our purposes.

Nathan Homan, Creative Director of Rouge Events, often uses Old Billingsgate, London as a venue because 'it has an excellent riverside location boasting views of Tower Bridge, City Hall, HMS Belfast and the Monument and is situated at the hear of what is called "iconic" London. The venue is Grade II listed Victorian architecture and plays host to several of London's most glamorous events. From the outside it is a grand, imposing venue that in itself creates an impact. Inside it is highly flexible and has lots of potential for creativity'. Figure 10.1 shows the natural interior in the top left corner. Working clockwise from there the images show how the venue can be transformed into a casino, banquet and fashion show. Nothing is more unique than such custom-made settings.

Nevertheless if we want to attempt to re-create the experience using similarities in setting then we need to understand the rational behind designing the setting in the first place. Take for example a circus Big

Figure 10.1   Design used to transform Old Billingsgate. Photograph courtesy of Rouge events.

Top where the internal physical setting never really changes over a series of tour events, although the geographic location does. Once we are inside this almost hermetically sealed environment then we are experiencing a very similar event to elsewhere, especially where the presentation format is scripted as opposed to interpreted. By scripted I mean that the format of the Circus show itself is very similar each time it runs and the variables for change are kept to a minimum. A more interpretative version would adapt the format in significant ways, suggesting a quite different event each time.

In this example we can see that we have different geographic locations (i.e. the 'tour') but where an event is created within an almost identical setting each time (the Big Top). The format of the show itself sometimes does change, but is often run to a similar script each time so the experience is similar for different audiences. What does fundamentally change is the interaction with audiences, as the audience is different for each and every show. And we know from many stage performers' shows that audience interaction and response can influence the experience significantly, offering both an upbeat and downbeat experience. So at this moment we have some knowledge of how interaction of and between people impacts on our event experience and also how physical location impacts as well.

Case study 10.3

The Oktoberfest, Munich

Case study focus

Location essential to experience

Oktoberfest 'the biggest fair in the world' or 'Wies'n' as it is called by Bavarians. The Oktoberfest combines fair entertainment with its own cultural and traditional links. It is also one huge 'beer' festival. Situated in Munich, it is an annual festival, and as a Hallmark event is commonly known as the Munich Beer festival. The appeal lies in the fact that the beer is specially brewed for the festival by the five breweries of Munich and no other beer is sold. Although copied elsewhere (Canada, USA, Australia, Brazil) the Oktoberfest retains its significance as the original, and the experience is based around the local people and culture of Bavaria. To visit it is to be a part of an historical occasion that dates back to 1810, when it was in fact a horse race to celebrate a wedding of Bavarian nobility. In 1819 it became officially organised as a city event and has remained so ever since. To add to the horse racing came beer, tents, food and a fairground. The traditions of the festival that give it its uniqueness include the brewers' marching into Munich, the costumes parade and the 'anstich' when the mayor of Munich opens the first barrel of beer. Once the beer is open and flowing, the mayor has to shout out aloud to the crowd, in a mock Bavarian accent, that beer is available. Even the style of beer drinking has a tradition to it that any visitor wanting the full experience should copy. Natives of Bavaria dress for the occasion in Dirndl or lederhosen. The main experience though is in the 14 beer tents, the largest of which the Hofbrau – Festhalle has a capacity for 10,000 people. The ambience of drinking in such a large collection of people is a main attraction, coupled with the opportunity to savour the Weris'n Marz, a beer brewed specially for the festival.

Objects

The next element to consider is that of objects. As noted earlier objects have three types and they act as representations for social, symbolic and physical meaning. The key to understanding them according to Rossman is to identify the key objects. These are the ones that will fill the setting and aid interactions. These objects we might also refer to as items, tokens, artefacts, even treasures as they serve to give meaning to an occasion. Up to this point this aspect of event management has been the area where design has been positioned, where the thematic and staging elements of the event are located. This tends to reduce event design to a rather singular component, that views it as only the tangible physical aspects of an event. So very often the objects within an event are the props, the floral arrangements, the lighting, the backdrops and decoration. Objects though can also be symbolic (or abstract).

I would argue that for events we need to be able to identify not only the key ones but as many of the others as are necessary for they are the very elements that enable a setting to be created. Where different events are being designed, or existing ones being re-designed, we need to carefully note what objects to include and exclude. The basis of decisions made here will directly influence how the experience is interpreted since the objects often provide the essential features that create that experience. Of course some objects would seem to be so obvious we barely give them a second thought but that does not mean that they cannot change or even be replaced. It is the implications of such decisions that must be considered though when looking at the type and nature of objects we use. We can see this in the way modern society has an ability to re-interpret and re-adapt older ideas and events to a new idiom, often referred to as post-modernism. Changes can be made for many reasons such as changing values in society, cultural development, changes to the law, advances in technology, rise in the events popularity, funding and out dated venue, and sometimes holding onto the key objects is not always possible or practical. Certainly in multi-cultural cities, where the re-interpretation of traditional events takes place to present them from more inclusive cultural perspective then the key objects can change significantly or the objects can be used in a different way such as the adaptation of Mardi Gras that Sydney's gay community has used to develop a different kind of 'carnival'. In some cases the objects of tradition are replaced and it becomes problematic to identify, examine and interpret what meaning the new objects hold. In others the critical objects are retained to maintain the link with previous events and to maintain the meaning of the event for the majority of people.

Case study 10.4

UK Celebration of Guy Fawkes

5th November each year
Case study focus

Changes in associated event objects

Changes in nature of celebration

The UK annually celebrates Bonfire Night or Guy Fawkes, an event also known colloquially as Plot Night, which occurs every year on November 5th. The transformation of this event since the mid-1960s to the present has been huge. The celebration and events associated with it relate to Britain's historical past when Guy Fawkes attempted, with others, to blow up the House of Lords, the visiting monarch James I and with it the seat of power in the country in 1605. This group of conspirators devised a plot to destroy Westminster with powerful explosives, in an attempt to devastate Parliament and kill the King. The now infamous Gunpowder Plot was intended to strike at the heart of the political system in London and give political power to the Roman Catholics. The Gunpowder Plot was organised by a group of five conspirators including Guy Fawkes. They failed in their attempt and were captured and subsequently tried and executed for their sins. Their plans though were very extreme possibly unknown to themselves since they had enough gunpowder to have blown up not only the Lords and Houses Parliament but also Westminster Abbey.

> In a report published in the New Civil Engineer, Dr Alford calculated that Fawkes and his fellow conspirators went for an overkill, filling the cellar beneath the House of Lords with 25 times the explosive necessary to bring the building down. On November 5, 1605, a solitary figure was arrested in the cellars of Parliament House. Although he first gave his name as John Johnson, a startling series of events gradually unfolded under torture. Guy Fawkes, as he was really called, was one of thirteen who had conspired to blow up the parliament, the King, and his Lords, thereby throwing the country into turmoil, out of which these traitors hoped to raise a new monarch, sympathetic to their cause, and return England to its Catholic past (www.suite101.com).

To celebrate this spectacular failure local communities build bonfires that are set alight, effigies of Fawkes are burned and fireworks are set off. The people do this to commemorate the country's most notorious traitor and have historically celebrated with quaint rhymes such as 'remember, remember the 5th of November'.

The year 2005 marked the 400th anniversary of the Gunpowder Plot, and as we shall see later in the section, offered some interesting developments in the way modern society remembers the period. What will also become clear is that the nature of the original celebrations were markedly different to today's centrally organised ones.

By the 1960s the celebration was a very local and community one that drew in children and adults alike. In the weeks' preceding the 5th, children would group together (in 'gangs') and go 'chumping', that is search for old wood to build a bonfire. An appropriate 'plot' of wasteland would be identified or claimed as a bonfire site. This was in the immediate community and was usually common or derelict land, or land attached to a cricket, football or rugby pitch and slowly a bonfire, as big as could be built would emerge as children scrounged for wood from all and sundry. Anybody who had wood to dispose of would contribute and local firms would drop a vanload of wood for the bonfire. An unspoken competition existed between local children and the aim was to have the biggest and best bonfire in the area. As a leisure time activity in itself the making of the bonfire often led to 'skirmishes' between 'bonfire gangs' as they scavenged for wood or invaded each other's territory either to check out their competitors bonfire or, more radically, burn it down. Adults (i.e. parents) oversaw this process in a casual manner, but there was always attention paid to the building of the bonfire itself (if only to ensure it didn't fall down) and to gathering larger trunks of wood. In the immediate week before 5th November children would cajole their parents to buy fireworks, in order to re-create the spectacle of explosion that Fawkes failed to achieve. They would also make 'guys', effigies of Fawkes, made from old clothing and propped up in a wheelbarrow. This would then lead to a trawl around local streets, knocking on front doors and asking for a 'penny for the guy', that is a request for money from the local residents, an acknowledged recognition of the efforts of the children in building the bonfire. Meanwhile parents would further be encouraged to prepare food for the bonfire night that mostly consisted of local favourites and universal ones such as pies and peas, gingerbread, parking (ginger cake) and toffee.

As MacWatt writes:

'As a young boy I joined countless other children during the preceding week begging from door-to-door for "a penny for the Guy". My "Guy" was a discarded old pair of pants and moth-eaten pullover stuffed with straw and newspaper. On Bonfire Night it joined the other children's "Guys" on the pyre of wood we had built in the neighbour's backyard or nearby field, to crackle and flare in the blaze when it was torched. If we were lucky our parents had bought some firecrackers for us to set off. The monster fireworks of today were unavailable just after the war' (MacWatt, 2003). On the 5th itself, and entirely through word-of-mouth, there were no marketing campaigns here, at an appointed time as many local residents as wished would descend upon the wasteland for the lighting of the fire. This was normally a task done by three or four of the children's parents as it could involve paraffin soaked paper to get the fire alight. Perched on top would be one, sometimes more, of the Guy Fawkes effigies. As the fire began to roar and the spectacle unfolded then fireworks would be let off. This was invariably an ad-hoc and unorganised affair as any family with fireworks let them off as and when they saw fit. After the fireworks were used and the bonfire began to lose its initial surge, if extra wood was available then it would be added. This was then the time for food and a combination of trays and plastic containers appeared. There was even a short visit to a nearby child's home for hot food, which was then carried back to the fire to be eaten. Finally as the evening progressed and the dying embers of the fire were reached someone would produce a bag of potatoes and these would be tossed onto the embers to roast. An hour or two later they would be retrieved, sliced in half and smeared in butter. Then, if not already gone, those remaining would head back home and Bonfire Night came to a close.

If we compare this slightly rosy-tinted view of the past celebration of bonfire night to the present, we can see how different today's celebration is.

In 2005 the community base that localised bonfire night has all but gone, and there are many reasons for this. Many of the objects that we can identify from the past have either disappeared or been replaced by contemporary versions and the setting for the bonfire has all but been erased in most parts of the country. Not all of these changes should be seen as bad ones but the social, emotional and physical objects of previous generations have clearly changed. Table 10.2 below indicates what some of those changes have been. One of the biggest changes has been to regulations controlling the use of fireworks and the making of bonfires (especially on wasteland). On the back of a very necessary safety campaign aimed at preventing some of the horrific injuries that occurred from the unregulated use of fireworks, the delivery of a bonfire has moved away from the casual ad-hoc one of yesteryear and into a more municipal controlled event. Public use of fireworks has not been made illegal but every effort is made to discourage it from happening. One of the mechanisms has been for local municipal authorities to organise their own fire and fireworks display operated in a safely controlled environment. Many take place in parks as local by-laws can be used to ban the use of fireworks without permission, and so the provision of a fire and display negates the need for individuals to purchase any. Modern bonfire night celebrations can attract 5–10,000 people.

As a result of the municipalisation of bonfire night, many of the associated activities of the past have also disappeared, simply because they are not based within the community. Children no longer, in any great numbers, organize to collect wood and build their own bonfire, parade their 'Guys' at front doors for a penny or indulge in homemade food on the night (there is case to suggest that this activity has now been displaced towards Halloween Night and the emergence of trick or treating). The backyard bonfires of earlier times have given way to spectacular bonfires and pyrotechnic displays organised by schools, municipalities or local Clubs, often raising money for charity. Whilst the main day for celebration remains 5th November, commercial and organisational reasons dictate that the event now be scheduled for the Saturday evening immediately before or after November 5th, whichever is the nearer, and over the passage of time the original significance of our celebration, the deliverance from such an act of treason that would probably have ushered in a Civil War, has been largely forgotten. Guy Fawkes Night shorn of its original political undertones is now much more organised, commercial and municipalised than in the past.

There does nevertheless remain some similarity of key objects but in many other ways the nature of Bonfire night has changed. Whilst some of these physical objects are still to be seen (fire, fireworks) many are not and the social and symbolic objects have often been dissipated or replaced.

We can see from the Table 10.2 the objects used to characterise a Bonfire celebration have significantly changed form a very local base to a more municipal one which has less close-knit social relationships as a result, and where some of the objects of the original celebration have been transplanted or removed. This is not to say the new celebrations are not spectacular in their own way but to highlight how they have been transformed. One of the most significant changes has been the very date of the celebration as stated earlier. Thus the social and symbolic impact of the 5th is often spread over a period of time rather than concentrated on the actual day itself.

What may have been regarded as essential objects for such an event have been in many cases displaced, rendering the celebration immaterial to its origins? MacWatt points out, any notion that there is recognition of the act of treason has pretty much disappeared. What we have instead is an official organised and controlled pyrotechnic display with a large fire, attended by in many vases, commercial traders selling food and assorted paraphernalia and where the cost of entry may or may not be free (often isn't). As a result of the safety processes being introduced the fundamental nature of the event has change, and the main object of celebration, the burning of the 'guy' is often omitted. The interactions that might have been readily apparent in previous generations celebrating GF night are no longer present, replaced by a combination of public and commercial ownership events and where the key objects have been gradually eroded. Ones from other cultures to give the 5th November a completely different slant have in some variants, replaced these objects. Cultures that have fire as part of celebration and ancient ritual (Aborigine, India, Peru, Chile) have seen some of their symbols and stories adapted for a western audience and incorporated into 5th November.

Table 10.2 Guy Fawkes objects past and present.

	Physical	Symbolic	Social
Past	Community/waste or garden land	Guy – used for street trawl and perched atop the bonfire	Local groups of children co-joined to collect and build
	Community wood collection/ donation	Bonfire – hand-built by children	Children's parents supporting through gathering/ provisions
	Homemade food/potatoes roasted in fire	Fireworks – ad-hoc, let off as and when	Free – spontaneous attendance but also very specific to an immediate area
	Penny for guy activity	Ownership – it belonged to an identifiable group/local area	
		Parental or min-imum supervision	
Present	Municipal or private ground	No guy	No children joined or collected wood
	Official wood collection/ donation	Bonfire – roped off	No parental involvement
	Burger/hot dog food stalls no roasting	Pyrotechnic display – ad-hoc letting off of fire-works illegal; especially if fire held in public park	Fee for admission – non-spontaneous and have to be brought in advance
	No guy activity	No ownership other than public authority	
		Security or official supervision	
		Alternative cultural form	

Therefore we have 5th November becoming a slightly dissipated celebration, as always though where there is development there is preservation. Recognising the erosion of the symbols and artefacts of 5th November has led to some attempts to re-instigate them. In the towns Lewes and Pevensey, Sussex, there is an attempt to mirror the escapades of children the past. A number of societies have been founded that seek to preserve the activities associated with 5th November and each competes against the other to see who can produce the best Fawkes effigy. The celebration itself is marked by fire, explosions, parades and brass bands, all bringing a sense of tradition to the event. Such community activity has occurred because the modern version of the celebration has become a civic display of entertainment rather than a community one. Fortuitously at a time when 5th November was beginning to lose meaning, and the social bonding and interactions of yesteryear were all being eliminated along with the objects of celebration 2005 marked the 400th anniversary of the Gunpowder Plot and to give significance to this, many civic organised events re-connected with the past. None did better than the celebration in East London at Victoria Park where the whole event took on a theatrical slant to connect past with present. Operating under the title Remember Remember the event became one massive outdoor theatre involving a pyrotechnic display, theatrics, a bonfire and a huge Guy Fawkes effigy. An essential part of the event was a dramatization of the Gunpowder Plot.

It is not unreasonable to suggest that were it not for the transfer of organisation of bonfire night from local to municipal, then such a major event and celebration would have never taken place. So despite the changes in bonfire night, where many of the original objects that made the experience have disappeared or been diluted, the newer approach provides possibilities for a different kind of celebration that can, in this instance, be as potent and object laden as the past, albeit in a different, less locally based way. What remains clear though is that the nature of organisation has been transformed forever, almost certainly without likelihood of returning, from a local to municipal and incorporating far more professional event and pyrotechnic skills in the process. This has also seen it move from a largely active event for children to one of almost total passivity.

Case study 10.5

Goodie bags

Focus of case study

Providing personal physical objects

The use of the goodie bag at events is widespread and applies to a wide range of event types. In fact such is their use in brand events that Chernushenko (1994) has drawn attention to what he says is the wanton waste that is produced as a result of events giving away free material that is then dumped at some later stage by the recipient. His argument also draws attention to the vast use and waste of resources that accompany such gifts, and he questions their ethical and indeed sustainable principles. Yet there seems to be no let up in the principle of a goodie bag being an effective way (a) to market products and services and (b) to provide event attendees with a tangible gift. They are used in all types of events from children's birthday parties to conferences and exhibitions through to product launches and brand events, the bags are offered as a physical thank you for attending. As and when they are handed out largely depends on the event type as some will contain little more than promotional material and factual information, which we may often feel we can do without whilst others however will truly be thank you gifts. In both cases they act as reminder of the event, a physical object that we can bring away with us that acknowledges our attendance. We see them everyday at business conventions, conferences and exhibitions where the first thing the visitor often gets on arrival either at registration or just after is a gift bag that is usually full to brimming with such things as promotional leaflets, flyers, booklets, magazines, exhibitor information, conference schedule, freebies and gifts. Goodie bags exists as objects in their own right, symbolic of a recognition of attendance, an almost tourist-type mentality that states 'I have been there and done it', they can be proudly displayed during and post the actual event as a cultural commodity that has value for the owner. Inside the bag there then exist the individual objects. A popular object to give away at business travel fairs in the mid- to late 1990s was the now seemingly essential stress ball or pad. More recently computer mouse mats have been in vogue. Indeed at one such event

I came away with 23 different varieties of anti-stress devices in all types of shape and sizes with only one real common denominator. They were all designed in the corporate colours of the company they were linked to and had styling to match e.g. a plane for Emirates, a red one for Virgin. Such objects are relatively cheap and easy to produce, they are harmless, and are a simple physical offering.

Children's birthday party

At a lower operational level, goodie bags for a children's birthday party, especially for those under 12, are common practice. Just like larger scale events, the range and variety of party bags is huge and is highly dependent on a child's preferences, their parents' deep pockets and/or their parents' creativity. A tour round many supermarket, gift store or toy shop will reveal that corporate branding is very much alive and well in this area too as almost any popular cultural form of the day is available as pre-packaged goodie bag. Some have longevity and are available most of the time such as Barbie, the Simpson's, or Action Man whilst others are a product of timing, that is the child's birthday in relation to current cultural trends in music, film, TV, games and so on with typical examples being Harry Potter, King Kong, Beyblades or Pokemon. The content of the bags is not normally a surprise other than in terms of branding as such bags normally contain a combination of sweets, crayons, toys, stickers, leaflets, comic books, jewellery and games. Homemade ones can be, literally, anything and is dependent upon the child's interests as much as their parents enthusiasm for making them. Homemade versions are different and may contain almost anything but typical inclusions are likely to be birthday cake, ball, badge, party popper, gum or streamer. They tend not to be 'themed' as such, so there is no uniform corporate image or logo and it is just as likely that we might find an NFL club badge, gum, pack of cards and toy soldier all in the same bag.

Whatever choice made though will act as a conscious representation of either re-affirmation of the role of and power of commodities and the appeal of popular cultural forms, the branded version, or the appeal of a bespoke version in which perhaps more personal traits are displayed and more time, care and meaning is invested. The branded version is designed and created for us, it nevertheless is our decision (to be made within the context of the overall event) to use it. Once we include the goodie bag it then exists as an object that ultimately has a role to play in the birthday environment in much the same way as the birthday cake and candles do. Its presence is there for interpretations to be made. In this way the goody bag itself is an object and the contents, as micro-objects, are looked upon by peers as a direct reflection of the birthday child's own interests and preferences and, we might also add, there credibility amongst those peers. The choice made will guide this interpretation and will be seen as culturally relevant and up to date or irrelevant and out of date. It is for these reasons that care has to be taken in the choosing of the 'right' reference point. Several points will guide this not least of which is the children's ages. What works at age 3–5 doesn't work for age 10–12 and equally what works for boys does not usually work for girls and so pitching the goody bag at the right level is an important consideration. From here, as I have suggested, the next reference point is going to be the children's own interests and that will draw upon current fads and trends as much as anything else. Here there is no universal guide other than awareness of what these may be. To illustrate the point we can use some popular myths and stereotypes so boys, for example, do not have goody bags based around Barbie, Power Puff Girls or Ponies and girls likewise do not have them based around Action Man, Ed, Edd and Eddie or Football. A mix of boys and girls adds a new dimension to the creative solution required. Of course, opting out, avoids this altogether, but runs the risk of being identified as offering a poor experiential end to the party. In the latter respect though this largely depends on what else took place during the birthday part and if other traditional prize giving activities were present, then the avoidance of a goody bag will probably pass without any observation of any kind. And so we are back to a design decision, in terms of how we plan out the birthday party and the stages we follow. At this level of gift giving the goodie bag is an extra, a pleasant offering by the hosts to thank children for attending the party and as a kind of quid-pro-quo for their gifts to the birthday child. However it doesn't occur as a consequence of the child's attendance, it is not a factor in them choosing whether to attend or not, nor is it a necessity. In this context the goodie bag has an air of innocence and pureness to it acting, amongst other things, to cement one child's relationship with another and to conclude a joyous, inclusive celebration.

There is though another context and level at which the event goodie bag operates with the ultimate gift now being the preserve of Hollywood and its film stars who are presented with prizes as a 'reward' for attending or featuring at an awards event. Lacking subtlety the gifts doled out to stars that turn up for certain events borders on bribery. And whilst all innocence and pureness is undoubtedly lost, there are similarities with those given out to children, albeit at a level that is incomparable in terms of cost and content. One target group for these gifts are the stars who give out the gongs and who, as a reward for doing this fairly functional but vital act, receive merchandise bordering on the obscene. The other target is the recipients of the awards themselves, who have to be likewise persuaded to attend. This perhaps tells us more about the real value of such award ceremonies.

The roll call of gifts is quite astonishing and includes items such as cashmere pyjamas, a $22,000 Tasmanian cruise, a Vespa motorcycle lease, two $500 bottles of Krug champagne and Kerstin Florian 'caviar facial' products. The latter two items formed part of a basket of goods handed out to the female contenders when the nominees for an Oscar were announced, and that is before the actual ceremony has taken place. The reason for such lavishness: 'It's our way of thanking them … it's all about branding. Everyone is trying to be the brand that the nominees use. It's about not getting lost in the crowd' Sarah Cairns PR for the Beverley Hills Four Season, venue for the Oscar nominations announcements (The Times 28/01/06). These objects of desire then become exactly that as the public reflect the 'tastes' of the stars in their post-event purchases. This is then fuelled by the endless paparazzi shots of stars, their outfits and their bags that appear on millions of TV screens and in 100s of print articles around the world.

The need for these objects though then becomes a necessary expectancy, an essential part of what we might well call the event brand-scape where desirable products are placed to attract maximum exposure and the attention of the public. And just to make sure that they achieve this then the event organisers have to design a means of promoting these objects, for in essence they are replacing the more traditional way of promotion through advertising. It has been suggested (Ayres, 2006) that a $10,000 product placement in a celebrity goodie bag can produce a very high publicity return, possibly in the region of $2 million. To ensure this exposure means that the media are then given a detailed list of contents. This activity appears to then make the event bigger than ever and, equally, extend its longevity as images drawn from the single event can re-appear several months (or even years) later. In turn the bar is lifted for each awards goodie bag. For example, the Golden Globes Awards gave away $62,000 of freebies to its presenters. As the largesse increases so it creates an organisational problem of where exactly to store them and how to transport them. One solution has been to create a kind of Santa's grotto 'goodie room', a side room storage area where celebrities can go and choose gifts of their choice to supplement their goodie bag. But it also creates a desire problem for organisers, what exactly 'them' should consist of in order to create the desired impact. Objectification amongst the public is the primary goal here, and we might even begin to question the intrinsic purpose of the event itself as brand exposure moves centre stage. Does it matter who won or received an award as long as the brand was exposed.

Rules

Rules play a part in guiding interactions and how those interactions unfold. Establishing rules sets out how the event will progress and develop in the course of its operation. Rules though are also codified and ceremonial and there are also rules of everyday discourse that require understanding. Rules as used here as a generic term that includes legal, ceremonial, relationship, administrative regulations and rules of games (Rossman, 2003). We can use rules to set parameters, to regulate and in some cases these are clearly essential to the meaning and purpose of the event (e.g. a sports event) based on the rules of the game and competition. Rules can be used and understood in many ways for example they can govern rules of behaviour, and there exist legal rules to effect our actions and interactions. But we can also have 'polite-ceremonial' rules, of which rituals forms a part, although I would split the difference between the two for events. Polite rules may also come into affect, for example, at an exhibition or conference where the engagement with the subject is a result of rules set out to behave and respond in a polite way, or the order of progression through an exhibition.

Such rules may influence the way we 'experience' the exhibition (e.g. in the case of art) there is often informal rules on noise and the need to be quiet. Ceremonial rules can be based on many things including the rules under which we conduct a wedding ceremony, an awards ceremony and a presentation. But they can also relate to ceremonial occasions where rules of tradition are laid down and followed by subsequent versions of the event. For example, the opening pitch of the USA baseball season follows a ceremonial rule by allowing the first pitch of the new season to be delivered by the President. In this case we may more appropriately call this a ritual rather than a rule. When talking about rules we tend to talk about either laws or administrative regulations that should be adhered to. The latter are those that have been used to establish a standard of operating procedures and can be most easily identified through sporting rules and regulations that come under the umbrella of a named activity or organisation.

Understanding sport rules, those that are written and prescribed, is a relatively simple task and all that really changes between any events is the method of administration. However the implementation of these rules can sometimes be open to interpretation and this can affect the event. Sometimes governing organisations issue instructions for stricter interpretations of certain rules that will influence the interaction of participants in sport. For instance every time the World Cup Finals are held the ruling body of football, Fédération Internationale de Football Association (FIFA) focuses on particular aspects of the game that it wants referees to pay attention to. This creates some uncertainty for players since actions that they have undertaken in the past are now being interpreted differently and so they are not immediately sure what will happen. To some extent this is the desired effect that the players alter their behaviour towards opposing players, and hence the interaction of the game changes as a consequence. However this change may not necessarily be for better, since the new interpretation has not been bedded in with the participants and so the rules may alter the nature of the event in a way not intended. Of course the 'new' interpretation may also be for the better. Either way the interaction within the event is affected by a change of interpretation.

Where rituals rather than formal rules have emerged then we must understand how they have been adopted and how they affect any interaction since they will then become an integral part of the design of the experience. Not all rituals, of course, can be perfectly designed but understanding them and their existence can help us at least frame an event in accordance with the rituals associated with it. There is also another element here to consider, for if we want to change or adapt or develop the ritual, then we need to know something about where it came from to begin with so we understand how the process of change will affect the experience.

Rituals are important for society. Rituals, as Durkheim (1965) argued, embedded in ceremonial gatherings are central to social integration. Using ideas of early anthropologists, Goffman (1967) looked at the role of ritual in everyday lives whilst subsequent later sociologists developed the concepts not in ceremonial exchange for its own sake, but ceremonial exchange such as traditional gift giving between kin and close friends and this idea itself was moved a step forward by suggesting that ceremonial exchange rituals between strangers should be important in the modern world. Shrum and Kilburn (1996) in looking at acts of nudity at New Orleans Mardi Gras then posed the questions: Where are the ceremonial exchange rituals in modern society? How do they develop and how are they organized? In helping us to understand rituals they ask that three factors be taken into consideration when interpreting rituals, namely: origin, structure and variation. For events these can be taken to refer to how particular forms of the ritual came into existence in the first place, the forms any ceremonial exchange between people actually takes and what, if any, accounts for the observed difference in the ritual performed (in comparison with previous versions). Drawing on these ideas we can begin to more concretely understand what is occurring and why and begin to see how in event design we need to pay attention to them and present an environment that re-affirms the place of ritual or, in some cases, develops it in a different way. Where the latter occurs we start to see the emergence of a paradigm shift, where we have moved from one way of thinking about the ritual to another. Such changes can be quite dramatic not to mention laden with anxiety over the response to them and they can be quite revolutionary in output for they are, in fact, bringing a metamorphosis to the event.

Rituals and ceremonial rules relate to our expectations and how we believe an occasion should be marked. Some are different between cultures especially in sport. In most European Union Competitions for example, the team winning the competition (say any sporting World Cup) the winning captain collects the trophy from a guest of honour and immediately holds it aloft to his own team's fans. In North America you are as likely to get the Coach receiving the trophy as much as the team captain or leader as in the case with the NFL Super Bowl. Some ceremonial traditions are essential to the experience (e.g. the oldest football cup), the FA Cup, has numerous ceremonial elements to it, many of which have been subsequently mirrored elsewhere. There is a roll out of ritual and ceremonial acts to be performed before the players take to the field of play. These give the event its gravities, its significance as a major event and provide the fullest possible experience at that point based on previous versions. Finals of professional sporting competitions, just like carnivals and other processional events, often have an order to them. The physical rituals are not the same for each sport (since different rituals are in place) but there is often commonality in the presence of a processional format that is recognised as a ritualistic occurrence.

This example draws mainly from Professional Football (Soccer) but not dissimilar rituals occur in cricket, rugby, American Football, hockey although each sports may have a different order:

- Special finals match day suit is worn.
- Coach arrival at venue.
- Team's pre-match walk on the pitch to soak up the atmosphere.
- Pre-match gathering in tunnel.
- Teams enter stadium arena side by side in a processional walk into stadium, lead by teams coach or manager.
- For the NFL an MC calls out the starting players from each team individually.
- Players line up in single file facing the main stadium grandstand, sometimes just off a red carpet.
- VIP guests shake hands with each player, manager and official.
- National anthem or other anthemia song is delivered/sung to the crowd.
- On completion respective teams break ranks and jog onto the playing field accompanied by a great roar from the crowd.
- Opposing teams captains meet the referee in the centre of the pitch and 'spin a coin' to see who will have first possession or kick-off in the game.

The role of the anthem or song is a characteristic ritual of these occasions and the tendency in modern sporting events is to have a special guest singer who would give a rendition of the national anthem or other appropriate composition. In the UK, for the FA Cup Final, the composition 'abide with me' was the song used, a bi-partisan selection that appealed to all spectators. In the USA, the opening ceremony of the Super bowl is symbolised by a rendition of the Star Spangled Banner sung by a special guest (Whitney Houston, Maria Carey, Diana Ross). Such elements of ceremony are seen as essential to the experience of such events and they must occur each time it takes place for they re-affirm those parts of the experience that can be, at least organisationally, replicated. A national anthem usually bestows on the event its import-ance as an occasion, the finale that, on conclusion, will bestow on the winning team the award of national (or international) champion. Other ceremonial occasions can rise directly out of culture, and serve the same purpose of re-affirming the integrity of the spectacle, by aligning the ritual with cultural determination.

Case study 10.6

The Haka

Case study focus

Regulated ritual

Perhaps one the most famous and visual rituals in sporting circles is the 'haka' as performed by members of the New Zealand Rugby Union team, or the 'all blacks' as they are known. This tribal routine of sound and movement issues forth a challenge to the opposing team and is the hallmark of any game of Rugby Union involving New Zealand.

The 'Haka' is the generic name for Maori war dance. It is an action chant, often described as a 'War Dance', but more a chant with hand gestures and foot stamping, originally performed by warriors before a battle, proclaiming their strength and prowess and generally ver-bally abusing the opposition. In modern times, the haka is used in a number of situations. The most famous modern use is its regular per-formance by New Zealand representatives in Rugby Union (the All Blacks), although there are similar editions given by Rugby League (the Kiwis), Australian Rules Football (the Falcons) and Basketball (Tall Blacks) teams before commencing a game. It is also performed at certain state functions, such as the welcoming of foreign dignitaries.

The haka dates back some 200 years and is generally attributed to Te Raupuarha, chief of the Ngati Toa tribe in 1810. Under attack by his enemies he managed to hide and escape capture whereupon emerging from his safe haven he was confronted by one of the local tribal chiefs. Rather than handing Te over, he allowed him to escape and out of sheer relief for his position Te is understood to have uttered the words, 'It is death, it is death: it is life; this is the man who enabled me to live as I climb up step by step toward sunlight'. The chant was fist used by the All Blacks in 1905.

To witness the haka is to experience a fearsome display of intent and aggression, doubtless bestowing on the team a bonding of culture and tradition that, indeed, no other team, at least outwardly, can show. The ritual format for performing the haka is established for international Rugby Union once the two opposing teams have met the dignitaries and broken ranks to their respective side of the pitch. At this point there is actually no reason for anyone in the ground to take notice of the haka or even to acknowledge it but you can be assured that every single person in a stadium, even the 75,000 at Twickenham, will have their eyes fixed on the All Blacks. Purposefully the team move into position occupying approximately the middle third of one half of the pitch. Having assembled in formation they then begin. All the spectators watch on in awe out of respect for the challenge that is being laid out before the opposing team, and almost like a minutes silence, very few move or make a noise.

What is interesting is the response of other nations to this challenge and the role they play in the continuation of this ritual. The haka is performed on the NZ side of the pitch and, although historically without rules, the opposing team usually either ignores it or locks arms someway inside their own half, facing inward in a joined circle, hence effectively turning their backs on the display. However in 1989 the Ireland team took the challenge head on, they linked arms and trotted over the half way line and stared face to face with the NZ players whilst chanting 'You'll never beat the Irish'. This was a tremendous show of fortitude on the part of the Irish and there is no doubt it took some of the impact out of the haka (unfortunately they still lost the match). This though is not the main point to draw attention to here instead it is the Rugby Football authorities response. In responding the way they did is seems that the Irish had also crossed the, hitherto, ceremonial boundaries but not rule based ones as the Irish, apart from their own supporters, were booed at this act of disruption. As a result a regulation was brought in forbidding opposing players from crossing the halfway line before the match had begun, effectively ensuring that the haka could be performed in future without intervention. As a rule, this is an odd decision for it has legitimised a ceremonial act in favour of one particular team since no other has the haka or a similar tradition to follow. And yet it has not rally met with universal complaint, because the ceremony of the haka is seen to be such an essential part of the experience of watching NZ.

Opponents react to the haka in different ways:

Staring wide-eyed at their opponents, the New Zealand rugby team launches into a foot-stomping, chest-beating, tongue-baring war dance. It's haka time. For more than a century, the New Zealand All Blacks have laid down a challenge to opponents with a pre-match performance of the Maori chant that lasts about 30 seconds. While former captains Wayne Shelford and Colin Meads say the ritual became devalued through overuse, Jonah Lomu, who scored the most tries at World Cups, said performing the haka would give him 'the rage'. For opponents at the current World Cup, the experience is mostly one to savour, not fear. Last night it was Tonga's turn to face the haka at the sport's showpiece, but with a twist. To the delight of the Suncorp Stadium crowd, at the same time as All Black fly half Carlos Spencer led the haka, Tonga issued its own challenge – called the kailao. 'Standing in front of them and watching them do the haka is a highpoint in a player's career', said Italy's New Zealand-born Matt Phillips, who scored a try in last week's 70-7 loss to the All Blacks. 'It's an experience few get the chance to have'.

'It's a wonderful tradition and still thrills me to see it', said Rod Kafer, who won the World Cup with Australia in 1999. 'I wasn't in fear of it, more a sense of awe'. Unlike New Zealand's 2003 group opponents Canada, Italy and Tonga, Australia plays the All Blacks at least twice a year. The Wallabies are among teams who've tried to counter the haka. Former Wallabies captain Phil Kearns would wink at the New Zealanders as they danced. Seven years later in Wellington, under coach Greg Smith's orders, Australia dropped its traditional approach of standing 5 m away and eyeballing its rivals. Instead, the Wallabies moved to the other end of the field and began practicing for the match – they then lost by a record 43-6. John Eales, captain that day, later said that he received angry mail from New Zealanders asking why the Wallabies hadn't stood and faced the haka. Some have tried a more confrontational approach. England forward Richard Cockerill went nose-to-nose with opposite number Norm Hewitt in 1997 at Manchester and a year later in Dunedin.

'I believe that I did the right thing', Cockerill later told reporters. 'They were throwing down a challenge and I showed them I was ready to accept it'. England lost both times.

The ritual holds most significance for New Zealanders. Shelford, who captained the All Blacks from 1986 to 1990, was so incensed by a lacklustre performance that he introduced practice to 'put some personality and meaning into it'. 'There's a real debate about whether it's overdone', said former All Blacks skipper Taine Randell, who learnt the words of the haka before he memorised the national anthem. 'As a New Zealander, I think it's a very special part of our heritage'. 'It's just show business really', said former England captain Bill Beaumont. 'You look at the haka and get on with the game' (rugbyheaven.com).

Clearly many events have this combination of ritual, ceremony and rules that result in a part of the experience remaining, at least conceptually, similar. We can see it at events like carnivals, awards ceremonies, state occasions, weddings, banquets, conferences, baptisms, funerals, swearing in of a head of state, trooping of the colour and so on. A typical event that has this feature would be a New Year celebration, where New York's dropping of the big apple in Times Square is now an essential part of the New Year celebration landscape. Another example would be that of carnivals, whether it is the one in Rio or Notting Hill or Mardi Gras in New Orleans or Sydney, we have what we can call ceremonial processions, displays or pageants as a feature of the carnival. Some of these are based on tradition and the origins of the carnival. In the case of Notting Hill the multitude of floats and costume displays that roll across the streets, are called the 'mas' and are part of year long effort by design and community groups to provide a spectacle. Such components are accepted as essential to the carnival and whilst there may be minor changes to the way these are displayed, they remain a part of ceremonial and ritual components of the event. These rituals though do not always remain static and can be re-interpreted and developed along different lines. Where they are open to adaptation, as in the case of Mardi Gras in the French quarter of New Orleans, according to Shrum and Kilburn (1994) they often undergo a new ceremonial exchange of ritual as a result. The three ritual paradigms identified are based on the (a) social and spatial relationships between actors and the (b) provision of symbolic goods and services. The central focus is public disrobement, a ritual interpreted in terms of cultural codes involving market relations, gender and hierarchy. What seems to be mere debauchery is an expression of moral commitment to an economic system in which conventional notions of gender and hierarchy are deeply embedded.

In this case ritual takes place that defines the ceremonial occasion sometimes with other similar events of the past and sometimes as a form of new ritual (although we may not know it at the time). In the past we would have seen new ships launched through the ceremony and ritual of cracking a bottle of champagne on the side as she is named and launched into the water. For leisure-based events where the perception of freedom is a vital element in the experience rules have to be applied that enable this perception to, if not flourish, at least exist. This is most viewed from the participant point of view, and effectively refers to amateur-based activity. In professional sports though the impact of rules can create interactions that impact not just on participant but also spectator and in turn shape the experience. There are rules that provide the core essential element of sport competition, that the contest is based on a set of rules equally applicable to all competitors and that the outcome of the contest is the test of skill in relation to those rules. From this the outcome of the competition is always uncertain, and it is the uncertainty of this that helps form a part of the experience and appeal of sport to spectators. Sport, as always, is an oddity within the event framework simply because such events do have rules that are as close to civil legislation as possible. Within the context of the sports arena any transgression of the rules results in a penalty of some description. Hence all sports events that are competitive have to be designed around rules and any re-interpretation of them has to be understood by all. Here I am thinking of say local events such as tennis event where the idea of a match lasting three or five sets is impractical and so adaptations of the rules are made. The game laws of play remain, but instead of three sets competitors may play one set of up to eight games instead of six. Any major variation though of the rules beyond that runs the risk of ruining the experience of competition, since it is no longer based around the known rules. If we run a tennis event that opted for a scoring system similar to badminton or table tennis where one game was played up to 15 points with serving changing every two points then the nature of experience changes of a designed rule changed. Once the competitors arrive and learn of this they may protest and be prepared to withdraw from the event. Why? Because the rules had changed to such an extent that they no longer see the event as representing tennis, it becomes a game of some other kind, a variant, and it would have no measurement of comparison with a 'proper' tennis event.

Activity 10.3

Graduation ceremony
Figure 10.2 shows the design of stage setting used for a University Graduation Award. The setting is described as follows:
The stage is at floor level, no rise. On the left is a lectern with microphone, on the right slightly obscured, is another one. The first row of seating consists of five relaxed armchairs. Behind these is one row of sixteen stacking chairs.

To balance the composition of the stage, there is a single row of four chairs at the far right. These match in length, but not depth, four chairs to the left where a small eight-piece brass ensemble will be seated. On the floor is the logo of the University and at the rear of the stage is a large screen flanked at either side by 'ceiling' banners. During the ceremony the screen will transmit live coverage of the event. Just visible superimposed on the left and right of the backdrop are images of stars.

1 What are the ceremonial rituals about to take place? List and explain them in chronological order of their occurrence.

Relationships

The next element requires thinking about what directed interaction may be required for an event. Where people interact we have to anticipate the relational history of those involved and this can only be achieved

Figure 10.2 The stage design of a Graduation Awards Ceremony.

if understand something about how it can influence the experience (Rossman, 2003). The level of designed interactions varies enormously depending upon what we know or understand about those involved in the event. Unlike leisure experiences based around a participant activity however, event experiences have much more complex relationships because, as we have seen earlier, there are multiple stakeholders at many events. Some events will require more designed interaction than other events both on a formal and informal level and the mechanisms employed depend on the extent to which interaction is required. Relational histories are not always necessary or required for an event to be experienced successfully, and it is clear that we do not need to have to develop any kind of relationship for many people who attend events. Equally, however, there are relationships that are quite essential to ensuring an event delivers a successful experience. As well as thinking about creating a relationship we have to also be sure we do not destroy pre-existing ones that would contribute meaningfully to the experience (Rossman, 2003). The most obvious relational history is the family relationship that includes children. The foci of family events is different to most others in that it requires much more careful design and planning to accommodate the needs of children and, in turn, their guardians who have to be appeased two fold, for themselves and for their children. It is, of course, impossible to pay attention to all the variables in relationships that are likely to attend an event, but to understand the complexity of how relationships may work, it is worthwhile considering the ranges of likely relationships for given types of events.

Activity 10.4

1 Make a list of event types that are different in terms of size, aim, and purpose.
2 Identify the likely groups of people that the event is aimed at and analyse the likely relational history of these groups.
3 Explain what particular relationship elements might be designed into the event to ensure an optimum experience.

We can say that events of a certain kind require more attention than others in terms of developing relations at the event, this approach works for those events that are based around people, both for their content and their success, such as conferences and meetings. Clearly meetings of industry bodies or representative organisations such as AEM, MPI or ISES, require some understanding of how new members can be integrated comfortably into the sessions and so obtain a satisfactory experience from their session. One academic conference, the Leisure Studies Association (UK), has a reputation in this respect of being open, friendly and inclusive for academics. Celebrating 25 years of Conference activity, it is both highly professional, academically rigorous but at the same time informal, relaxed and conducive to supporting and integrating new delegates. There is little room for the formation of cliques or professional clusters that can affect other academic conferences. The three-day event functions on the basis of openness and transparency where LSA Committee members and internationally renowned researchers all mingle and interact in all the same areas and at the same times. Planning socialisation opportunities to create relations is a vital component in such situations and although it should not necessarily be a difficult element to identify there are still too many conferences that misunderstand how to manage them. Problems of interaction can occur when there is an uncertain message and mix. Designing interactions that involve suppliers, retailers and the general public needs careful handling. Here misunderstanding what relations need to exist for an event to thrive can result in a poor experience for all.

In 2004 an event called the Cycle Show took place at the Business Design Centre, London that provides an illustration of this point. The event, a showcase for cycle-related businesses manufacturing and/or selling bicycles, clothing, equipment, accessories, media, supplements and fitness consultancy was spread across 3 days. Day 1 was a trade day and for retailers to meet suppliers for exchange of ideas, information and, of course trade sales. The nature of this day differs from others in terms of not only the programme of support activities but also in the type of approach suppliers take to the design and layout of their stands and the product they display. Industry retailers arriving are there to 'trade' to do business with suppliers and make bulk orders at trade prices. They come with a 'cheque book' and possibly a list of products they want to order, as well as discovering new ones that appear to have potential. However when, due to low initial ticket sales for the day, the event organisers decided to let in the general public, this relationship between purchaser and supplier is derailed, to the annoyance of both. Suddenly the relationship that existed in respect of price sensitivity is fractured and numerous stalls during the trade day were extremely reluctant to discuss prices with people until they were certain that they were 'trade' buyers as opposed to the general public. In fact more than a few stand holders were incensed that the general public were allowed access to a session where business deals were being conducted for quantity as opposed to single item purchase enquiries from the public. In fact one company were so enraged that the supplier would not even discuss prices until evidence was provided of ability to purchase in some bulk. In this example the relational history, that of supplier and buyer, whilst not destroyed is fractured because the event has allowed a clash of interests and aims that are significantly different. Visiting members of the public have a completely different idea to trade visitors about the type of event experience they want and also about how they go about business. The former are invariably there to 'gaze' in some wonderment at new products and to be impressed by new ideas and development, but they are also there to bag a bargain, usually of single item products, and are not there to deal in quantity. They are limited purchasers who often arrive waiting to discover all and everything. As a result they demand more time from those working on the stands, time that invariably does not lead to any sale, let alone a bulk purchase. At such events stallholders will often come armed with two types of product, those for retail trade that are then supplemented or exchanged for others that serve the public trade. It is not uncommon for several exhibition stands to be completely overhauled and re-displayed overnight to account for the two different visitors. Indeed some events such as the fashion event Clothes Show live have historically dealt with this by having a trade day followed by a public day, in the latter the content of display stands is often changed 100%, sometimes with new exhibitors arriving who then display not the latest seasons' garments, but the sell-off items of previous seasons at discounted prices.

> *'Understanding the role that relationships play in the interaction of a programme and anticipating how they may contribute to or detract from client satisfaction is an important element of place. Programmers cannot simply assume that the best course of action is always to foster or create a relationship between individuals who attend an event'.*
>
> Rossman (2003, p. 38)

Animation

The final element to consider, and perhaps the most difficult, is that of animation. This idea relates to the 'action' of any occasion and where the planner must structure the event, sometimes to make it appear spontaneous, and to affect movement for those in attendance. Animation is concerned with the experience of motion and how people will move in, through or around a given space. Examples from theatre and dance can be insightful here where scenarios are planned in advance to direct movement, for example in the choreographing of a sequence of occurrences, in order to reach a desired point (Rossman, 2003). Applied to events we can see this animation overlapping with previous elements as we consider not only how to choreograph but also who and where? The timing, pace and delivery aspects of an event come into consideration here also, so we can see how this impacts upon our ideas of ceremony and ritual and the order of procession. People or objects can guide animation. In particular we can think about animation in relation to exhibitions where we are predicting and, often controlling, how people will move through the exhibition, predicting the sequence of interactions that will take place. This might be guided not by actors but by physical signposts such as the layout of the exhibits, the separation of the exhibiting space and the timeline of the artist and nature of communication. A chronological ordering of text as the visitor moves from each section helps to order them and direct them in the preferred route. Understanding this process means we have to design and direct a structure that will deliver our event experience as we have planned. Where people are moving through passages or sections of an event, we need to understand how to animate their experience.

The most glaringly obvious way of illustrating this would be in the way people enter an occasion or event and the experience they get from this. As we have noted earlier the initial 'wow' factor can set our experience off on a positive note. This initial choreographing of the guests entrance to an event, possibly also providing an animated sequence of interactions and happenings, and constructing the order and nature of those happenings, provides an immediate experiential moment. We can regard this as the first phase of the tangible experience of our decision to attend. The design of an entrance to an event is not just about visual style, it also relates to such things as movement, running order, sequence of arrival, even ceremony. It can, but does not have to, provide the first stage in the attainment of an optimal experience, the beginning of the flow that will lead to this point. Animation can be seen as a tool for providing the very uniqueness of an event that marks it as different from other events. It can be used throughout the entirety of an event or it can be used for specific aspects of the event. A more common usage is to direct people to move from one segment to another such as from entrance into reception, from reception into main area, from one zone to another within a main area and from main area to exit. This is simply an indicative list of uses; in practice animation can be incorporated into almost any aspect of an event. The key to its use is to understand exactly why you wish to animate something and then how you wish to design the animation. It doesn't have to be active either, by that I mean there doesn't have to be physical movement in order to animate. It can be achieved via signs, not directional signs bit signs of transference that encourage someone to move into, through or beyond a certain zone. By designing particular settings we can encourage and direct people to move in a certain way if we are trying to get them to sample as much of the event as possible. Providing attractions or signalling a gateway helps to do this and draws people's attention.

We can of course replicate the scenario as well, and rather than ensuring its uniqueness we can attempt to ensure its portability as an event experience concept. Being able to do this depends very much on how we choose to animate something. The TiLE (Technology in Leisure Entertainment) exhibition and conference which originally took place in London but more recently in Stuttgart has had some memorable moments but perhaps none more so that when new arrivals to the Business Design Centre, London were met by a towering 25 ft high mechanical Dinosaur, reputedly from the set of Jurassic Park. As guest entered they had to move directly under the giant creature and between its enormous legs, at the same time bearing witness to a moving head that growled at them. It fitted perfectly with the concept and theme of TiLE. This type of animation though is largely static, once guests have passed through and beyond then they are into another segment of the event and another experience, and so we can then begin to think about how we might animate their experience from this point. Again different event types will require more than others. Charity balls, fundraisers and similar events often rely on very personal animation to make them work. In this respect an individual can be the single most unique factor of the event. Events that rely on personal relationships being developed on site require considerable more attention to the animation aspects, since not only do we need leaders we also need plants (or players) to instigate contacts and we need to provide the right environment for it to take place. Having 'plants', people who have a specific function to perform within the event but all intents and purposes are guests, helps initiate contact. Plants are different to event 'hosts', who act in that capacity almost by default at dinner parties, celebrations or even galas and balls.

Animation then is thinking about the way an event unfolds through a series of linked sequences. The extent to which we consciously want to include animative actions very much depends on what we are setting out to achieve for the event, and the type of experience we want to give people. There is no getting away though from the fact that it is a problematic conundrum for events people, knowing how much or how little you need to animate an event. There are no clear rules, since we have established that each event is going to be different, although we may be able to develop some guidelines that might helps us understand the level of animation required. There is such a thing as too little or too much animation. The former may lead to some feelings of anxiety amongst guests or visitors simply because they are unsure of what to do or where to go next. To fully assimilate the level of animation needed we can return back to the characteristics of different events and reflect on the way each event requires animation and assign a level we feel is required. We can also explore whether or not the animation should be upfront or discreet, whether or not we should have a defined leader (such as a compere, celebrity) or an invisible one (plant). There is no magic formula for ascertaining what levels of animation are needed but a simple exercise can be undertaken by using a 10-level animation plan.

Table 10.3 Ten-level animation plan.

Level	Extent of animation
1	None
2	Little or self-directed
3	Minor animation (entrance)
4	Amenity – food, drink, toilet, etc.
5	Occasional user – technical
6	Information – advice on usage
7	Entertainment – amusing distraction for ambience
8	Guided – develops event flow but may be avoided
9	Guided specificity – essential for full section experience
10	Guided event – essential for total concept

Activity 10.5

1 Using the 10-level animation plan below conduct a study of five events you are familiar with. Assign a 'level of animation' to each event as it is experienced by you.
2 Critically evaluate the event and analyse whether there is too little or too much animation and suggest how the level of animation should change and in what ways.

The types of animation we are all readily familiar with occurs through events such as the Academy Awards, BAFTAS, Britannia Music Awards, MTV Awards and similar high-profile events. They are also ones that have multi-experiences not only in terms of those present at them but also because they are (a) live and (b) on television, and have to cater for at least two types of audience. There are also layers of animation required due to the composition of those attending which includes media, public, performers, presenters, award winners and invited guests. As we shall see in the example of the BAFTAS later, the need to understand what animation is required for these different groups holds the key to the events ultimate experience and success. Perhaps the key role is that of the compere, whose job here is to link the different sequences on stage, the awards and ad breaks as they unfold and they do this by providing the fills and entertainment for the audience. In 2002 at the MTV European Awards Christina Aguilera did this quite memorably by using the TY advertisements breaks to change costume resulting in something like 15 changes throughout the course of the evening. As animator and compere she beguiled both TV and live audiences with her provocative, risqué routine. She animated, quite literally, the event, directing it through its different phases linking live performances to awards presentations to winners acceptances to television ad breaks in a multi-repeated cycle. Her performance was not spontaneous, it was a choreographed journey across several stage settings with deliberate timing to ensure that her 'slots' fitted in with the event timing as well. Using animation in this way helps make connections between the different features of an event and the different elements within it.

Case study 10.7

Celebrating Peter Pan

Kensington Palace Gardens, London

Details on environment creation and event information supplied by: Alexandra Munroe, Theme Traders, London

Case study focus

Event animation and interaction

In 2004 the 100th anniversary of Peter Pan took place to celebrate the first time the story appeared which was on 27 December 1904 at the Duke of York's Theatre, London. To celebrate this, the Great Ormond Street Hospital Children's Charity (GOSHCC) held numerous Peter Pan themed fundraising events throughout the year. One of the main events took place in Kensington Gardens, London and provided an opportunity to acknowledge this milestone but also provided a chance for fundraising and awareness raising about the Peter Pan story. This fundraising event was especially interesting because the author J.M. Barrie left the rights to the Pan stories with the Great Ormond Street Children's Hospital and so every time something is bought money goes to the hospital. To celebrate the 100th anniversary the charity used the design and props company Theme Traders to create the environment, in this case a characterisation of Neverneverland, the magical land in which the story is mainly set. One of the main aims of the event was to create the experience of the Pan story around the original locations where J.M. Barrie was inspired. This in itself was a challenge as these locations were situated within a park that had public access. This alone presented challenges since the park could not be closed off, public access had to remain at all times, and because it is public the entire list of items and subjects that would be used in the event had to be listed in advance for the park managers.

The story of Pan is known to millions but the origins of all the characters and places developed in the book are not so well known, although there is no secret to the sources of Barrie's inspiration. J.M. Barrie lived on the edge of Kensington Gardens and it was while walking his dog there that he met the Llewelyn-Davies family of five boys, who were the inspiration for Peter Pan. The play was first performed in December 1904, and J.M. Barrie gave the copyright of his classic play to Great Ormond Street Hospital in 1929. Ever since, the timeless children's story has brought magic to countless sick children from around the country whom the hospital has treated. The locations that influenced him are however strewn across the grounds and present a formidable task for anyone attempting to connect the separate locations and turn them into Barrie's magical Neverneverland. So to begin with the event planning had to take this problem on board and work around the locations in the park together with the fact that it was impossible to close the park to the public. There was also a need to balance pre-booked access and on-the-day access to the event. In the first instance this led to an understanding that the event had to unfold within a public realm and where some members of that public visiting the park would not necessarily be aware of the event or want to be involved. Others though would and this presented an opportunity to attract spontaneous visitors. The event was billed as fun and family day out and, above all else, it had to be a safe environment.

The Pan story has a number of realms and characters and the idea of the event was to re-create these in, or as close to, the original locations in the park that inspired Barrie. This meant there were going to be seven different areas based on the narrative of the book, so each area or zone had to re-create the fantasy. For example, one spectacular zone was built around Captain Hook's ship and created by television design figure Laurence Llewlyn-Bowen who stated, 'in designing

Captain Hook's Galleon I have tried to stay broadly faithful to the Edwardian feel of Peter Pan. It is very much inspired by Edwardian book illustration, and particularly those of Arthur Rackham, which I have taken very much on board'.

One of the most important parts of the event was the animated feature used to link each area and also to provide a net of safety. This was done through the use of costumed 'animators' representing the different characters in the book. These became central to the events' purpose, as they served to 'direct' pre-booked visitors across the park and between each zone and also to 'attract' and 'distance' spontaneous visitors on the day. In all a total of 110 people were used and each one was dressed in costume representing one of the seven different thematic zones. In the zones themselves there were eight characters permanently stationed who guided visitors through that particular zones attractions and activities. The remainder of the actors were used to 'animate' the park, appearing to wander loosely between each zone. Their role was to animate, firstly, pre-booked visitors moving between each zone to ensure that the Neverneverland fantasy was continued throughout the course of their journey between zones and, secondly, to interact with potential visitors who had arrived at the park but not booked for the Pan celebrations and if, necessary guide them towards the zones and the central area where tickets for the day could be purchased.

Although appearing to the public as a loose and flexible operation the animated efforts of the actors was in fact a carefully scripted and designed operation. Every one of the 110 character actors was given a 'direction' sheet and a short biography for the part they were playing. The sheet reminded the actors to engage and interact with all visitors and suggested phrases and exchanges they could make to do this. For main characters, such as the Lost Boys, each one was given a name and profile description based on their particular character in the book. They were directed to act out this profile throughout the course of the day. On top of this an elaborate timing sequence was put together so that all actors circulated across the whole of the Neverneverland environment, ensuring that the same ones were not in the same place all the time and that no zone or connecting path was left unanimated for any length of time. From this example we can see how a difficult problem of location, space, access and safety was overcome by designing a very well scripted animated environ-ment that engaged visitors throughout the course of the event and maintained the magical appeal of being in Neverneverland even when people were moving between zones. In incorporating char-acters and language from the book, a sense of continuity was made available to everyone even if they 'dropped out' of the zones for break or rest.

Summary

To conclude this section it is now possible for us to understand some more of the complexities that lie behind an events creation. We have looked at ideas on symbolic interaction and Rossman's advocacy for it as a way of anticipating what will occur but also as a way or then reviewing what does occur. These are tools needed that can be used to control the experience of a designed programme. The emphasis is on the designer anticipating how an experience will unfold, and then accommodating or manipulating this circumstance, anticipating the scenario of actions that will take place. As a tool it can act as a guide to preview how interactions will occur and how experiences will result. Whilst this approach is applicable for designing events, the purpose of examining it here, is to use it as a tool to reflect on how those event experiences have unfolded in reality and we would ultimately ask the question of whether our foresight in the perception of the experience was correct or not. Managers of experiences need to have the ability to analyse and reflect on what they have created and be able to identify and determine how the combination of elements worked. Especially important is an ability to understand the balance between each of the elements, whether the combinations blended together or whether there was over importance placed on some and not enough on others. Adopting this kind of analytical framework enables events to be stud-ied meaningfully from a design and experiential perspective. What I have attempted to illustrate to this point is that the design experience of events is recognised in most approaches to the study of event but there is a limited amount of conceptualisation around the nature of the experience and the designing of those experiences. The predominant issue is that events need to be recognised as providing opportunities for experiences where people will look for both meaning and interpretation. Such a way of studying events will give much greater depth to what an event experience is and truly begin to tell us something about the interactions that occur during all phases of the event.

Chapter 11

Studying the significance of event design

Learning objectives

- Understand the importance of communications for events
- Understand how communications help set the experience agenda
- Be familiar with basic semiotic principles
- Understand how semiotics can be used to analyse event design and experiences
- Establish a link between theatricality and event experience

Introduction

In the previous chapters we have seen how events, design and experience can be understood and analysed via concepts in experience and symbolic interaction. Both provide frameworks for looking within the event experience and understanding what is taking place. They have enabled an insight into specific component elements within events to be explained and evaluated via methods that enable specific experiences to be studied. Symbolic interaction provides a mechanism for interpreting how any envisioned event experiences have occurred, offering a route to a potential critical review of any one event. Each of these approaches has also indicated that events use symbols and images to convey meanings, evidenced through the symbolic use of artifacts for example, and that these artifacts can be exposed to further study. Preliminary analysis has already been made of some of the signs used in events to convey such meaning but we now need to elaborate on this further and attempt to explain how detailed meaning is derived form event experiences.

Event communication and meaning

Events use symbols and images in many different ways to convey a message to the audience as part of a general communication process. In the section on experiences and experiential marketing we looked at how events have a pre-, actual and post-phase. The pre-phase is concerned with communication strategies adopted for the events, resulting in a presentation of images and symbols that a prospective audience can extract meaning from. This process involves a number of stages of a communication model that originates with the event organiser as the sender of the message (Masterman & Wood, 2006). The model then moves onto encoding and the selection of images to be used, followed by the message delivery itself via the event, then onto decoding of the message and its interpretation as this reaches the intended receiver who responds either with interest or disinterest. The key point to note is that the decoding of the message can be subject to noise or clutter that subverts the original message, so there is the potential for uncertainty in the meaning. This presents some difficulties since the communication strategy is designed to provide shared meanings so that the message is clear to all. However as we shall see the message can also become cluttered by interactions at the event itself, so even if the original communication remains intact, the reality of the experience may not.

At this of initial communication we have the pre-experience phase in operation where a combination of different stimuli is used to present the message about the event. This will largely depend on the chosen methods of communication but will most likely feature words, images and sounds. The purpose of any marketing communication is to engender response in attitude whether it is towards an organisation, a product, a service, an experience or a brand and to precipitate action. The action, of course, for products is the purchase of it. In the case of the event it is to attend. The underlying assumption of any such message however is that there is also a promise message which is that the product lives up to the communication. Whether it does or not is something we will evaluate once we have tried it out and will either form a negative or positive attitude about it. With many products though we can at least try them or sample them before purchasing and sales promotions are designed to achieve exactly this. We can, for example, take a test drive in a car or ride a bicycle, we can watch a television, listen to a CD, play a video game, even sample food although we usually cannot see a fridge in operation nor a washing machine. However with events there is really no option at all to sample or try it out before it happens. We have therefore an implicit, and we might add ethical, promise that if we respond to the communications about the event and decide to attend then we will experience an event that correlates to the communication messages we have received. This of course is not an exact promise since it very much depends on the event type and the extent to which we have a passive or active involvement in the event. There is no set rule to guide this simply because events are so varied but if we were to pay to attend a particular celebratory event based on the communication we had received about it, we would expect the event to resemble the experience promised. There is though an interesting twist here and that is if we buy the product and it doesn't live up to the promise then we may be reticent in the future to either buy the product or brand again so there is a two fold attitudinal response. We can be selective in this because we know the product name and, more often than not, we know the brand. However with events this is different, we know the event name but we very rarely know who has organised it and though we can extend our negative feeling to not attending the specific event again, unless we choose to conduct research into the event, we are unlikely to extend this to the event management company.

Case study 11.1

Robot Wars Goes Live

Case study focus

Where experience fails to live up communicated promise

Robot Wars is a popular, television programme that is screened in the UK and across some 15 nations worldwide. The rationale of the programme is simple; you have to build a robot that is more powerful than your opponent's robot. Powerful in this context means to be able to move quicker, sharper and either withstand or inflict damage in relation to another robot. There are some fairly lengthy rules and guidelines to building the robots but in essence this is the result: a radio-controlled robot that has mobility via wheels or traction of some kind has to engage in 'battle' with another robot. The construction of the robot can include offensive or defensive materials. A common offensive device is a hydraulic heavy-duty hammer or pick, another is a flipper device. The object of the exercise is to destroy or immobilise your opponent's robot before it does the same to you. To make the event more interesting the battle arena has a number of 'house' robots that can at certain points engage with the competing robots. The actions take place in a fenced-off arena (similar in concept to a Ice hockey arena but much smaller) so any destruction is contained within a small area and the audience is protected. And destruction there is as these home-assembled robots do battle. In some cases the machines are obliterated, in others pieces fly off, or they are set on fire or have wheels and/or body parts crushed and mangled. Generally there is some carnage and destruction.

The TV programme has had a number of modifications over various years but normally consists of eight robots battling through a knock out round before the final two go head to head. In the course of the TV programme some other activities may be included such as a robot football match or assault course. A presenter who announces the robots, the teams of operators and usually interviews winners/losers oversees the 'wars'. In the UK the person who does this is called Craig Charles. It is a linear programme with strong appeal to the 25–40 audience and the under 16s. Currently no new series of the show has been commissioned (2006) but in the past it has achieved audience viewing figures of 5 m.

The announcement of a UK 'live' Tour of the show in 2001 attracted lots of public interest and was expected to play to near full audiences. Communication about the tour events relied, naturally, on the TV programme to deliver its' message to a would be audience. Here was excitement, adventure, creativity, competition, destruction and battle all set in one arena, presided over by, what was regarded as a cult, Craig Charles.

Analysis

At this point we should be clear that the homemade robots symbolise the show, these are the central elements in the robot wars experience. The event did represent the TV show in principle. The symbols associated with the show the enclosed arena, house robots, homemade robots, presenters' tower, operator booths and so forth were all present. In fact the 'stage setting' itself was a fairly accurate and effective 'authentic' representation of the show. However several scenes were developed within the event that, whilst not rendering this representation pointless, severely undermined it.

These were:

Gross under-use of the homemade robots, that appeared for approximately 10% of the event in 'battle'. Whilst there were some additional activities included the central point of robot wars was dissipated by their brief appearances.

Over machined robots meant that no destruction occurred. The 'bouts' consisted of semi-final and final and there was next to no damage to any robot. As a result the 'battles' were little more than choreographed exchanges with all the excitement of a blunted can opener.

A second presenter – Craig Charles appeared for only certain scenes, amounting to about a 30% presence. Someone else presented majority of the show.

Significant gaps in action

Audience whipped frenzy via 'roller girls'. Three leather clad roller girls, who straddled a thin line between acceptable show poses and inappropriate erotic dress and poses, headed attempts to fill-in the event. At every available opportunity the girls were wheeled out to get the audience cheering and whooping. Whilst this has it's place, the sheer over use and monotony of it quickly became a burden so that by the time the event entered it's second hour at least half the audience were totally disinterested in these faux attempts to whip up audience participation.

Limited action. As a consequence of all of the above the robot activity itself was limited, replaced by more human forms of engagement. In this way the meaning of the event, as we would have interpreted from the show, was changed. The original communication based on the programme failed to fulfil its promise in the live event on almost every count by providing too little action and too much choreographed peripheral entertainment.

Activity 11.1

Event communications

Do certain event types make it difficult to fully live up to the promise of the advance communication?

Conduct research amongst friends/colleagues/relatives or the general public and ask them for recollections where the event did not live up to the communication. From the results see if there are any patterns that show certain event types are more likely to fail to live up to the promise.

We can analyse these communication strategies and dissect the different methods used to evaluate the success of the message in whichever medium is used. Masterman and Wood (2006) provide a comprehensive list of possible methods that includes public relations, lobbying, direct sales, personal selling, exhibition, promotion, advertising, celebrity endorsement, sponsorship, etc. The next stage is to then select the choice of medium for conveying the message such as cinema, TV, radio, print media, Internet, mails, text and so on. At this point we can begin to deconstruct these messages and analyse some of the ways that people see them. This analysis enables us to identify the meaning of the message as originally intended but also the way meaning is shaped by different interpretations of the message. This will tell us about responses to the communications but not the event itself. It is at this junction, the representation of the image of the event compared to the reality that studies of events now needs to develop so that we can begin to interpret what it is that actually takes place at the event. As suggested in discussions around design and experience there are a number of tools that can enlighten what occurs during an event, but one of the things we need to reflect on is the meaning of the signs (messages, symbols and images) used within event settings. One of the most appropriate tools for doing this is semiotics, the study of signs, since its primary aim is to focus on representation. As we have discussed earlier, events contain a large dose of representation from the initial communication about the event through to its delivery and the creative elements used within the event.

Semiotics

Semiotics is a field of study that uses a number of different theories and methodologies and draws exponents from several subject disciplines such as linguistics, philosophy, anthropology, sociology, aesthetic and media theory and psychology (Chandler, 2002). It is also a subject that has received considerable attention as a tool for interpreting the meaning of signs, that is the combination of stimuli expressed through words, sounds, images and objects (Barthes, 1977; Eco, 1976; Fiske, 1982; Culler, 1985; Baudrillard, 1988; Danesi, 1999; Sebeok, 1994; Hartley, 2002). As a result of a wide range of scholarship interest, any definition of semiotics is, a bit like events, inevitably broad. But whereas events are moving towards an accepted understanding and definition, semiotics remains elusive. The very scope and methodology for studying signs is not universally agreed and as a critical practice it is not a unified method for analytical research and study and has no widely agreed theoretical assumptions, models or empirical methodologies (Chandler, 2002). The aim of semiotics is though to understand the meaning behind signs, as a field of study it is 'concerned with everything that can be taken as a sign' (Eco, 1976, p. 7). This in practice means studying words, sounds, images, gestures and objects to understand what they mean and, equally importantly, what they can mean. Understanding meaning though is not an isolated activity, semiotics is conducted via sign systems of a particular medium or genre that is film-horror. Approaches to the study of semiotics have emerged from several theoretical viewpoints such as structuralism and post-structuralism (Foucault, 1970; Derrida, 1987), culture (Turner, 1992), language and literature (Eagleton, 1983), mass communication

(Hall, 1980), advertising (Williamson, 1978); cinema (Eaton, 1981; Stam, 2000) and television (Fiske, 1987). As a field of study it is highly theorised and readers looking for more critical insight into the development of semiotics should seek out those texts that provide a study of semiotic discourse.

Signs

In explaining semiotics Chandler (2002) suggests that we are all driven by the desire to make meanings and that these are made through interpretation and creation of signs. Such signs take many forms and in addition to those indicated above they also include odours, flavours, acts or objects. However Chandler stresses that signs such as these have no intrinsic meaning and they can only become signs 'when we invest them with meaning' (p. 17). Anything in fact can be a sign with the proviso 'as long as someone interprets it as signifying something, and something other than itself'. A sign then 'stands for something (it's object) to somebody (its interpreter) in some respect (its context) (Pierce quoted in Masterman and Wood, 2006). Semiotic study and interpretation is built around two models and it is in this act of interpretation that they differ with one offering what is called a deterministic meaning whilst the other offers an open meaning.

Passive interpretation

There are a range of theories attempting to explain meaning, focussing on where meaning begins to emerge in any relationship between readers and texts. The suggestion is that this can be illustrated as a continuum and that there are two extreme positions that reflect the above models (Chandler, 2002). Formalist semiotics maintains that any meaning is contained entirely in the text and that readers can only extract it from that. In this model meaning can be transferred from the sender to the receiver, the latter is entirely passive and has no role to play in shaping the meaning, it is determined by the text and by nothing else. This is the view of Saussure and what is commonly called a structuralist approach to semiotics and is deterministic in meaning, that is the sign is not open to any other interpretation than the one that gives it meaning which is a result of social and cultural conventions. It is these conventions that give the sign its meaning and, whilst those using them maybe familiar with the meaning, it still requires an explanation (Culler, 1985). This approach to semiotics does not engage with any other factors that could influence interpretation of meaning. There is no subjective interpretation of the sign. So the reader is passive and unable to interpret the meaning beyond what was intended by the sender. No allowance is made for the social, political or cultural context of the reader or that may influence their interpretation. This is deterministic, also called denotative meaning and there is little allowance made for any variation either between or within texts, signs have the same meaning for everyone.

Active interpretation

The opposite of this approach is to consider that any meaning is negotiable and that the sender alone cannot determine the interpretation. This is the model put forward by Pierce which stresses that individuals will interpret meaning depending upon their own experience and attitude and this may lead them to accept or reject the sender's meaning. Alternatively they may just simply choose to ignore or partially modify it to their own way of thinking. This is called connotative meaning. If the interpretation can be a variable it means, as Hall (1980) argues, that no meaning is inevitable or uniform. In rejecting the one interpretation for all model, he gives emphasis to the decoder (interpreter) of the sign rather than the encoder (sender). This raises the question of how we decode something. In order to do it we need, first of all, to have some recognition of what is being communicated, we then begin to interpret it and make an evaluation of it. This evaluation is made via reference to the interplay of conventions and codes that we are normally unaware of and that creates in our mind a sign, our initial interpretation of the message. There are various phases in decoding and encoding that Hall calls 'moments'. Such moments occur as encoding, developed in the practices of the organisation for example, as text when it takes the form of something and as decoding when we receive or consume it (Corner, 1983).

Barthes (1977) argues that there are three levels in this process of signification. The first one is the denotative, this is what it is for example a star, the second is the connotative, the star connotates space and the third is the mythical, space is mysterious so the image of a star can signify mysterious space.

Physical signs

Studying the meaning of signs requires a signifier and a signified, there is no such thing as a meaningless sign or signifier. It is this meaningful use of signs that is at the heart of the concerns of semiotics. In modern semiotic study the signifier has moved from Saussure's psychological version to a more physical form that can be seen, heard, touched, smelt or tasted (Chandler, 2002). Semiotics also has an interesting relationship with reality with some studies considering the role signs play in the construction of reality. This has some implications for event experiences as they are about trying to create a reality where there is satisfaction of need as expressed through the event environment. The extent to which this is achievable is a bi-product of the signs used in designing that environment. In this case signs can stand for other things, they can act as a representative of something else for users. These help to explain what the signs themselves mean in the context of the medium or genre. The idea is to construct meaning out of the signs as they appear in the immediate reality or setting. Many theorists refer to this as 'text' reading, where the text can take almost any form and is itself an amalgam of signs. These signs are created (or constructed) from reference to the genre and the conventions that might be applied to it (Chandler, 2002). One of the more popular uses of this approach is through film analysis where the conventions of the genre such as horror, are used to send a message to the viewing audience. This can be achieved by sound, scene and photography that transmits a sign that, via the genre conventions, we interpret as a moment in the film that is meant to signify fright, fear, intrigue, shock and so on. But it doesn't always work that way simply because we are attempting to understand the meaning within the genre. The signs may be poorly constructed and they may also be linked to conventions that are themselves open to interpretation. In this way we can, say through the Scary Movie film series, see the conventions in a different light where the horror conventions are used humourously or ironically to signify the very fact that they have become conventions and, as the films, suggests, clichéd and stereotyped to the point of absurdity and mimicked as such. Semiotics offers then a qualitative methodology for analysis and 'encompasses the relationship between a sign and its meaning/s, the way in which signs are combined into codes, and the wider culture within which signs and codes operate'. It can be efficiently applied to the analysis of visual texts and is also a particularly useful methodology for deconstructing aspects of cultural representations and experiences (White, 2006).

Semiotics and events

Why can we apply semiotics to events? In earlier chapters I have expressed the view that events are created settings and that they can be scripted as a consequence of seeing them as this series of designed environments. This view of events explains them as pre-planned and designed experiences. The occurrences and occasions that make up an event are the result of foresight and perception where the event manager or planner has envisaged how the event will unfold during the period of its occurrence. In this way the components of the event experiences are shaped and can be understood through a theatrical paradigm (Jackson, 2005). The use of a theatre analogy as a base for analysis is, incidentally, not uncommon and is included in the symbolic interaction theory of Goffman who uses the idea of dramaturgy to help analyse human behaviour.

Theatricality

Theatre like film operates from a script that presents a series of linked scenes where the narrative is acted out for the audience. It is a view that is a fundamental part of Pine and Gilmore's study of the experience economy in which they explain that performance, as a staged process, is an essential part of experiences. Using Schechner's 'performance theory' as a model they argue that it enables a perspective to be developed that explains performance as some activity that is carried out either by a person or persons in the presence of another person or persons. This performance has four parts to it: drama, script, theatre and performance (Pine & Gilmore, 1999). The significance of the work of Schechner is the extent to which it is applied to the analysis of areas other than theatre. Examples are drawn from several activities such as sport, play, games, dance, music and also ritual to illustrate the key points. Significantly it also draws back to the work of Goffman and points out that performance is not restricted to theatre, that it is not limited to a 'fenced-off genre' but can occur in any situation. This provides us with a direct link to Rossman who also uses Goffman extensively in developing a model for experience design and, equally importantly, advocates that scripting experiences is the most useful tool for their development. Theatrical scripting has been linked to events and experiential marketing via parallels of engagement where there is relationship, performance, fantasy and role occurring within the setting (Jackson, 2005). Jackson also argues that not only are characters and story line likely to have the biggest impact upon audiences but the 'metatext' (Harris et al., 2003) is a important task that 'needs to be undertaken for events if they are to reach their experiential goal (2005, p. 8)'. The theatrical service experience framework of Harris et al. shows how to develop the holistic experience as a result of what is referred to as dramatic script development. This incorporates metatext (experiential goal) as expressed via experience design and experience performance. This is most likely to be achieved when guests are provided with experiences that are personally relevant, memorable, sensory, emotional and meaningful (Garbutt, 2006).

Just like theatre, events need to engage their guests in such a way that the experience of attendance becomes one that is immersed and absorbed within the created environment. Theatre via its language, performances and settings attempts to do exactly the same by drawing its audience in and, momentarily, placing them in another environment (the plays setting) where they become engaged with the unfolding story. Attempts to relate this to service creation have shown how similar approaches to non-theatre experience settings can equally engage customers (William & Anderson, 2005). Contemporary event management practice also shows an awareness of how to utilise these aspects of the theatrical in designing customer experiences (Ulfers, 2005; White, 2006). Applying these ideas to analysis of events through firstly experience marketing and secondly theatrical experience can now be seen as a result of at least this two-tier process that involves analysis of the original communication that persuaded someone to attend the event, followed up by a comparative analysis of the reality of the event experience.

Case study 11.2

Santa's Kingdom and Winter Wonderland

Case study focus

Signs and signification

This case study focuses on two events run over the Christmas and New Year and are designed to appeal to all the family, although the emphasis, especially Santa's Kingdom, is on the under 12s. The first thing to observe is the text used to draw attention to the events. Both use text that is signified and interpreted in relation to a specific calendar period. One does it directly, Winter, the other uses Santa and extrapolates recognition via a more mythical code. Winter is to most people a period of cold, harsh weather, dull skies and prevalent with wind, storms, rain, ice and snow and where there are no leaves on the tree. It can be drab as a result and in the western hemisphere the days are short with daylight hours operating between 8 a.m and 4 p.m. In Northern Europe some towns do not see daylight for several months. However this is not necessarily what we understand by 'winter'. Only in news bulletins and, one should say, reality is this version of winter on offer. Elsewhere the idea of winter is represented by one distinct image, snow. Snow itself is a strange substance but appears to have a degree of purity to it in most eyes. Most people love snow, they like to see it fall, land and they like to catch flakes and gaze upon its strangely ethereal quality (before it quickly melts) and there is a degree of mystique about the snowflake with its varied and complex pattern structure that is all but invisible to the naked eye. Snow also represents play and happiness for some, spontaneous activity in the form of snowballs and sledging. It also gives rise to another great fictional character, the Snowman. The epitome of the presence of snow is the creation of the snowman. This is another image that helps cement our notion of winter. So the word winter sends a message of a time and place that is, dare we say, universally understood. We might argue that using the word Santa is more specific, it is also iconic, to not only winter but a definite time period, for myth has us believe that Santa only appears on 1 day of each year, 25th December. Santa holds a special meaning for the stories that surround this person are special. Children under a certain age know who Santa is and what he represents to them namely joy, suspense, happiness, surprise and presents. Parents (and some adults) are in league with children to maintain the belief in this fantasy figure, each in their own way coercing the other to maintain the charade (unknown of course to the child) that Santa exists.

The second word in each draws further on myth. Wonderland suggests somewhere special, a place of wonderment that is drawing upon the association the word has with one of the most fantasy based children's stories of all time, Alice in Wonderland. As we know from Lewis Carroll's story Alice's adventures are magical, fantastical and even surreal at times. Although there are daunting moments for Alice they are few in comparison to the wonderful, fun packed adventures she has. So a Winter Wonderland sends a potential message to a receiver that here is a child's place that is snowy, fun and full of adventure. Kingdom is altogether a different proposition for it sits squarely as a natural accompaniment to Santa. It is the kingdom where Santa and his sleigh, the reindeer and the elves live and is the place where all the toys for Xmas are made. It is also, let we forget, located at the North Pole but it is invisible to human eyes. It is there but it doesn't physically appear. Its depiction in storybooks and films is of a bright, utopia type environment where happiness rules, happiness generated in the making of toys for children.

So in these event titles we have much to attract us, especially if we are a child or a parent. Of course there are further accompanying texts and images that complete the communications about these events and they assist, as we discussed earlier in the chapter, in providing the pre-experiential phase that leads to our decision to go. Like all communication strategies there are several different ways of delivering this message. Here is an example from each:

Santa's Kingdom

Santa's Kingdom boasting real snow, real reindeer, a massive play area hosting 'Snowball Alley' and a giant Snow Slide, Santa's Village and, of course, Santa himself. Lasting approximately two and a half hours, this experience for the whole family to enjoy replicates a visit to Lapland. On arrival families will be greeted by personal flight attendants who will escort them on a simulated flight carrier to Santa's Kingdom. Upon landing they will be welcomed by real snow, real reindeer and elves within Santa's Village. Visitors will have the opportunity to roam freely into Santa's Workshop, play in a large snow covered area, pick up presents in the shops and, of course, visit Santa.

Winter Wonderland

It will be packed with family entertainment including cutting-edge theme park rides, a giant Santa's workshop, the largest temporary ice rink in the UK this Christmas and Cartoon Network's Supercinema, characters and games. Winter Wonderland offers magical attractions for little kids and big kids alike, all under one roof, including: The 12 rides of Christmas – including a giant big wheel, log flume and a fantastic new inverted roller coaster, the Tsunami, which drops, loops and twists at speeds of 55 mph and which has never been seen in London before! Other children's favourites include a super-sized traditional carousel and a space train ride. The UK's largest temporary fully facilitated ice rink accommodating 300 people at any one time with access for disabled visitors – plus a kids' skate zone exclusively free for the under 12 seconds.

A statement from the organisers of Winter Wonderland was included in press releases:

'We know children love Christmas, and we wanted to bring that magic to life in what remains a fantastic entertainment facility. We are no strangers to staging successful events and we are confident that this super-value extravaganza will be the best yet.'

Having absorbed the communication about the events, the next step is to make the decision whether or not to attend.

In conducting the analysis of the experience there is one point of note. Whereas Santa's Kingdom was a timed and programmed event Winter Wonderland was not. The former was 'directed' by Santa's helpers and visitors went round in discrete groups of 30, usually at 15 minute intervals following a set route and the whole journey took 2–2.5 hours. The latter was a free environment, with no guidance and no route to follow and visitors stayed as long as they wished. We discussed earlier in the book how venue can add to the experience in a number of ways. The location of the two events studied here was Winter Wonderland at the Millennium Dome, London and Santa's Kingdom at Wembley Exhibition Centre, London and both carry different connotations for any potential audience. Since the closure of the Millennium Exhibition, the Millennium Done has had a chequered history as a number of ideas for permanent usage have fallen by the way side. The site has only been used as an occasional venue for events and because of this it adds to the appeal for Winter Wonderland. There is a curiosity amongst people who had not been to see what all the fuss was about in building the Dome in the first place, and its appearance on the London skyline acts as a reminder of what some critics see as an ultra expensive white elephant. Yet it is a

Figure 11.1 Entering Santa's Kingdom after the shuttle ride. Photograph courtesy of Lindsey Mellor.

spectacular building that is like no other in London and, since it's limited use since 2001, offers people a rare chance to see inside it. There is also curiosity to see what could be done with the venue post the Millennium. Harnessed to a highly topical theme event the appeal is two fold.

The venue for Santa's Kingdom has different connotation as Wembley is a renowned multi-site complex, capable of hosting major events and exhibitions. The Exhibition Hall building itself has little appeal from an architectural or visual point of view apart from it's entrance and there is no elusive quality attached to it, unlike the Dome, and most people would not even recognise the building since it is, as befits many large exhibition halls, functional. What it conveys though is a venue of assurance since it is part of a larger complex that includes Stadium (now being rebuilt), Arena (recently refurbished), Exhibition and Conference Centre (recently refurbished) and Exhibition Halls. Wembley is known as a complex for a host of major events and we might think that this would give a sense of assurance to would be visitors. But the word 'Wembley' also holds a special place in UK hearts and minds since it is home to the famous football stadium. Whilst not immediately relevant to any event taking place in the Exhibition Hall, it does add a sense of status to all events taking place there as they stand in the shadow of the stadium, at least until its recent demolition.

Adopting White's (2006) approach we can consider the event as a whole (the 'ceremony', or in this case exhibition), and then discuss individual sections within that. We could also deconstruct specific individual settings or zones within the events and this would allow us to analyse specific experiences. This would enable us to understand how particular elements within an event related to the over arching theme or concept. Making an initial impact at any event is always a good ploy, it instils in the guest an immediate sense of excitement and anticipation of what else will follow.

The entrance to Santa's Kingdom was, firstly, little more than a queue of people outside a building that had a Santa's Kingdom sign on it, in truth it could have been for anything (burger, chips, cinema). However once the ticket check had been negotiated, the entrance to the event itself was multi-staged. By this I mean it was composed of a series of staging areas designed to draw out any large queues to offer a series of sequenced settings that would unfold systematically and be interpreted as the beginning of a journey into the Kingdom. The pre-entry section where tickets were checked was decorated in a vibrant deep red with green floor lines to direct the queuing system. Entrance to section one was via a theatre style entrance of gold colonnades and velvet curtain. This theatrical setting is no accident; the intended message is that we are about to enter a story where actors will play out scenes for us in the context of the Kingdom. Using red and green draws attention to this by reference to traditional styling of old theatres and it is also a colour combination often used to depict presents in Xmas cards and adorns other festive artefacts. The message is, just like in a theatre, to build up suspense before it all begins. The design presentation was relatively neat and a clear attempt had been made to create a self-absorbing environment.

In through the curtains and another staging area was encountered this time to tell the story for our journey. A clever design, because it helps suspend disbelief, and that we are going somewhere other-worldly (the Kingdom) and in fact leaving the exhibition centre behind. Transport was via 'flight' in a 'magic shuttle ride' where all 'passengers' were seated in rows and a screen showed the route, not quite IMAX, but it got the journey done. Where is the journey to – Lapland of course? There is no practical need to include this but it helps to tap into the general feeling people have about travel journey's to somewhere nice, it's excitement, there is anticipation and there is the 'are we there yet' factor, we simply cannot wait to arrive. Here there is a universal connotation for it carefully taps into the codes we know about leisure journeys, that they, by intention, head off to places of pleasure. However the text suggests flight and the connotative of flight is motion but there was no actual motion. This was fake motion and an artificial experience of travel so it was not a motion adventure like that of a simulator so we can critically dispute that the segment provided the experience it communicated. Exiting the shuttle (via another red curtained doorway) provided the third stage and it was a passageway with the North Pole tantalisingly at its end. The passage design was completely enclosed by a dense layer of fir (or commonly known Xmas) trees that swept up the sides and over the heads of everyone. Hung among the trees were masses of 'fairy' lights, bright coloured baubles, fake candles, tinsel and streamers that give the look of starry night. The depiction of such a dense Xmas tree scene is obvious, but there is also a nod in the direction of the northern lights that are so visible from the North Pole. On the ground, and laying out the route were stacks of gift-wrapped boxes, presents, and at the end of the passage Santa's Kingdom. The final chapter in this entrance procession is that which was promised all along, Lapland or the North Pole. A bright white tiled floor lead up to the North Pole itself. The setting was bordered by snow scenery, four white painted backdrops with doorways (to enter into the new world?). Waiting to greet were the animators, an elf and a snowman. We cannot but recognise this as the beginning of an enchanted journey for it is offering us a fantasyland, a real make-believe experience. There is one last connection to make before we got down to the business of each zone, and that is the walkthrough a starry night sky, a dark passage lit only by distant stars and that brought each visitor to the real start of the Kingdom adventure. Here there was ice realm with real (fake) snow and the Snow Queen appeared magically in a slightly up-lighted perch on top of an ice platform and introduced us to Santa's Kingdom. This last section prolonged the excitement and, by using a starlit setting, once again sent a message of magical land. Starlit imagery is a sign that something else is out there, something we cannot explain but we would like to experience. It is used to provoke a thought of what might have been and, in this case, what could be in a far off distant land. This connotes to space and is interpreted as a mysterious place, a place where we are not sure what can or will happen but where we hope something (good) might. Although the North Pole is not space it is represented by it because we believe in the purity of the night sky around the North Pole, the clean unpolluted access to the stars.

The remainder of the journey through Santa's Kingdom followed similar plot lines as the visitors moved from segment to segment sometimes via conduits such as the night sky other times via simple doorways that directly connected one to another. Along the way the fake plastic scenery was used to maintain the illusions of being enclosed within the Kingdom as we went passed each experience such as the Post Office (a chance to send a letter to Santa), the Toy Factory or Santa's House where 'real' reindeers are found. Finally visitors emerged into the Village square itself and the journey was near its end. The Village was a merchandise opportunity mixed in with food service (a carvery, mulled wine) and some play zones where real buckets of ice were on hand to make snowballs and with a real snow toboggan ride. The Village also served as the final staging post as visitors wandered through it, distractedly stopping off, before moving onto the final segment. This is the exit from the Kingdom but first there is the visit to Santa. Elves guided you through another red fabric doorway that led onto a lane where there is 'open' booth or house, and inside a 'real' Santa. The end is Santa's grotto, a last parting shot to re-affirm the myth, to meet Santa and to get a present. Multiple Santa's are available here but the design of the setting ensured that visitors were screened from really seeing that there is more than one.

Post event verdict: 'That was the best thing I've ever been to'.

Winter Wonderland

By contrast the entrance to Winter Wonderland was totally different. Queuing was again staged but not one suspects by design. Visitors had to first of all queue to get tickets, and then queue to get into the

Dome. There was very little to signify that inside the Dome structure there was, in fact, an event at all. Nominal dressing on a few pillars was the extent of the thematic effort. Furthermore this was, naturally, winter and apart for the basic protection offered by the Dome's original entry system, there was little to protect the queuing crowd from the weather. This meant that large numbers of visitors were waiting for 'something to happen' with little or no distraction to the wait. To a certain extent there was, at this point, no message. However we can also say the lack of any excitement building was a message, that it may be tiresome to wait, but once inside there would be unbounded joy. This we can interpret as a bottling of the sense of anticipation, keeping the visitor in state of alert because they don't know yet what is going to unfold before them. But it also runs the potential of antagonising visitors, keeping them waiting in the cold without any visible form of entertainment or amusement.

Nevertheless as the doors opened and visitors entered the usual buzz of first appearance was apparent. This, after all, was a 'wonderland'. The immediate entry point was marked out by two sets of white firs, forming a passageway into the main arena. Artificial snow was used on the floor entrance. So the symbols of winter were evident and the association with snow. However this was no closed interpretation and, where in Santa's Kingdom it was possible to suspend disbelief and fall in line with the signification of the various signs used, the result here was different. The firs were little more than guideposts, never high or dense enough to make an impact. They were also negotiable; the visitor did not have to follow the route they formed. But the most ineffective aspect of this design was the floor covering which could be, at best, described as discoloured at worst just plain dirty. No apparent attempt had been made to spread the 'snow' out and ensure it covered the floor, not that it seemed possible to do that anyway because there simple was not enough of it. Snowflakes are not easy to replicate, but the essence of this event was 'winter wonderland' and on both accounts the initial entrance impression here was dismal. From this point on the whole 'wonderland' experience could be viewed as a general arena, unlike the Kingdom that had a labyrinth approach. Wonderland was open and it was possible to gaze across a large part of the event and see what there was. The immediate impression sadly, was not one of winter or wonderland, but of a slightly beefed up fairground. The ambience was very low and there was no real design intent apparent that would convey a message of wonder and fantasy. In many ways the event resembled expo entertainment zones in that it appeared unconnected. Was there any sign of 'wonderland'? One of the problems faced here was the venue. The Dome is incredibly large and it is a single stage arena, not a series of separate halls that can be used to divide the space. So the event had to fit into this and to be fair most of the floor space was taken up. But there was very little of the 'magic' promised by the original communications in the design and layout. No real attempt was made to disguise the Dome and present an environment conducive to 'wonder'. This meant that the stark interior of the Dome was the backdrop and one of the problems inherent in this is that there were four huge pieces of machinery built to provide heating when the Dome was used for the Millennium (incidentally they weren't in use). So we have the design of event providing little in the way of denotative signs that could connotate 'wonderland' as an interpretation of the overall effect. Too many of the attractions were unconnected and this gave no impression of a unified environment. One strange aspect of the ambience was the cold. As mentioned above the heating system did not appear to be in use, and so the idea of winter was, intentionally or not, transmitted. However considering the vast numbers of people entering the building in just t-shirts, there was little comprehension on their part that this environment would be cold. Hence we have an indoor venue effectively presenting outdoor conditions.

At nighttime the illusion of a wonderland was marginally improved with light rigging used to draw a veil over the central attractions and because it was dark outside, the impact of the Dome interior was less noticeable.

Post event verdict: 'Worse than a cheap funfair'

To summarise we have two different approaches to events in the Festive Season. The intention is not to decide which of the two provided a better or worse experience, the readers can do that for themselves, but to look at the signs used within the event to support the original communication and concept of the event. It is not about simply promises of what rides or zones or attractions would be present, it is about how design and creativity provided signs that linked to the event theme. Signs, as we have discussed connotate meanings and the intention of the signifier is to try to get those meanings interpreted as intended. The context in which we interpret, to use Pierce's ideas, suggests an interpretation is open, hence we can reasonably argue that in these examples the context of the venue effects the interpretation. Equally though we can say that the profusion of credible linked signs – snow, winter, fir, white, for example – gives one event a higher possibility for appropriate experience in comparison to the other.

Analysing events this way allows for a specific type of insight into particular component elements that is different to the social study of mega events that is the focus of the work of Roche (2000). Such large events like the Olympics can therefore be discussed not only in relation to modern culture but also via their component parts such as the specific sports and arenas. This is almost like looking at separate events since the Olympics itself is so big. One of the most recognised features of any large global sports tournament is the opening ceremony and it is often regarded as the most important component event, especially for a global audience. A study of the Sydney Olympics opening ceremony demonstrates how signs can be used to deliver event experiences that both presents universal signification and allows some interpretation of meaning as well but which was designed to show Australia, Australians and Australianness (White, 2006). Using a mixture of semiotics and content analysis White draws out the meaning of the different design themes used in the ceremony and sets these in the context of public apprehension, apprehension that was based on early exposure to some of the possible images likely to be shown. The study paints an interesting portrait of the public being concerned that the signs and images used in the ceremony would be embarrassing clichés and stereotypes.

> 'Some of the Australian signifiers included in the Opening Ceremony were: Akubra hats, Driza-Bone coats, Australian flags, Australian native flora, Victa lawnmowers, the Southern Cross, the performance of the national anthem Advance Australia Fair, and Australian songs such as Waltzing Matilda and Click go the Shears. Australian signifiers that were incorporated into the Closing Ceremony included: a blow-up kangaroo on a bicycle, the Australian flag, Hills clothes hoists, Bondi life-savers, Australian celebrities such as Kylie Minogue, Elle Macpherson and Paul Hogan, and the performance of Australian songs such as Island Home, Treaty, Down Under and again, Waltzing Matilda'.
>
> White (2006, p. 124)

The ceremony was divided into different segments each using a theme (awakening; arrival; tin symphony; nature; fire; eternity) within the overall theme and many of the images used drew on cultural codes that many Australians could interpret as a sign for Australianness. Interestingly, White observes that some commentators found the images to be 'schmaltzy and tear jerking' especially in the way they were used to depict reconciliation between black and white, an acknowledgement of Australia's uncertain treatment of indigenous aborigines. Using signs that can convey mixed messages was evidence, says White, in the Awakening segment.

> 'With the Awakening segment, Stadium Australia was symbolically cleansed with the burning of eucalyptus leaves. Some may have even wondered whether white Australia's black history could be just as easily cleansed in the nation's collective consciousness. It certainly seemed that the organizers of the Opening Ceremony at least were trying to convey a message along those lines'.
>
> White (2006, p. 127)

The conclusion is that the ceremony avoided old clichés of Australia that are otherwise so prevalent in other sectors of industry, especially tourism. White summarises that the repertoire drew from a much wider selection of references to depict Australia/ns/nness and these were: flags, colours, landscape, landmarks, artefacts, pre-1788 references, post-1788 references, clothes, plants, animals, words, music and songs. In the final analysis the design of the ceremony used images that carried significance nationally.

Art meaning

Another way of attempting to analyse events is to use theories of art that help explain the nature of the design ideas used. Using art theory helps establish an initial meaning for the event signs so audience or guests can interpret their experience in the context of art conventions. In the section on design we looked briefly at design as art as well as problem solving and laid the foundation for an analysis of event design. Creating a setting that is themed enables a decoding to take place where we can denote a sense of place. Pine and Gilmore contend that experiences must happen in places, and that by theming a place we are offering potentially better places. Theming follows typical populist lines drawing heavily from contemporary culture and is mostly an attempt to create universal meaning for all guests. Malouf (1999) suggests a range of themes for when an event requires 'atmosphere and fantasy' – Alcatraz; Fabulous Fifties; Australian Adventure; A night in the Orient; Moulin Rouge; Rio; Italian Affair;

Las Vegas; Great Gatsby; Broadway; Evening at Ascot; Big Band Swing. We might regard these as populist theming. Interpreting the design of such events would appear to be relatively straightforward since the signs used to create the event setting appeal universally. This suggests a reading of the event along deterministic lines since there is a little need for meaning to be interpreted. However what we must remember is that any themed event is, by its very nature, a representation of something that is already known. The question for event study is what signs are used to denote the theme and how are they connotated by recipients. When we attend a themed event we are looking for the signs that re-affirm the theme but these do not have to be immediately obvious to us.

An alternative to popular theming is something we might call art theming which means employing artistic theory and where the event design is not just based not on popular representation. In this situation there is duality in design, where the basic underpinning concept of the setting stems, not from a thematic concept, but rather an artistic one or where a thematic idea is developed using artistic theory. Art theory presents challenges for the designer simply because the guest might not understand the references. For example how many of us can honestly say we can define and explain cubism or surrealism or renaissance let alone know the conventions and codes that will enable us to interpret them. Denoting such concepts requires some daring by the event team if their efforts are not to be wasted. However they also offer the opportunity to provide dynamic and vibrant settings that are not trapped in well-known and obvious signs. The difference can be explained by comparing a Star Wars theme to an abstract one. Consider what signs might be used to denote a Star Wars theme and for the vast majority of people a number of recurring ones would probably spring to mind – Obi – wan, Luke, Yoda, R2D2, C3PO, light saber and so on. Now think about an abstract theme and what comes to mind. It is less obvious what connotation we are going to be able to make for two reasons. Ones is that abstract theory is less understood by the public, and two is that it is concept that can use any subject matter for reference and create design unlike a Star Wars theme which is limited by definition to the images drawn from the series of films. If we are to use art theories as the basis of event design how might we interpret them?

A series of short articles in Special Events magazine attempted to show how inspiration from art concepts and theories could infuse events with creativity, imagination and appeal. There are some insightful evocations produced from the different ideas on art where the theory is given representation in terms of the feeling/expression it emits. Each event then has a theme or sub-theme around or within which the theory has been utilised. The list of art theories with their expressive features is:

Abstract – emotional, moody, provocative – an outward expression of the designer's soul

Assemblage – raw, unorthodox, poetic – the transformation of non-art objects into sculptures

Pop Art – witty, celebratory, larger-than-life – elevating the ordinary into the extraordinary

Impressionism – suggestive, unbound, fluid – design that captures the spirit and soul of them. Borders are blurred and ambience is everything.

Kitsch – campy, tongue-in-cheek, nostalgic – design that begs us to laugh at our past

Regionalism – topical, urban, representative – reconnecting with the familiar. Literally painting the town.

Realism – natural, faithful, true – life as it is without exaggeration. Design that take sits cue from the world around us, creating scenes that ring resoundingly true in our hearts and minds.

Surrealism – dreamy, ethereal, make-believe – the transformation of dreams onto canvas, stage or room

Traditionalism – classic, tried and true, original. Design that gives and teaches, offering a springboard for creativity.

Narrative Art – literary, embellished, eternal – design that suggests a past and tells a story, leaving just enough to the imagination.

(Specialevents.com)

Using these art concepts to influence event design ideas gives the event experience an additional aesthetic along the lines suggested by Pine and Gilmore (1999). What is not clear however is if these concepts of art are understood or shared by people attending the event. This raises questions about the level of experience they will get. If they are understood then we can say at least on one level, that of artistic concept, the optimal understanding of the experience has been attained. If they are not understood then, by contrast, at the level of concept, the optimal experience has not been attained. Apropos of this, can we say the experience is any more or less satisfying if we do or do not understand the concept.

Meaning and experience

In reflecting on the use of semiotics and art theory we can begin to appreciate the link that takes us from meaning (of an event) to experience. If we consider the range of events that are communicated to us the choice of what to attend is huge. The decisions we make are the result of a myriad of factors that influence us. Attempting to use a semiotic analysis of event communications and event settings offers a framework to help identify some of the meanings that the communication and setting 'texts' might hold. In the Wonderland and Kingdom studies a case was made for the meanings of the events formed through initial communications and the event titles. It was also suggested how the reality of the actual experience is then shaped by the extent to which the event re-affirms the pre-experience interpretations. This link between initial meaning and event experience is worthy of further study since it is not only complex but also prone to huge variables. What we should see in the relationship is at least two factors. One, the signs, in the form of the original communication, are interpreted in a way that is generally understood by most likely event attendees, is re-affirmed by the design and experience of the event. The meaning we thought they had, with allowances for differences depending on context, is present in the recognisable images and physical forms used in the event, ala Australianness as discussed (White, 2006). The second, that element of the event so associated with the special and unique aspects of events, the 'wow' factor. This is where we get something more than any meaning we had interpreted to begin with. At this point we should be able to attribute 'wow' as factor that can also be applied at different levels within an event and that it does not have to be such an expression of astonishment or exclamation that it is usually seen as, that is it doesn't just have to be fantastic scene setting it can be something special in a different way such as individual presence, speech, award, food, greeting and so on. A sense of wow can be attributed to a

Case study 11.3

Charity fund-raiser

Case study focus

Personal interaction 'wow'

Using a recognisable name can help interactions at events, especially if the person chosen is there within context and not just a 'hire for the day' celebrity. A fundraising evening was held to raise money for the London Community Cricket Association (LCCA), an urban cricket development organisation in London. The venue was Lord's Cricket Ground, London, probably the most famous cricket ground in the world. For guests there was an option of pre-evening tour of the ground itself, including an opportunity to visit the famous 'long room' home to a number of cricket memorabilia. There were several guests of honour, people from radio, TV and entertainment a few of which occasionally played cricket in charity matches for the LCCA. One of those was a well-known 'raconteur' who would oversee the fundraising session towards the end of the evening. However the biggest feature of the event was kept secret from guests and delivered, in this context, the 'wow' factor. After guests has checked in and entered the reception area each one was greeted by the words 'Hello, good evening. My name is Colin Cowdrey, and I would like to thank you for attending', subsequently followed by several minutes chat and discussion. Mr Cowdrey then 'did the room' exchanging stories and anecdotes with as many people as possible prior to the dinner and fundraising session. Why was this a 'wow'. The first thing to say is that it may not have been so for everyone who attended. Every nation and every sport has its heroes and in England Sir Colin Cowdrey is one of those sporting heroes from yesteryear, especially for those over the age of 50 who made up the majority of the guests and, whilst he is no global figure like Shane Warne, he is highly respected and one of England's finest past exponents. It was not only his presence at the event but his willingness to mingle and exchange pleasantries with the assembled guests that gave the event an added experiential moment. In this case we can see how an evening already signalled as special via its aim and audience, was extended further via a surprise personal experience. It shows how the signs denoted by the event had been surpassed by the actual experience. Numerous events buy in so called 'celebrities' these days but their level of interaction with anyone other than a small group of selected guests is at best derisory. Many of them of course are only attending because they have been paid a fee. A popular way of describing these type of arrangements is the 'VIP cluster' where VIP's are separated from the main event and guests, cordoned off in a separate area or even room, are provided with special courtesies, and have little or no interaction with the main body of people attending. This doesn't mean to say they do not provide any wow, simply to illustrate that it can operate at a different level, it doesn't have to be based on some wonderful creative setting, but it remains a designed experience albeit one that is not based on meaningful interaction. To illustrate the point further, at a University Graduation Ceremony VIP recipients of Honorary awards were not only kept away from mixing with students they were also separated from non-management staff. Their reality of the event was little more than an entry onto the stage.

specific section or element within an event, it can be something that appeals only to a portion of guests or audience. Event signs can convey several messages and be open to interpretation along several avenues of meaning, the connotations are therefore affected by the context of the interpreter (Chandler, 2002). In some cases meaning and interpretation can change by simple change in image and sign. In this way we can begin to find deeper meanings in what, on the face of it, may appear to be simple enough design images.

Activity 11.2

This activity has a description of a venue, its themed setting and several possible explanations for choosing the venue. It will be used for a lunch party for a particular product. Read through the information and then reflect on the questions at the end.

The venue is the Royal Courts of Justice, London. Airy with high ceilings, replete with colonnades, cornices and facades, portraits, detailed architectural masonry work, the building's overall architectural design is Gothic. The interior resembles a small church, with its intricate pattern of colonnades and arched doorways. It also has stained glass windows. The venue is chosen because the organisers want to signify something about the event itself, they want to perhaps give the product an association with respectability, maybe social acceptance. Or maybe the venue is daring because it is the main civil court in the UK. It is certainly unusual. The venue signifies tradition, and can be interpreted as such. It doesn't mean to say the tradition is one we wish to upheld or even like but it is one that is understood. Why do we need such venues to hold events? Do they suggest safety, assurance; we know what we will get? Do they represent prestige, especially those with a Royal stamp? The venue was opened by Queen Victoria in 1882, and was designed by GE Grant. It is regarded as the last major Gothic revival building in London. The venue may have been chosen for its Victorian heritage, an age in British history that might be regarded as a golden age of empire, art, investigation, philanthropy, science, achievement, industry, austerity, suffrage, posterity, exhibitions, discipline or discovery. So although we can relate to this tradition of Victorian, the type of tradition is formed by our own experience or knowledge of the period, the sign of Victorian is given meaning by our own understanding of it. The same applies to it being a Gothic building, a style of architecture that is visually strong. In choosing such a venue the organisers may be trying to send several messages, we simply don't know for certain. We can suspect that it is linked to prestige, maybe even grandeur (Royalty) and it is unusual (Justice courts) and possibly daring or challenging (Gothic) but for any other we cannot be at all sure. The room where the launch will take place is re-decorated with temporary furnishings designed to signal luxuriousness, quality, splendour, modernity and reflects modern styling that compliments the Gothic elements of the venue. The chairs, for example, have a grilled backrest and the table furnishings reflect some of the shapes and lines of the building arches and windows. Each guest has a personal card adorned with the product logo and image. There is a colour theme (see Malouf (1999) for ideas on colour, also Ittens) used in the place settings with plates being a mixture of colours from red to yellow to green. The main colour used in the table décor is white and silver, and there is a reason for this. The lighting is capable of several different colour projections and so can be used throughout the launch to create different moods. The colours used are subtle versions of the colour of the plates and the product logo. There is also intermittent use of a dominant shade of red to uplight some areas and to provide intensity to others Hanging from the ceiling is a trapezoid projection screen.

Question:

Ask yourself what you feel about this setting as it is described?

What sign or message is it trying to convey to me?

Would I be comfortable or happy attending this launch event?

Try and write clearly your comments, whether they are negative or positive.

At the end of the References there is a note that explains what product is being launched here. When you see the name of the product re-visit this description of the event and your own view of it. What do you think the message is now that you know what is the product and has it changed your view, in anyway, about the event?

Summary

There are often complex signs associated with events stemming from them having a multi-layered and multi-phased experience. So although

Figure 11.2   Sample of promotional material distributed at the 2005 Tour De France. Photograph authors own.

we may interpret the initial communications these may not always be able to signify the required range of messages as they are so varied. Events that can be lengthy, complex and are open to so many potential experiences can also have meaning that is variably and openly contested. We can look at the event as a whole or single occasion and analyse in general how it works. We can also though begin to focus on particular sections of an event, on specific artifacts or components, and specific experiences and examine how they work. The former gives us an overview and a general interpretation of the event, whereas the latter allows for interpretation of some of the very specific moments within the event. Most initial communications presents us with the general event messages, with (depending on the vehicle for communication), restricted highlights of key sections. In some cases we can reasonably argue that whilst the event failed to deliver its overall promise, there were separate elements that were successful. The context of interpreter is also going to effect how we see it. For example a group of men, celebrating a 21st birthday, would probably view the 'Weekend at Dave's event as a hugely successful day out with lot of 'male' attractions helping to create the promised experience. The fulfillment is based largely on the expected interactions and the extent to which the event provides the setting for such a celebration to occur in relation to the meaning extracted from the original communication. Dave's though is an event that, a bit like a Monopoly game card, carries an element of chance with it, as it is something new and untried. It has no association in itself other than those that have been denoted by the event communications and design. In comparison, there are other events where the meaning of something is imbued with significance as a result of past versions of the event. Event signs can convey several messages and be open to interpretation along several avenues of meaning, the connotations are therefore affected by the context of the interpreter (Chandler, 2002). In some cases meaning and interpretation can change by simple change in image and sign. In this way we can begin to find deeper meanings in what, on the face of it, may appear to be simple enough design images.

Case study 11.4

Tour De France

For this final case study we will eschew the 'essay' style of previous ones and replace it with a list of the key event design and experience elements of the event.

The Tour de France is the largest and most important cycle race event in the world. It is also one of the most arduous, as it requires riders to race for three continuous weeks on the roads of France. There are 21 teams of 9 riders all supported by back up support in the form of motor cars and a motorhome/bus and numerous personnel than can number in excess of a dozen or more. It is an event of high complexity since each day riders will travel in the region of 200 km moving from one town or city to another. The huge variation in terrain from sea level to 3000 m in the course of the event adds to this complexity. In addition the roads en route have to be closed not just for the race itself but also for the touring sponsors carnival that precedes the race and the official's vehicles and team support vehicles. Apart from corporate boxes at the finish of each stage, it is a free event to spectate at. In actual fact it is 20 different events taking place one after another as there are 20 daily stages to the race, and each one has to be created from scratch. A snapshot of a typical flat stage of the race would include:

Start area and riders sign on zone, official sponsors banners and display areas

Race route incorporating special 'sprints', indicated by roadside banners, sometime offering special prizes to reflect the region where the sprint occurs and also featuring as one of the events sub-category competitions, the points jersey.

Finish area normally near the centre of a town. Requires barriers to separate riders from spectators at least 3 km from the finish but often can be longer.

Town has to accommodate all the 21 teams support vehicles plus all the sponsors requirements. To add to the logistical challenges the start of the next days stage is usually in a different town to the preceding days finish.

Events like the Tour De France can be understood as 'large–scale cultural events, which have a dramatic character, mass popular appeal and international significance' (Roche, 2000, p. 1). They can also be understood via analysis of individual component elements and an event of this nature needs to be considered as one that provides an experience that is multi-phasic and multi-dimensional across many interlinking and overlapping sections.

Here are a few thoughts on the Tour De France using a selection of key experential indicators previously discussed:

1 *Sign.* The tour. There are many other national cycling tours, notably of Spain and Italy but there is only one tour, or 'le tour'. Its presence in cycling is omnipotent. It represents the geographic variation and beauty of France, it is a symbol of unbearable hardship for the riders cycling over 3000 km in 21 days. Upon entering Paris the riders follow a route that enables them to see the Eiffel Tower, and this acts as a symbol of achievement for those who finish it, irrespective of where they are positioned in the race. The yellow jersey, worn by the raceleader, has become a ubiquitous symbol of the race leaders jersey for many other cycle events, although Italy's Giro d'Italia admirably retains its own version, the maglia rose, or pink jersey.

2 *Cohesive theme.* A cycle race tour of France visiting various regions and travelling anti-clockwise in even years and clockwise in odd years, always finishing on the champs elysees in Paris.

3 *Interaction/engagement/participation.* Unlike almost any other sporting event, and one that occurs on several levels. To follow in the footsteps of giants might be one slogan attached to the tour since anyone on a bicycle can ride a stage of the tour, the day before or the day after and, in the case of mountain stages, on the very day itself before the peloton arrives thus immersing the participant in the event. Simultaneously people are participant and spectators who consume the tour as an event and as a participation activity. Thousands of people come out to the tour when it reaches the mountains just to ride the route that the professional riders will take. For spectators absorption is varied, but again for key alpine stages many fans camp out several days in advance creating mini roadside camps and become absorbed by the experience of being there, on the side of the road, eating, drinking, flag waving and painting out elaborate messages or slogans on the road for their heroes.

4 *Relationships.* These form with other spectators and with spectator participant riders who revel in their collective sense of achievement at, for example, riding up and over an alpine col. There is a hugely popular sub-event called the etape du Tour which follows the route of a stage of the race a day or two prior and is open to amateur cyclists. Entry figures for such an event are close to 8000 and it spawns countless web forum discussions and blog pages as

participants share their actual and post event experiences. Local villages and towns thrive on the collective relationship of celebrating the tour passing through their region.

5 *Emotions*. Appealed to on many levels, but epitomised by the nature of the competition in the event itself. For French nationals this is 'their' event and a sense of emotional pride is felt, in a similar way as described above. During the course of the race Bastille Day is celebrated and provides a poignant and additional emotional and celebratory element. The finish to any stage generates a degree of euphoria amongst the riders, especially those who win a 'key' stage.

6 *Authenticity*. This is the authentic event and not a created experiential copy, yet there are times when the race goes into other countries (Belgium, Germany, Switzerland, Holland, UK) that the element of authenticity appears lost until the race enters or returns to France.

7 *Objects*. The event is overwhelmed with them from natural to created. Landscape plays a major part in characterising the race as it travels through the different regions of France. Monuments to French life are constantly featured en route. There are the more visible objects of the competitive jerseys (yellow, white, green polka-dot) presented to the leading rider in each category at every stage finish. The stage winners often receive an additional regional prize in the form of a local good or produce such as a giant cheese. Preceding the riders is the sponsors carnival, 45 minutes of travelling promotion. Some have special floats, special cars or something that attracts spectator attention. They all do the same thing though and that is distribute product and there is an almighty scramble amongst spectators to acquire whatever is being given out. The objects seen in Figure 11.2 represent around 50% of those that are distributed along the route of a stage.

8 *Visual imagery*. Too much to mention. The design of the winner's podium on the Champs Elysees with the Arc de Triomphe in the background frames the final act of the tour, the final podium that awards the winner their final yellow jersey. The Arc signifies victory and its selection as a backdrop is an appropriate physical setting to celebrate victory in the Tour.

References

Adcock, D., Halborg, A., Ross, C. (2001). *Marketing: Principles and Practice.* Financial Times Prentice Hall.

Addis, M. (2005). New technologies and cultural consumption – edutainment is born! *European Journal of Marketing,* 39, 7/8, 729–736.

Aitchison, C., Jordan, F. eds. (1998). *Gender, Space and Identity.* LSA 63, LSA Publications.

Aitchison, C. (2003). *Gender and Leisure: Social and Cultural Perspectives.* Routledge.

Allen, J., O'Toole, B., McDonnell, I., Harris, R. (2002; 2005). *Festival and Special Event Management,* 3rd edition. Wiley.

Anderson, J., Lawrence, L. eds. (2001). *Gender Issues in Work, Leisure and Culture.* LSA 68.

Arcodia, C., Reid, S. (2004). Event Management Associations and the provision of services. *Journal of Convention and Event Tourism,* 6(4), 5–25.

Argyle, M. (1996). *The Social Psychology of Leisure.* Penguin.

Arnould, E.J., Price, L. (1993). River magic: extraordinary experience and the extended service encounter. *Journal of Consumer Research,* June, 20, 1, 24–45.

Ayres, M. (2006). Oscar goodies worth less than $100,000 would be lacking in taste. *The Times Newspaper,* 28/01/06.

Badmin, P. (1992). *Leisure Operational Management. Vol. 1: Facilities Management* 2nd edition. Longman/ILAM.

Badmin, P. (1993) *Leisure Operational Management: Vol. 2: People,* 2nd edition. Longman/ILAM.

Barthes, R. (1977). *Image-Music-Text.* Fontana.

Baudrillard, J. (1988). *Selected Writings* (ed. Mark Poster). Polity Press.

Bayle, S. ed. (1985). *The Conran Directory of Design.* Conran Octopus Limited.

Berridge, G. (1996). Designing Leisure Experiences. Unpublished paper presented at *WLRA Conference,* Cardiff.

Berridge, G. (2004). Adopting sustainable ethics: voluntary practice amongst event organizers in Stebbins, R.A., Graham, M., eds. *Volunteering as Leisure: Leisure as Volunteering*. CABI Publishing.

Berridge, G., McFee, G. eds. (2002). *Partnerships in Leisure: Sport, Tourism and Management*. LSA 78.

Beverland, M.B. (2005). Managing the design innovation–brand marketing interface: resolving the tension between artistic creation and commercial imperatives. *Journal of Product Innovation Management*, 22, 193–207.

Bitner, M.J. (1990). Evaluating service encounters: the effects of physical surroundings and employee responses. *Journal of Marketing*, 45(2), 69–82.

Blumer, H. (1969). *Symbolic Interactionism*. Prentice-Hall.

Bødker, S. (1991). *Through the Interface: A Human Activity Approach to User Interface Design*. Lawrence Erlbaum Associates.

Bond, C. (2005). Better Days Ahead. *Event Magazine* October 2005.

Botterill, D. ed. (1989). *Leisure Participation and Experience*. LSA 37.

Botterill, T.D., Crompton, J.L. (1996). Two case studies exploring the nature of the tourist's experience. *Journal of Leisure Research*, 28(1), 57–82.

Bowdin, G. (2003). *Resource Guide in Events Management* for LTSN Hospitality Leisure Sport and Tourism available at: http://www.hlst.lstn.ac.uk/resources/events.pdf extracted 12/10/04.

Bowdin, G., McDonnell, I., Allen, J., O'Toole, B. (2001). *Events Management*. Butterworth Heinemann.

Bowdin, G., McPherson, G., Flinn, J. (2006a). Identifying and analysing existing research undertaken in the events industry, People, 1st edition. (Online report available at http://www.people1st.co.uk/research/themes).

Bowdin, G., McDonnell, I., Allen, J., O'Toole, B. (2006b). *Events Management*, 2nd edition. Elsevier Butterworth Heinemann.

Breckenridge, C. ed. (1993). *Body Matters: Leisure Images and Lifestyles*. LSA 47.

British Design (2003). *Interiors, Retail and Event Design*. BIS.

Brown, S., James, J. (2004). Event design and management: ritual sacrifice in Yeoman, et al., eds. *Festival and Special Events Management*. Elsevier.

Buswell, J. (2004). Sport and leisure service encounter in McMahon-Beattie, U., Yeoman, I., eds. *Sport and Leisure Operations Management*. Thomson.

Button, G. ed. (1993). *Technology in Working Order: Studies of Work, Interaction, and Technology*. Routledge.

Byars, M. (2004). *The Design Encyclopaedia*, 2nd edition. MOMA.

Campbell, F., Robertson, A., Brown, S., Race, R. (2003). *Essential Tips for Organising Conferences and Events*, Kogan Page.

Cannon, T. (1996). *Basic Marketing: Principles and Practice*, 4th edition. Cassell.

Carpenter, G.M., Howe, C.Z. (1985). *Programming Leisure Experiences: A Cyclical Approach*. Prentice-Hall.

Chandler, D. (2002). *Semiotics: The Basics*. London: Routledge.

Chernushenko, D. (1994). *Greening our Games: Running Sports Events and Facilities that Won't Cost the Earth*. Centurion Publishing and Marketing.

CHI2002/AIGA *Experience Design Forum Case Studies* (Extracted from http://www.aiga.org/content.cfm/2002_case_studies. 01/03/06).

Clawson, M. (1963). *Land and Water for Recreation*. Rand McNally.

Climb Meru. *An Integrated Brand Experience*. (Extracted from www.aiga.org/resources/content/7/6/2/documents/FORUM_davison_case_032102.pdf on 04/02/06

Collins, M. ed. (2000). *Leisure Planning in a Transitory Society*. LSA 58.

Collins, M.F., Cooper, I.S. (1998). *Leisure Management: Issues and Applications*. Wallingford: CAB International.

Collins, P.H. (2004). *Race Class and Gender: An Anthology*, 5th edition. Wadsworth.

Cooper, R. (1995) *The Design Agenda: A Guide to Successful Design Management*. Mike Press.

Corner, J., Hawthorn, J. (1983). *Communication Studies: An Introductory Reader*. Edward Arnold.

Cowell, D. (1984) *The Marketing of Services*. London: Heinemann.

Critcher, C., Bramham, P., Tomlinson, A. (1995). *Sociology of Leisure*. E & FN Spon.

Crompton, J.L. (1979). Motivations for pleasure vacations. *Annals of Tourism Research*, 6, 408–424.

Crompton, J.L., Lee, S. (2000). The economic impact of 30 sports tournaments, festivals, and spectator events in seven US cities. *Journal of Park and Recreation Administration*, 18(2), 107–126.

Crouch, G.I., Timmermans, H.J.P., Uysal, M. (2003). *Consumer Psychology of Tourism, Hospitality and Leisure: Vol. 3*. La Trobe University, University of Colorado.

Csikszentmihalyi, M. (1991). *Flow: The Psychology of Optimal Experience*. Harper Perennial.

Culler, J. (1985). *Saussure*. London: Fontana.

Cunningham, M.H., Taylor, S.F. (1995). Event marketing: state of the industry and research agenda. *Festival Management and Event Tourism*, 2, 123–137.

Danesi, M. (1999). *Of Cigarettes, High Heels and Other Interesting Things: An Introduction to Semiotics*. Macmillan.

Davis, S. (1996). The theme park; global industry and cultural form. *Media, Culture and Society*, 3, 18, 399–442.

Decio, G., Carugati, R. (2003). *Brionvega: Designing Emotion*. Electra.

Deem, R. (1986). *All Work and No Play? A Study of Women and Leisure*. Milton Keynes: Open University Press.

DeGraaf, D., Jordan, D., DeGraaf, K. (1999). *Programming for Parks, Recreation and Leisure Services: A Servant Leadership Approach*, 3rd edition. Venture.

Denzin, N.K. (1978). *The Research Act*, 2nd edition. McGraw-Hill.

Derrida, J. (1987). *Positions*. Athlete Press.

Druin, A., Bederson, B., Boltman, A., Miura, A., Knotts-Callahan, D., Platt, M. (1998). Children as our technology design partners in Druin, A. ed., *The Design of* Children's *Technology: How We Design and Why?* Morgan Kaufmann.

Dumazedier, J. (1974). *Sociology of Leisure*, translated by Marea A McKenzie. Elsevier.

Durkheim, E. (1965) [1912]. *The Elementary Forms of the Religious Life*. Free Press.

Eagleton, T. (1983). *Literary Theory*. Blackwell.

Eaton, M., ed. (1981). *Cinema and Semiotics (Screen Reader 2)*. Society for Education in Film and Television.

Eco, U. (1976). *A Theory of Semiotics*. Indiana University Press/London: Macmillan.

Emery, P.R. (2001). Bidding to host a major sports event: strategic investment on complete lottery in Gratton, C., Henry, I. *Sport in the City: The Role of Sport in Economic and Social Regeneration*. Routledge.

Event Magazine (2004). News item. October 2004.

Events Continue to Grow In Importance Among Corporate Marketers Globally Press Release July 11 2005 www.gpjco.com accessed 12/1/2006.

Face-to-face Events Deliver Greatest Marketing ROI According to Global Executive Perspective (2004). The George P. Johnson Company/MPI Foundation 2004 Global Event Trends Survey Finds Increased Confidence in Event Marketing's Power, Value.

Farrell, P., Lundergren, H.M. (1991). *The Process of Recreation Programming: Theory and Technique*, 3rd edition. Venture.

Featherstone, M. (1990). *Consumer Culture and Postmodernism*. Sage.

Fiske, J. (1982). *Introduction to Communication Studies*. Routledge.

Fiske, J. (1987). *Television Culture*. Routledge.

Fletcher, M. (2005). London Bounces Back. *Event Magazine*, October 2005.

Fletcher, M. (2006). Reasons to be Cheerful. *Event Magazine*, March 2006.

Foucault, M. (1970). *The Order of Things*. Tavistock.

Gale, T.J. (1996). Changing holiday Cultures and the Production and Consumption of the British Seaside Experience, paper at *VVS/LSA/ATLAS Conference*. Wageningen.

Garbutt, J. (2006). *Experiential Marketing Vs Field Marketing: Experience the Difference*. Jack Morton Worldwide.

Gardner, L., Terpennin, S., Froger, N. (1989). *The Art of Event Design* (Paperback) Miramar.

Getz, D. (1991). *Festivals, Special Events, and Tourism*. Van Nostrand Reinhold.

Getz, D. (2005). *Festivals, Special Events, and Tourism*. 2nd edition. Van Nostrand Reinhold.

Getz, D. (1997). *Event Management and Event Tourism*. Cognizant Communication Corporation.

Getz, D. (2005). *Event Management and Event Tourism*, 2nd edition. New York: Cognizant Communications Corporation.

Getz, D., Cheyne, J. (1997). Special event motivations and behaviour in Ryan, C., ed. *The Tourist Experience: A New Introduction*. Cassell, pp. 136–154.

Getz, D., Wicks, B. (1994). Professionalism and certification for festival and event practitioners: Trends and Issues. *Festival Management and Event Tourism*, 2(2), 108–109.

Gibson, H. (2005). Understanding sport tourism experiences in Higham, J., ed. *Sport Tourism Destinations*. Elsevier.

Goeldner, C., Ritchie, J.R.B. (2003). *Tourism Principles Practices and Philosophies*. Wiley.

Goffman, I. (1967). *Interaction Ritual*. Anchor Books.

Goldblatt, J.J. (1990). *Special Events: The Art and Science of Celebration*. Wiley.

Goldblatt, J.J. (2005). *Special Events: Event Leadership for a New World*, 4th edition. Wiley.

GOSCHH at http://www.gosh.org/news/2004/peter-pan-picnic2.html extracted on 24/11/05.

Grainger-Jones, B. (1999). *Leisure Management*. Butterworth Heinemann Peter Pan at www.gosh.org extracted from www.gosh.org http://www.gosh.org/news/2004/peter-pan-picnic2.html on 24/11/05.

Gratton, C., Henry, I. (2001). *Sport in the City: The Role of Sport in Economic and Social Regeneration*. Routledge.

Green, E., Hebron, S., Woodward, D. (1990). *Women's Leisure, What Leisure?* Basingstoke: Macmillan.

Growing Role of Events Evident in Both Automotive and Technology Sectors November 2, 2004 Press release.

Gummeson, E. (2002). *Total Relationship Marketing*. Butterworth-Heinemann.

Hall, C. (1997). *Hallmark Tourist Events: Impacts, Management and Planning*. Wiley.

Hall, C.M. (2005). Selling places: hallmark events and the reimaging of Sydney and Toronto in Nauright, J., Kimberly, S., Schimmel, P., eds. *The Political Economy of Sport*. MacMillan, pp. 129–151.

Hall, S. ([1973] 1980). Encoding/decoding. In Centre for Contemporary Cultural Studies, ed. Culture, Media, Language: Working Papers in Cultural Studies.

Hargreaves, J. (1994). *Sporting Females: Critical Issues in the History and Sociology of Women's Sport*. Routledge.

Harris, R., Harris, K., Baron, S. (2003). The future of service marketing: forecasts from ten services marketing experts. *Journal of Service Marketing*, 17(2), 107–121.

Hartley, J. (2002). Communication, Cultural and Media Studies: The Key Concepts, 3rd edition. Routledge.

Haywood, L., Kew, F., Bramham, P. (1989) and 2nd edition (1995). Understanding Leisure. Hutchinson Education. The Henley Centre (1996) Hospitality into the 21st Century – a vision for the future. The Henley Centre.

Hochshild, A.R. (1997). *The Managed Heart: The Commercialisation of Human Feeling*. Metropolitan Books.

Horner, S., Swarbrooke, J. (1996). *Marketing Tourism, Hospitality and Leisure in Europe*. International Thomson Business Press.

Haworth, J., Veal, A.J. eds. (1977). *Leisure and the Community*. LSA 4.

Hoyle, L.H. (2002). *Event Marketing: How to Successfully Promote Events, Festivals, Conventions and Expos*. Wiley.

Hull, R.B., Michale, S.B., Walker, G.J., Roggerbuck, J.W. (1996). Ebb and flow of brief leisure experience. *Leisure Sciences*, 18, 299–314.

Iso-Ahola, S.E. (1980). *The Social Psychology of Leisure and Recreation*. Wm. C. Brown.

Iso-Ahola, S.E., Allen, J.R. (1982). Dynamics of leisure motivation: the effects of outcome on leisure needs. *Research Quarterly for Exercise and Sport*, 53(2), 141–149.

Iso-Ahola, S.E. (1999). Motivational foundations for leisure in Jackson, E.L., Burton, T.L., eds. *Leisure Studies: Prospects for the 21st Century*. Venture.

Itten, J. (1975). *Design and Form*. Thames and Hudson.

Jackson, B. (2000). Experience Design, July 18 *A List Apart Magazine*. No. 77.

Jackson, C. (2005). The Experiential Impact of Events. Unpublished paper presented at *LSA Conference*. Edinburgh.

Jago, L., Shaw, R. (1999). Consumer perceptions of special events: a multi-stimulus validation. *Journal of Travel and Tourism Marketing*, 8(4), 1–24.

Jensen, R. (1999). *The Dream Society*. McGraw-Hill.

Johnston, R., Clark, G. (2001). *Service Operations Management*. Prentice Hall.

Kaplan, M. (1975). *Leisure: Theory and Policy*. Wiley.

Kelly, J. (1982). *Leisure*. Prentice Hall.

Kelly, J. (1990). *Leisure*, 2nd edition. Prentice Hall.

Kelly, J., Godbey, G. (1992). *Sociology of Leisure*. Venture.

Kelly, J. (1994). The symbolic interaction metaphor and leisure: critical challenges in *Leisure Studies*, Vol 13, No. 2, pp. 81–96(16).

Kelly, J.R. (1999). Leisure behaviours and styles: social, economic, and cultural factors. In Jackson, E.L. & Burton, T.L. eds., *Leisure Studies: Prospects for the Twenty-first century*. Venture Publishing, pp. 135–150.

Keynote Report (2004). *Exhibitions & Conferences Market Report*. Keynote.

Kotler, P., Armstrong, G. (2006). *Principles of Marketing*, 12th edition. Prentice Hall.

Krug, S., Black, R. (2000). *Don't Make Me Think! A Common Sense Approach to Web Usability*. New Riders Publishing.

Kuhn, H.M. (1964). Major trends in symbolic interaction theory in the past twenty-five years. *Sociological Quarterly*, 5, 70.

Kuhn, S., Muller, M. (1993). Special issue: participatory design. *Communications of the ACM*, 36, 4.

Lawson, F., Bovey-Baud, M. (1998). *Tourism and Recreation Handbook of Planning and Design*. Architectural Press.

Lee, Y., Dattilo, J., Howard, D. (1994). The complex and dynamic nature of leisure experience and leisure services. *Journal of Leisure research*, 26(3), 195–211.

Lentell, B. (1995). Missing services: leisure management textbooks and the concept of services management in Lawrence, L., Murdoch, E. Parker, S., eds. *Professional and Development Issues in Leisure, Sport and Education*. LSA 56. Eastbourne: LSA, pp. 273–287.

Lentz, J.L., Weinman, L. (1998). *Deconstructing Web Graphics: Web Design Case Studies and Tutorials*, 2nd edition. New Riders Publishing.

Lepp, A., Gibson, H. (2003). Tourist roles, perceived risk and international tourism. *Annals of Tourism Research*, 30(3), 606–624.

Lipton, R. (2002). *Designing Across Cultures*. HOW Design Books.

MacWatt (2003) retrieved from http://www.suite101.com/article.cfm/food_travel_UK/104285 06/07/05).

Malouf, L. (1999). *Behind the Scenes at Special Events: Flowers, Props, and Design*. Wiley.

Mannell, R.C. (1999). Leisure experience and satisfaction in Jackson, E.L., Burton, T.L., eds. *Leisure Studies: Prospects for the Twenty-First Century.* Venture.

Mannell, R.C., Kleiber, D.A. (1997). *A Social Psychology of Leisure.* Venture Publications.

Marcus, G.H. (2002). *What is Design Today?* HN Abrams.

Masterman, G. (2004). *Strategic Sports Event Management: An International Perspective.* Elsevier Butterworth Heinemann.

Masterman, G., Wood, E. (2006). *Innovative Marketing Communications: Strategies for the Events Industry.* Elsevier Butterworth Heinemann.

Middleton, B. (1996). *BTEC HNC/HND Business – Option Module 5 Marketing.* BPP Publishing.

Monroe, J.C. (2006). *Art of the Event: Complete Guide to Designing and Decorating Special Events.* Wiley.

Morello, A. (2000). Design predicts the future when it anticipates experience. *Design Issues,* 16(3), 35–44.

Morton, J.L. (1998). *A Guide to Colour Symbolism.* Colorcom.

Mullins, D., Lowe, P. (1999). *Millennium Celebrations Toolkit.* EEA.

Murphy, J.F., Williams, J.G., Niepoth, W.E., Brown, P.D. (1973). *Leisure Service Delivery Systems: A Modern Perspective.* Lea and Febiger.

Nielson, J. (2000). *Designing Web Usability: The Practice of Simplicity.* New York: New Riders Publishing.

Neulinger, J. (1981). *To Leisure: An Introduction.* Allyn and Bacon.

Newark, Q. (2006). *What is Graphic Design for?* Roto vision.

Nichols, G. ed. (2003). *Volunteers in Sport.* LSA 80.

Nijs, D. (2003). *Imagineering: Engineering for the Imagination in the Emotion Economy in Creating a Fascinating World.* NHTV. Breda University.

Nijs, D., Peters, F. (2002). *Imagineering, Boom* (in Dutch).

O'Sullivan, E., Spangler, K. (1999). *Experience Marketing: Strategies for the New Millennium.* Venture.

Parry, B. (2004). Facilities planning in McMahon-Beattie, U., Yeoman, I., eds. *Sport and Leisure Operations Management.* Thomson.

Pearce, P. (1985). A systematic comparison of travel related roles. *Human Relations,* 38, 1001–1011.

Petkus, E. (2004). Enhancing the application of experiential marketing in the arts. *International Journal of Nonprofit and Voluntary Sector Marketing,* 9(1), 49–56.

Pine, J., Gilmore, J. (1999). *The Experience Economy: Work is Theatre and Every Business is a Stage.* HBS.

Potter, N. (2002). *What is a Designer: Things, Places, Messages.* Hyphen Press.

Ransley, J., Ingram, H. (2004). *Developing Hospitality Properties and Facilities.* Elsevier.

Ries, A., Trout, A. (1984). *Positioning: The Battle for Your Mind*. Forbes. McGraw-Hill.

Riordan, J.J. (2004). Sports and leisure experiences in McMahon-Beattie, U., Yeoman, I., eds. *Sport and Leisure Operations Management*. Thomson.

Roberts, K. (1970). *Leisure*. London: Longman.

Robinson, R. (1990). The art of seeing; an interpretation of the aesthetic encounter. J Paul Getty museum and the Getty museum for education in the arts.

Robinson, L. (2005). *Resource Guide in Sport and Leisure* (internet). Available from http://www.hlst.heacademy.ac.uk/resources/resource_guides.html accessed 02/10/05.

Roche, M. (2000). Mega-Events Modernity: Olympics and Expos in the Growth of Global Culture. Routledge.

Rogers, T. (2003). *Conferences and Conventions: A Global Industry*. Elsevier Butterworth Heinemann.

Rossman, J.R. (2003). *Recreation Programming: Designing Leisure Experiences*. Sagamore Publishing.

Rugbyheaven.com at http://www.rugbyheaven.smh.com.au/articles/2003/10/24/1066974312130.html extracted 12/12/05.

Ryan, C. (1995). Island beaches and life stage marketing in Collins, M., Baum, T., eds. *Island Tourism: Management Principles and Practice*. Wiley.

Ryan, C. ed. (1997). *The Tourist Experience: A New Introduction*. 2nd ed. Cassell.

Ryan, C. (2002). *Tourist Experience*, 2nd edition. Thomson Publishing.

Salem, G., Jones, E., Morgan, N. (2004). An overview of events management in Yeoman, I. et al., eds. *Festival and Events Management*. Elsevier.

Samdahl, D.M. (1988). A symbolic interactionist model of leisure: theory and empirical support. *Journal of Leisure Research*, 24, 391–400.

Schrage, M. (1999). *Serious Play*. Harvard Business Press.

Sebeok, T.A. (1994). An Introduction to Semiotics. London, Pinter.

Sharpe, D. (1982). *The Psychology of Colour and Design*. Nelson Hall.

Shaw, S. (1994). Gender, leisure, and constraint: towards a framework for the analysis of women's leisure. *Journal of Leisure Research*, 26.

Shebroff, N. (2001). *Experience Design 1*. Prentice Hall.

Shebroff, N. (2004). http://www.nathan.com/ed/glossary/index.html).

Shibli, S., Gratton, C. (2001). The economic impact of two major sporting events in two of the UK's National Cities of Sport in Gratton, C., Henry, I, eds. *Sport in the City: The Role of Sport in Economic and Social Regeneration*. Routledge.

Shone, A., Parry, B. (2004). *Successful Event Management*, 2nd edition. Thomson.

Shrum, W., Kilburn, J. (1996). Ritual disrobement at Mardi Gras: ceremonial exchange and moral order. *Social Forces*, 75, 423–458.

Shukla, N., Nuntsu, N. (2005). Event marketing in Tassiopolous, D., ed. *Event Management*, 2nd edition. Juta Academic.

Silvers, J. (2004a). EMBOK http://www.juliasilvers.com/embok.htm#The_Proposed_Knowledge_Domain_Structure extracted 07/01/06.

Silvers, J. (2004b). *Professional Event Coordination*. Wiley.

Smith, V. ed. (1989). *Hosts and Guests. The Anthropology of Tourism*, 2nd edition. University Pennsylvania Press.

Snape, R. (2004). *Resource Guide in Leisure in Society* (internet) available from http://www.hlst.heacademy.ac.uk/resources/resource_guides.html accessed 11/10/06.

Sonder, M. (2004). *Event Entertainment and Production*. Wiley.

Stabler, M. ed. (1989). *Tourism and Leisure (Part 1): Models and Theories*. LSA 39.

Stam, R. (2000). *Film Theory*. Oxford: Blackwell.

Sterne, J. (1999). *World Wide Web Marketing: Integrating the Web into Your Marketing Strategy*, 2nd edition. Wiley.

Sukaviriya, N., Podlaseck, M., Kjeldsen, R., Levas, A., Pingali, G., Pinhanez, C. (2004). *Augmenting a Retail Environment Using Steerable Interactive Displays*. IBM T.J. Watson Research Center.

Supovitz, F. (2005). *The Sports Event Management and Marketing Playbook*. Wiley.

Tassiopoulous, D. ed. (2005). *Event Management*, 2nd edition. Juta Academic.

Thames Valley University (2006). Annual Course Report for Event Management.

Tinsley, H.E.A. (1997). A Psychological Perspective on Leisure. *Leisure Sciences*, 19(4), 291–294.

Toffler, A. (1971). *Future Shock*. Pan books.

Tomlinson, A. ed. (1983). *Leisure and Popular Cultural Forms*. LSA 20.

Tomlinson, A. ed. (1990). *Consumption, Identity and Style: Marketing, Meanings and the Packaging of Pleasure*. Routledge.

Torkildsen, G. (1995; 2005). *Leisure and Recreation Management*, 5th edition. London: Routledge.

Tum, J., Norton, P., Wright, N. (2006). *Managing Event Operations*. Elsevier Butterworth-Heinemann.

Turner, G. (1992). British Cultural Studies: An Introduction. Routledge.

TVU (2006). *Annual Monitoring Report, Event Management*. TVU.

Tyrrell, B.J., Ismail, A.J. (2005). A methodology for estimating the attendance and economic impact of an Open-Gate Festival. *Event Management*, 9(3), 111–118.

UCAS (2006). Search 06 Entry. (Internet) University College Admissions Service. Available at: <http://www.ucas.com/search/index06.html> (accessed 02 Feb 2006).

Ulfers, E. (2005). *Designing the Customer Experience.* Jack Morton Worldwide.

Ulrich, K.T., Eppinger, S.D. (2004). *Product Design and Development*, 4th edition. McGraw-Hill.

Urry, J. (1990). *The Tourist Gaze.* Routledge.

Urry, J. (1995). *Consuming Places.* Routledge.

Van der Wagen, L., Carlos, B. (2004). *Event Management for Tourism, Cultural, Business and Sporting Events.* Pearson Prentice Hall.

Veal, A.J. (2002). *Leisure and Tourism Policy and Planning.* CABI Publishing.

Velarde, G. (2001). *Designing Exhibitions: Museums, Heritage, Trade and World Fairs*, 2nd edition. Ashgate.

Wahlers, R., Etzek, M. (1985). Vacation preferences as a manifestation of optimal stimulation and lifestyle experience. *Journal of Leisure Research*, 17, 283–295.

Wakefield, K.L., Blodgett, J.G. (1996). The effect of the service scape on customers' behavioural intentions in leisure service settings. *Journal of Services Marketing*, 10(6), 5–15.

Waterhouse, R. (2000). Are you experienced? *Sunday Times*, 3 December.

Watt, D. (1992). *Leisure and Tourism Events Management and Organisation Manual.* Longman.

Watt, D. (1998). *Event Management in Leisure and Tourism.* Addison Wesley Longman.

Watt, D., Stayte, S. (1999). *Events from Start to Finish.* ILAM.

White, L. (2006). National identity and the Sydney 2000 Olympic Games Opening Ceremony in Robertson, M. ed. *Sporting Events and Event Tourism: Impacts, Plans and Opportunities.* LSA.

Wickens, E. (2002). The sacred and the profane: a tourist typology. *Annals of Tourism Research*, 29(3), 834–851.

Wilkinson, D. (1998). *The Event Management & Marketing Institute* 1, IBD.

Williams, J.A., Anderson, H.H. (2005). Engaging customers in service creation: a theatre perspective. *Journal of Service Marketing*, 19(1), 13–23.

Williamson, J. (1978). *Decoding Advertisements. Marion Boyars Cultural Studies, 1972–79.* London: Hutchinson, pp. 128–138.

Wills, A. (2005). New Talent in the Classroom. *Event Magazine*, February 2005.

Wilmshurst, J. (1995). *The Fundamentals and Practice of Marketing.* Butterworth Heinemann.

Wolsey, C., Abrams, J. eds. (2001). *Understanding the Leisure and Sport Industry.* Longman.

WorldTrans   http://www.worldtrans.org/whole/wholedefs.html extracted 02/02/06.

World welcomes millennium at http://www.wndu.com/news/ 121999/news_1059.php extracted 2/02/01.

www.wndu.com. Millennium Commentary retrieved from http:// www.wndu.com/news/121999/news_1059.php on 06/07/03.

www.wordnet.princeton.edu at http://wordnet.princeton.edu/perl/ webwn?s=design Extracted 4/08/05.

Wynne, D. (1998). *Leisure Lifestyles and the New Middle Class*. Routledge.

Yeoman, I., Robertson, M., Ali-Knight, J., Drummond, S., McMahon-Beattie, U. (2004). *Festival and Events Management*. Elsevier Butterworth Heinemann.

Yiannakis, A., Gibson, H. (1992). Roles tourist play. *Annals of Tourism Research*, 19, 287–303.

Zoels, J.C., Gabrielli, S. (2003). Creating Imaginable Futures: Using Design Strategy as a Foresight Tool. DFFN Case-Study Technical Report, edited by Interaction Design Institute Ivrea for the European Commission, Brussels 10–11 December 2002.

The event in Activity 11.2 was held to launch the Pirelli Calendar that traditionally shows photo images of scantily clad women for each calendar month.

Index